Water and Ritual

The Linda Schele Series in Maya and Pre-Columbian Studies

This series was made possible through the generosity of William C. Nowlin, Jr., and Bettye H. Nowlin, the National Endowment for the Humanities, and various individual donors.

Water and Ritual

The Rise and Fall of Classic Maya Rulers

LISA J. LUCERO

University of Texas Press   *Austin*

First edition, 2006

Requests for permission to reproduce material from this work should be sent to:
Permissions
University of Texas Press
P.O. Box 7819
Austin, TX 78713-7819
www.utexas.edu/utpress/about/bpermission.html

♾ The paper used in this book meets the minimum requirements of ANSI/NISO
Z39.48-1992 (R1997) (Permanence of Paper).

Library of Congress Cataloging-in-Publication Data

Lucero, Lisa Joyce.
    Water and ritual : the rise and fall of classic Maya rulers / Lisa J. Lucero.— 1st ed.
        p.   cm. — (The Linda Schele series in Maya and pre-Columbian studies)
    Includes bibliographical references and index.
    ISBN 978-0-292-72611-6
    1. Mayas—Politics and government.   2. Mayas—Kings and rulers.   3. Mayas—
Rites and ceremonies.   4. Water rights—Central America.   5. Water rights—
Mexico.   6. Water—Religious aspects.   7. Central America—Economic conditions.
8. Mexico—Economic conditions.   I. Title.   II. Series.
    F1435.3.P7L83   2006
    305.897'42—dc22
                                                                            2005028167

For my parents, Jim and Ida Lucero

Contents

Preface

In 1999 I published a paper (Lucero 1999b) on water systems and Maya ruler-ship at Tikal and other comparable centers (large centers in areas without per-manent water sources such as lakes and rivers). This paper, as well as questions from colleagues and students and a perusal of cross-cultural cases, made me wonder about the role of water at other centers in the southern Maya lowlands, particularly those located in areas with rivers and lakes. I realized that the level of reliance on and scale of reservoirs had a significant impact on the degree of rulers' political power. The more I delved into research on water issues and Maya rulership, however, the more I also realized that water management is inadequate in and of itself to explain completely the ability of a few to exact tribute from the majority. One only has to look around each Maya center to no-tice a missing piece of the puzzle—monumental public architecture and large plazas. These settings served as competitive arenas to integrate people through ceremonies and feasts, particularly during the dry season. They also served to highlight the fact that the average commoner was an active participant and had some say in the amount of tribute paid as well as to whom. Commoners were willing to contribute surplus because rulers offset problems that arose as a re-sult of seasonal vagaries—not enough or too much water.

Annual water shortages in the tropical jungles of the southern Maya low-lands dramatically affected the livelihood of the Maya like no other natural re-source shortage. Even in areas where water was plentiful, seasonal water issues impacted settlement decisions and agricultural practices. By about 1000 BC Maya had relocated to interior areas away from the major rivers and coastal ar-eas. Pioneers found plentiful fertile agricultural land but not much permanent surface water. The first farmers had a definite advantage over succeeding gen-erations of immigrating families who needed to farm to support themselves. The first settlers or founders—the earliest elites—did not offer the use of their land for free. In return for homestead privileges, they demanded, and were paid, a percentage of the crops; and new arrivals worked elites' land, built their homes, and provided other services (e.g., as craft specialists). Elites soon organized the construction of small public temples and plazas, where they sponsored ceremonies and feasts to thank ancestors and gods for providing rain and bountiful crops. This scenario occurred throughout the southern lowlands. In some areas, however, rulers emerged—why in some areas and not in others?

The interior can sustain many people with the major staples of maize, beans, and squash. But the annual 4- to 5-month drought posed challenges to the Maya, especially in areas without lakes and rivers. They met this challenge by building water catchment systems to provide water that would last until the rains began again. Elites organized the construction and maintenance of water retention features. At first they were small-scale. Later they became much more complex and larger to supply water to increasingly greater numbers of people. Although there always seemed to be an abundance of land, there never seemed to be enough water in many areas. Families lived in farmsteads dispersed throughout the jungle; and rulers had to convince them that it was to their advantage to supply labor, goods, and services. Many farmers did not necessarily have to work for a particular ruler, because they could choose to build their own small-scale water systems or contribute to the coffers of other nearby rulers. Powerful rulers also arose along rivers. People still relied on reservoirs and other water systems in such settings, and rulers provided capital to repair water or agricultural systems damaged by heavy rainfall and flooding. In times of shortages (drought, rain damage) rulers also may have supplied food from their fields, located in several areas to spread the risk, and perhaps allocated water.

A major means that rulers used to bring together Maya farmers was traditional rituals writ large, including dedication, ancestor veneration and termination rites, prayers for abundant water, and other household and community rites. Maya kings also created special rites highlighting their divine qualities; some of these were performed in public venues, and others for a private or restricted audience. By sponsoring public rituals, rulers demonstrated their close ties to the supernatural world. They showed people that their affiliations and influences with ancestors and deities resulted in plentiful rain and crops. If they were successful, it was only natural that they should receive some form of payment—labor and goods.

The more people kings integrated, the more powerful they became, particularly in areas with plentiful agricultural land and noticeable seasonal vagaries. A long-term drought at the end of the Classic period, however, demonstrated that rulers had lost their ability to intercede with supernatural forces and failed to bring enough rain. Consequently, farmers looked elsewhere for survival and discontinued contributing to political coffers. Rulers had no choice but to abandon royal trappings: civic-ceremonial centers with palaces, temples, inscribed monuments, and ball courts. Farmers either remained in the vicinity outside of centers or left the southern Maya lowlands altogether. What did not change was that all Maya continued to perform rituals in the home.

This book documents this story and expands on ideas published earlier (especially Lucero 2002a, 2003). I detail commoner, elite, and royal ritual histories in the southern Maya lowlands from the Late Preclassic (ca. 250 BC−AD 250) through the Terminal Classic periods to illustrate their role in the emergence of Maya rulers and eventually their demise.

Acknowledgments

The completion of this book would not have been possible without the support of various agencies, friends, and colleagues. A grant from the National Science Foundation (BCS-0004410) made the 2001 field season at Saturday Creek possible, as did support from Robert Vitolo, Robert Vannix, and Berniece Skinner, all of which is much appreciated. John Yellen, director, NSF Archaeology Program, has been particularly supportive. Permission from the Belize Department of Archaeology (now the Institute of Archaeology) is greatly appreciated, and I want to give special thanks to acting archaeology commissioner George Thompson.

Completion of the fieldwork would not have been possible without an excellent staff, including field director Andrew Kinkella and lab directors Jim Conlon and Jennifer Ehret. Jim and Jenn spent much time conducting ceramic analysis and generated a ceramic chronology critical for our goals at Saturday Creek. I also appreciate Jane Arie Baldwin, Natalie Smith, and Jennifer Kirker for taking time from their busy schedules to help me with New Mexico State University 2001 field-school students, whose assistance was critical: David Brown, Sean Graebner, Julie Jeakle, Gaea McGahee, Joseph Bergstrom, Nick Chamberlain, Yvette Coral, Sarah Field, Patrick Graham, Charles (Sonny) Hartley, Elizabeth Pugh, and Gabriela Sanchez. We all learned much about burial excavation techniques and analysis from David Lee and Jennifer Piehl; their input was crucial and appreciated. Gaea McGahee and Rachel Saurman are responsible for the fine artwork.

The field season would not have been possible without the help and friendship of our Belizean excavation assistants: Cleofo Choc, Zedikiah Scott, Stanley Choc, Juan Antonio Lopes, Vicente Cal, Besi Alvarez (Rodríguez), Isabel Ascencio (Don Luna), Joel Portillo, Jeremías Portillo, Rene Penido, Rafilo Sansores, Julio Rodríguez, and Rafael Magana. The Martínez family at Saturday Creek provided delicious breakfasts every morning and welcomed us into their home. Our living and lab quarters were kindly provided by John, Carolyn, and Lisa Carr at Banana Bank; they and their staff always made us feel at home. The Carrs also gave me permission to excavate on their property, for which I am grateful. I want to thank Bob and Nettie Jones and Paulita and Ramón Figueroa for their friendship; they made Belize feel like a second home.

Several colleagues have provided invaluable input in the long process of writing this book, especially William H. Walker, Timothy Earle, Jeremy Sabloff, and Vernon Scarborough. An anonymous reviewer's comments were also of much assistance in revising the manuscript. Much of the writing took place at the Bean in Mesilla, a coffee shop that provided the necessary caffeine and atmosphere to complete this project, especially in the person of the owners, Debbie and Mary. The final revisions took place at the University of Pennsylvania while I was a research associate in the University Museum of Archaeology and Anthropology and a visiting faculty member in the Department of Anthropology. I want to thank museum director Jeremy Sabloff and department chair Greg Urban for setting the stage for the warm welcome I received at Penn. I would like to thank Jane Arie Baldwin and James Arie for providing comments on the preface. Finally, I want to thank everyone at the University of Texas Press for all their support and guidance, especially Theresa May and Allison Faust.

Water and Ritual

The Rise and Fall of Classic Maya Rulers

A key goal of this book is to explore how ritual and material factors articulate in the development and demise of political complexity. I attempt to do so using two factors: water and ritual, specifically short-term and long-term seasonal vagaries and traditional rituals writ large. I illustrate this model by examining the emergence and demise of Classic Maya rulers (ca. AD 250–950) in the southern Maya lowlands. My focus is on the way in which Maya kings used their wealth to offset seasonal problems (e.g., provisioning of dry-season water supplies) and integrated people by sponsoring large-scale traditional rituals. These factors are crucial in revealing not only how political agents appropriate the surplus of others but also eventually how such a strategy can fail (Lucero 2002a, 2003; cf. Tainter 1988:31; see Toynbee 1972:223). I concentrate on the Late Classic period (ca. AD 550–850), when the most powerful Maya rulers arose in areas where they could integrate large numbers of farmers and exact tribute—that is, areas with noticeable seasonal water issues and plentiful agricultural land. When seasonal vagaries became more drastic and long-term (decreasing seasonal rainfall), beginning in the late AD 700s, commoners no longer were obligated to pay tribute to kings who clearly had lost the power to propitiate the gods and supply water.

While each Maya center has its own particular history, long-term climatic change set in motion a series of varied, sometimes related, events in the Terminal Classic (ca. AD 850–950) and/or exacerbated local problems (e.g., political competition and warfare). Basically, the most powerful kings lost power; many secondary rulers followed suit, while others (for a brief time) experienced what it was like to be a primary ruler. Climate change, however, was too drastic to support a royal lifestyle for long; soon people largely abandoned their rulers and civic-ceremonial centers—the heart of royal life. A permanent political vacuum resulted, and it is this fact that needs explaining. In the aftermath, there was a major restructuring that focused at the community level.

There the Maya continued to conduct the traditional rites that they always had performed.

I illustrate the process of how the politically ambitious replicate and expand traditional rituals as a means to attain and maintain political power using dedication, ancestor veneration, and termination rituals. These rites concern life, death, and renewal—factors key in the lives of all Maya. Other rites undoubtedly were just as important in social and political life, such as community, agricultural, water, and other domestic and traditional rites. They are more difficult to identify in the archaeological record, however—community rites take place in open areas and plazas; agricultural rites in fields; water rites at the edge of *aguadas* (rain-fed natural sinkholes), reservoirs, and rivers; and so on. In contrast, dedication, ancestor veneration, and termination rites leave clear evidence in the archaeological record, particularly in structures, consisting of caches, burials, and burned surface deposits. Most rituals likely were replicated and expanded by elites to allay conflict in the face of wealth differentiation and later by political leaders to promote political agendas.

To document ancient Maya political histories, I detail ritual histories at minor, secondary, and regional centers before, during, and after the appearance of rulers. The Maya case studies, especially Tikal and Altar de Sacrificios, illustrate the ritual process of how rulers initially emerge but do not necessarily represent the earliest southern lowland Maya kings, who likely arose in the Mirador Basin in northern Guatemala (Hansen et al. 2002). The minor river center of Saturday Creek (another case study) did not have rulers, but its inhabitants conducted the same rites as did those Maya beholden to rulers; this pattern indicates that appropriated rites have a long history (before rulers) and that they never left the home (during rulers).

Before focusing on the Maya, I begin by presenting a general model that articulates the critical role of water and ritual in political systems. Political power is defined here as the ability to exact tribute in the form of surplus goods and labor. Whatever the route to political complexity, a material basis is required to support it, and ritual is key to explaining it. The amount of surplus available to leaders relates to where and how people live. Basically, densely settled people are more easily integrated, whereas dispersed people are less so. My intent is to show the process of how people get other people to contribute to their political coffers, step by step. Rulers need not own critical resources or even control their access per se. What they do need to provide, however, is water during drought, food during famine, and capital to rebuild water or agricultural systems damaged, for example, by flooding. They also need to have the wealth or means to perform the necessary rites of continuance and plenty. When agricultural regimes yield less food for whatever reasons, people abandon their leaders, whose rituals have failed to bring forth prosperity.

Chapter 1 presents the major factors used to distinguish different political systems (community, local polities, and centralized and integrative polities) to provide a backdrop for the political model with ritual at its core. I also define my use of the concept of "collapse" and discuss how political systems fail. Chapter 2 details political histories at southern lowland Maya centers and briefly presents the major factors that distinguish different Maya centers. Chapter 3 describes ethnographic, colonial, and prehispanic evidence of traditional Maya ritual practices to demonstrate their long history. I also present the methods to reveal ancient ritual activities as well as the expectations regarding ritual histories in commoner, elite, and royal contexts. I begin Chapters 4, 5, and 6 with a general discussion of community organizations (Chapter 4), local polities (Chapter 5), and centralized and integrative polities (Chapter 6) and use cross-cultural cases to illustrate them. In addition, Chapter 4 defines Late Classic minor Maya centers and details the history of ritual activities at Saturday Creek. Chapter 5 does the same for secondary Maya centers and Altar de Sacrificios, and Chapter 6 for regional Maya centers and Tikal. Chapter 7 discusses how water and ritual articulated in the rise and fall of Classic Maya rulers. Chapter 8 concludes with a general discussion of the role of ritual and water in ancient political systems.

CHAPTER 1

Water and Ritual

The environment in its largest sense creates the context in which choice is made, but the choice is made by individuals.

LEACH (1970 [1954]:259)

I focus on economically stratified (including incipient) agricultural societies, and how and when wealth differences transform into political power. Specifically, how do a few people get others to contribute their labor, goods, and services without compensating them equally? My definition of political power reflects the focus on surplus appropriation, and therefore my perspective is necessarily materialist. Thus, I view resources as a condition for, not a cause of, political complexity (cf. Fried 1967:111; Russell 1938:31) and focus on the way people interact with their natural and social surroundings. My approach is not environmentally deterministic but acknowledges the key role that resources play in surplus production, especially rainfall dependency and the degree to which people rely on water or agricultural systems. Long-term climate change (e.g., rainy seasons begin later than usual or are shorter than usual, temperatures drop slightly, and so on) has various, and sometimes drastic, impacts on agricultural and political systems (see Fagan 1999, 2004). After all, no matter how unique people are in terms of how they think, act, and create, they still need to survive and interact with the material and social world. The way in which surplus is appropriated, however, is another matter; and this is where the role of ritual is crucial.

I discuss water (especially seasonal vagaries) and ritual separately, because to appreciate the whole we must first understand its constituent parts. In doing so, individual factors can only appear as static entities. Nevertheless, my goal by the end of this work is to discuss them as an integrated, dialectical, and dynamic system. Edmund Leach (1970 [1954]:63; emphasis in original) said it best when he explained the challenges of detailing structural change between *gumsa* and *gumlao* organization in highland Burma:

> I assume that the system of variation as we now observe it has *no* stability through time. What can be observed now is just a momentary configuration of a totality existing in a state of flux. Yet I agree that in order to describe this totality it is necessary to represent the system *as if* it were stable and coherent.

This being said, it is important to acknowledge that the model presented does not and cannot account for all the varied political histories; instead, I attempt to provide an idealized general organizational framework from which to evaluate under what material and social conditions political leadership develops and fails. The defining traits of each political type are not static and impermeable; they are fluid and part of a continuum and only a heuristic device. The use of types is simply an attempt to separate the constituent parts of complex and dynamic systems (see Klejn 1982:17, 52). My goal also is to avoid the baggage that usually comes with using traditional terminology that implies stages through which all societies must pass in the drive toward complexity (such as tribes, simple chiefdoms, complex chiefdoms, and states). The systems I describe thus can be viewed synchronically (nested hierarchies), diachronically (changing political histories), or as separate entities (autonomous); different political systems can apply to societies in different times and places or to a single culture during a specific period. In the Maya case, various southern lowland centers are evaluated either as separate polities or as nested hierarchies during the Late Classic period.

People interact with natural and social forces in various ways, resulting in varied political histories. Given that there are a limited number of responses (Friedman and Rowlands 1978), however, similar processes must be at work (Earle 1997:193). The model thus provides a useful construct to illuminate the inner mechanisms of political systems and how they emerge, expand, and fail.

There is no doubt that many types of relations can and do exist within social systems (e.g., kinship, alliance, marriage); here I focus specifically on how seasonal water issues and ritual bear on political systems. Finally, while the cross-cultural case studies that I use to illustrate the varied political systems are well known, what is different is the way in which I discuss and situate them.

In this chapter I introduce the different types of political systems (community, local, and centralized and integrative polities) and the factors that distinguish them. I then detail the step-by-step process of how rulers emerge and the crucial role that ritual plays in their rise, maintenance, and loss of power. I define political collapse and discuss the relationship of short-term and long-term seasonal climate change and resource stability with political power. Finally, I discuss ritual and collapse and present a scenario illustrating a political history.

Political Systems

The distribution of critical resources affects how people settle across landscapes, which in turn bears on the ability of aspiring leaders to communicate ideas and to conduct large-scale activities (political rallies, feasts, and work parties) (Roscoe 1993). Densely settled areas where people are tied to the land through investments in subsistence technology (e.g., plowed fields, canals, dams, agricultural terraces, fish ponds, transportation, storage buildings) facilitate the consolidation of power (Carneiro 1970; Gilman 1981; Hayden 1995), because political aspirants can more easily access critical resources and surplus (Earle 1997:7). Dispersed populations that rely on scattered resources are more difficult to organize, regardless of surplus potential. Aspiring leaders thus need to bring people together physically, and they accomplish this through funding and conducting integrative events and providing some type of material benefit. Political demands (e.g., corvée labor), however, are superimposed onto existing economic and social institutions that may or may not be affected by the waxing and waning of political power.

Surplus funds the political economy. Without it everyone would be concerned only with household and community obligations. This scenario would not leave much time or money for emerging rulers to recruit followers; organize military campaigns; sponsor public works, monumental building projects, and public spectacles such as feasts and ceremonies; support royal family members, retinues, or administrators; and fund artisans (see Sahlins 1972:101; Wolf 1966:4–9). Without surplus production, farmers could not take time off from working in their own fields to labor in the fields of their patrons or of the political elite, not to mention provide corvée labor to build the material manifestations of political power (e.g., Sahlins 1968:92). And even if rulers owned or controlled, for example, large plots of agricultural land, they could not benefit from the fruits of the land if they could neither afford to pay laborers nor implement labor demands on others. Access to labor, thus, is more critical than resource control—surplus labor, that is (cf. Russell 1938:31). The point is this: whatever the source of surplus, it is a must for anything political.

For the sake of simplicity, I define four kinds of political systems—community organization, local polity, and centralized and integrative polities. Each is detailed in Chapters 4, 5, and 6 and described in terms of resource distribution, subsistence strategies, seasonal issues and resource stability, presence of water or agricultural systems, settlement patterns and relative density, internal differentiation, leadership, resource access, territorial extent, external relations, political economy, conflict, interaction sphere, type and scale of monumental architecture, scale of integrative events, public iconography, the presence of writing or recording, and duration (Table 1.1). While I discuss some factors more than others, I include them all here to provide a more complete backdrop.

RESOURCE DISTRIBUTION: Water supply and critical resources (concentrated, dispersed, or extensive agricultural land and other resources) bear on population size and density, as well as whether or not resources potentially can yield a surplus.

SUBSISTENCE STRATEGIES: This factor relates to the amount of surplus produced, as well as how it is distributed and for what purpose it is used (e.g., to procure prestige items, to contribute to political coffers, and to build monuments and public works).

SEASONAL ISSUES AND RESOURCE STABILITY: Seasonal food scarcity and/or water shortages, transportation problems, heavy rainfall resulting in property damage, flooding and erosion, hurricanes, water allocation, and other natural disasters (e.g., blight, hail, crop diseases, and pests) are factors that the political elite can use to their advantage (for example, store food and repair flood-damaged subsistence technologies) (e.g., Scarborough 2003).

WATER OR AGRICULTURAL SYSTEMS: Reservoirs, check dams, canals, terraces, and other subsistence technologies reflect local adaptive strategies as well as the number of people they can service. Their location and scale typically reflect their role in politics (e.g., water allocation). Small-scale systems are built and maintained at the household and/or community level; large-scale systems are funded or built, or at least maintained, by a political body.

SETTLEMENT PATTERNS AND RELATIVE DENSITY: The number of people and the way in which they are distributed across the landscape affect the ability of leaders to incorporate and communicate with people, not to mention their ability to tap the surplus of others.

INTERNAL DIFFERENTIATION: This factor distinguishes wealth differentiation from political power. In the former, wealthy people equally compensate others for goods and services; in the latter, the political elite exacts tribute without equal compensation to fund the political economy.

LEADERSHIP: The number and the type of leaders are significant factors relating to who has access to the most surplus (e.g., several clan leaders or chiefs versus one institutionalized ruler).

RESOURCE ACCESS: Garnering the means of production is key in any political system (Fried 1967) for gift giving and to fund public works, ceremonies, and feasts. Wealth provides the means to sponsor integrative events and create obligatory relations (debt). Political leaders also provide capital to repair public works damaged by weather gods (flooding, hurricanes, hailstorms, etc.) and food when necessary from their own stores or acquired via trade (e.g., Scarborough 2003:96–99).

TERRITORIAL EXTENT: This involves community, local, or regional territorial extent, or how many people rulers incorporate.

EXTERNAL RELATIONS: This includes equal or unequal external relations and the nature of ties with other groups (e.g., peer political alliances, subjugated polities or communities, and heterarchical relations).

POLITICAL ECONOMY: This involves the ability to exact tribute. The amount of surplus that rulers extract corresponds with the degree of political power. Paying taxes does not negate resistance on the part of farmers, who use various strategies to avoid paying onerous demands (e.g., Adas 1981; Joyce 2004).

CONFLICT: Incorporating more people via conquest results in more tribute and hence greater political power. Rulers also provide protection from outsiders and keep internal conflict under control. Conquest differs from raiding, in which the goals are to steal food and kidnap women (and acquire land, if possible) (Johnson and Earle 2000:249) and which involves feuding among lineages.

INTERACTION SPHERE: This involves prestige-goods exchange, political alliances, and royal marriages. The way in which and degree to which elites and royals distinguish themselves reflect wealth and extent of power. It also involves the exchange of goods between commoners, typically free from elite interference.

TYPE AND SCALE OF MONUMENTAL ARCHITECTURE: These features reflect labor organization (compensation versus tribute), restricted (royal) versus public activities, and the number of participants (e.g., size of public areas; Moore 1996).

Table 1.1. Political systems

Scale	Community Organization	Local Polity	Centralized Polity	Integrative Polity
Resource Distribution	Varied, plentiful resources	Varied resources, some concentrated	Concentrated resources	Dispersed key resources
Subsistence Strategies	Horticulture/agriculture extensive/intensive; mixed	Mixed; intensive agriculture, hunting, fishing	Intensive agriculture	Intensive agriculture
Seasonal Issues/Resource Stability	Seasonal rainfall important	Rainfall dependent; differential rainfall and distribution; flood damage; storage important	Rainfall dependent; heavy use of resources; cycles of plenty and famine; flood damage, crop failure, periodic drought; storage important	Rainfall dependent; heavy use of resources; cycles of plenty and famine; flood damage, crop failure, periodic drought; conditions prevent large-scale storage
Water/Agricultural Systems	None	Small-scale irrigation	Large-scale (responsibility of communities), water allocation	Large-scale (some aspect is the responsibility of the ruler—usually related to potable water)
Settlement Patterns and Relative Density	Farmsteads, small villages	Villages—dispersed and dense	Nucleated villages, towns, cities	Dispersed villages, towns, or regal-ritual centers
Internal Differentiation	Household wealth differences	Household wealth differences and some political surplus—enough to provide capital; stratified	Household wealth differences and political surplus-capital; stratified	Household wealth differences and political surplus-capital; stratified

Leadership	Managerial, more than one leader (chief), kinship-based (ranked), hereditary, somewhat institutionalized	One major leader (chief), hereditary, institutionalized	One hereditary, institutionalized ruler	Hereditary, institutionalized rulers
Resource Access	Corporate land ownership, chiefs can control/own other means of production (e.g., canoes)	Chief controls/owns major means of production and has access to enough resources to offset famine	Ruler has access to resources to offset food shortages and other problems	Ruler has access to key resources in the immediate vicinity to offset seasonal fluctuations
Territorial Extent	Localized	Central place and immediate hinterlands	Central place, immediate hinterlands, and local polities	Central place, immediate hinterlands, and local polities
External Relations	May interact or be part of a political system; alliances/exchange with other villages	Hierarchical relations with larger polities, and equal relations with other local polities; alliances/exchange with other villages	Equal and unequal interpolity relations; alliances/exchange with other villages	Equal and unequal interpolity relations; alliances/exchange with other villages
Political Economy	No tribute; surplus acquired through other means; equal compensation	Some tribute	Tribute	Tribute
Conflict	Feuding, raiding for food, land, and some political reasons; endemic but regulated	Small-scale conquest for land and labor during agricultural off-season; protection	Conquest for labor; protection	Conquest for labor when possible; status rivalry; protection
Interaction Sphere	Elite interaction; prestige-goods exchange and trade of subsistence goods	Elite and royal interaction; prestige-goods exchange, alliances	Elite and royal interaction; prestige-goods exchange, alliances, trade/markets	Elite and royal interaction; prestige-goods exchange, alliances, trade/markets

(continued)

Table 1.1. (continued)

Scale	Community Organization	Local Polity	Centralized Polity	Integrative Polity
Type and Scale of Monumental Architecture	Small-scale public architecture	Public monumental architecture	Large-scale public and private monumental architecture	Large-scale public and private monumental architecture
Scale of Integrative Events	Household rites, community events (ceremonies, public works); intervillage; involving ancestors	Household rites, community events, involving chiefly ancestors (descendants of gods), fertility gods (and others)	Household rites, community events, large-scale royal political/ceremonial events involving royal ancestors and supreme gods (mandate of heaven)	Household rites, community events, large-scale royal political/ceremonial events involving royal ancestors and supreme gods (mandate of heaven)
Public Iconography	Stylized spirits (ancestors), clan totems	Gods of war, fertility, chiefly ancestors	Gods of war, fertility, royal ancestors, hierarchy of gods; rulers depicted	Images of war, fertility, royal ancestors, hierarchy of gods; rulers depicted
Writing or Recording	None	None	Economic, political, and religious writing/recording	Political and religious writing/recording
Duration	Stable, long-lasting	Political system tied to external conditions; subsistence system stable	Politically and economically (subsistence) stable as long as resources are stable	Required continual maintenance (feasts, ceremonies, display); affected by fluctuations; subsistence system relatively stable
Examples	Trobrianders, Nuer, Tellensi, Logoli Bantu, Marajo Island, and other Amazonian river societies	Zulu, Ngwato, Bemba, Banayankole, Kede, Kedah, Hawaii	Egypt, Aztec, China, Inka, Central México, Mesopotamia	Bali, Classic Maya, Angkor Wat, and many other Southeast Asian polities

SCALE OF INTEGRATIVE EVENTS: This includes household rites, small-scale community ceremonies, and large-scale public ceremonial and political events. Successfully propitiating supernatural entities guarantees material rewards for both intermediaries and participants.

PUBLIC ICONOGRAPHY: This represents what is significant in political, social, and religious life, which is visible for all to witness and absorb.

WRITING OR RECORDING: The presence of a writing or recording system indicates the need to keep track of important royal and supernatural events, economic transactions (taxes and trade), and ideas, usually for an exclusive few (Postgate et al. 1995).

DURATION: This factor highlights differences between political and occupational histories. The length and stability of political systems relate to specific circumstances and surplus availability. Changing political fortunes typically do not affect daily living (settlement, subsistence practices)—political collapse often results in people abandoning their kings, not their land and homes.

In brief, community organizations have several leaders (e.g., lineage heads, village chiefs) who are unable to implement tribute demands but who use their wealth to distinguish themselves materially. Farmers are extensive and/or intensive agriculturalists who rely on seasonal rainfall but do not rely on water/agricultural systems. People honor ancestors through public ceremonies. Local polities differ from community organizations because they have denser settlements, rely on small-scale water/agricultural systems, and have one major institutionalized leader (e.g., a paramount chief). In exchange for what leaders provide in times of need, such as providing food during famine and capital to repair water/agricultural systems damaged by heavy rains or flooding, people contribute labor and goods to political coffers. Their power to acquire surplus from others is conveyed in public ceremonies which thank chiefly ancestors.

Centralized polities represent the pinnacle of political power, and there is little doubt that rulers' capital and abilities to reach the supernatural are necessary in situations where dense regional populations rely on rainfall, intensive agriculture, and large-scale water/agricultural systems. Their success is publicized in large-scale ceremonies with roots in traditional rites. In integrative polities, the ruler has a similar role. The distinguishing features are that key resources and settlement are more dispersed, two factors that pose a challenge for rulers to integrate people. They succeed in doing so through frequent ceremonies, feasts, and other displays as well as playing a major role in funding large-scale water systems. A greater reliance on large-scale water/agricultural systems in the face of changing climate patterns, however, can also be a formula for disaster.

The question is, who superimposed political demands? How were people able to accomplish this feat and in many cases expand the political economy? Clearly, material resources are critical. Just as critical, or even more so, is ritual; simply put, those persons interested in acquiring power use ritual as a means to achieve their ends.

Ritual and Political Power

Ritual is not in good odour with our intellectuals. . . . In their eyes only economic interests can create anything as solid as the state. Yet if they would only look about them they would everywhere see communities banded together by interest in a common ritual; they would even find that ritual enthusiasm builds more solidly than economic ambitions, because ritual involves a rule of life, whereas economics are a rule of gain, and so divide rather than unite.
HOCART (1970 [1936]:35)

This section and the following one address the question of how a few people get others to contribute labor and services without compensating them equally. There are many pathways to political power, all of which have several common elements (see Godelier 1978). For example, Michael Mann (1986) argues that economy, ideology, military force, and politics are the four sources of social power or the means of social control. Similarly, Timothy Earle (1997) views economy, ideology, and the military as sources for political power or the expansion and domination of the political economy. Richard Blanton (1998) distinguishes two major sources of power: an objective base (material) and a cognitive-symbolic base (shared ideology). While alternative pathways to power exist (e.g., Flannery 1972), more centralized political systems develop when more sources of power are controlled and integrated (Earle 1997:210 – 211). Local circumstances (cf. Fried 1967:37–38; Trigger 1991) and how people interact with other people and adapt to their surroundings affect the ultimate success and duration of different political strategies, as well as the amount of goods and labor that political leaders can extract from others (e.g., Earle 1997:15). Further, "these generic sources of power may in fact be universal to the political process in human society, but the outcomes are highly variable" (Earle 1997:193).

A common factor in all political success stories, whatever their origins, is ritual. Political aspirants integrate people, promote political agendas, and situate political change within known cultural constructs through the replication and expansion of traditional rituals. They incorporate new elements in such a way as to make them seem as timeless and natural as the original rites. Emerging leaders not only take on the role of ritual specialist but, more significantly, serve as intermediaries between people and gods. Consequently, rituals reflect this new role, but in traditional formats.

Edmund Leach (1966) notes that ritual pervades all aspects of society and life, and thus it is not surprising that the politically ambitious transform ritual action into political fortune (e.g., Bourdieu 1977:41). Ritual integrates religious, social, economic, and political life, including, for example, creating and maintaining alliances through marriage and long-distance trade (e.g., Friedman and Rowlands 1978), warfare (e.g., Carneiro 1970), and integrative activities such as constructing public works (e.g., Service 1975:96) and sponsoring religious ceremonies, political rallies (e.g., Kertzer 1988), and feasts (e.g., Hayden 1995; Hayden and Gargett 1990). How these various factors intersect largely determines the pathway to power. Through ritual, political actors involve active participants in political change rather than passive observers (e.g., Joyce 2004).

Leaders, by rights as lineage elders and heads of military societies, kinship groups, and religious sodalities, often promote political change through ritual (Kertzer 1988:30) in which they show that their success benefits all members of society (Godelier 1977:111–119). They organize the building and maintenance of religious structures, subsistence technology including irrigation systems, and canoes or roads for trade and craft production facilities and lead raiding parties—activities that typically involve ritual. Their role presupposes their abilities to lead and provides the opportunity for expanding their influence outside their particular group. Often successful aspirants are descendants of founding families, who have closer ties to original ancestors—another predisposition in their favor.

Each group has special ties to an aspect of the supernatural world, which political aspirants appropriate to highlight their special abilities (Bloch 1986). Emerging political elites claim closer ties to the supernatural world (particularly ancestors), using the same means employed by kinship lineage heads, who themselves often are politically ambitious (Friedman 1975). As descendants of founding ancestors, they connect with more people (Bloch 1986:86). As intermediaries, they receive offerings that once were made directly to the ancestors (Friedman 1998; e.g., Friedman and Rowlands 1978; Helms 1998; Joyce 2004; McAnany 1995) and other supernatural forces.

> . . . this development is an internally determined evolution, the outgrowth of the operation of the political economy within a pre-structured kinship system. Thus, the transformation to ranked hierarchy can be explained without any external references. Nothing new has been added, but certain relations have

emerged as dominant on the social level which were previously only latent in the supernatural realm. A headman becomes a chief by taking on some of the properties formerly possessed only by the deities. (Friedman 1998:129)

For example, among the Kwakiutl, Eric Wolf (1999:103) notes:

Since chiefs are represented as "iterations" of the founding ancestor or donor, they are equated with the creators or progenitors of the human groups over whom they exercise authority. Because the original donor or ancestor first occupied the resource area that will subsequently be utilized by his group, the chief is also "owner" or manager of that resource base. Since the original donor was endowed with valuables—houses, crests, masks, songs—the chief also keeps and wields these prerequisites.

Maurice Bloch (1986:117–119) explicitly details how the circumcision ritual in nineteenth-century Madagascar, in which every Merina male took part, was transformed into a state ritual using the same rules of descent and authority. "The state took on the appearance of a large descent group, the descent groups took on aspects of being a constitutive part of a small kingdom. As a result, at the same time as the child renewed the blessing of the ancestors through cir-cumcision, he also became a subject of the king," whereby he basically made a declaration of his allegiance (pp. 117–118). The entire kingdom is thus repre-sented as one descent group. The king also takes on the authority structure of kinship; earlier it was elder to younger; later, and in addition, it became king to subject, as the king took on the role of elder (p. 192). The Merina king also was able to keep an accurate count of men for taxation purposes (p. 144): he required a specific time (every seven years) for the circumcision ritual to take place (p. 126). The ritual itself was performed privately in houses that involved family and community members (p. 115). Afterward, the king traveled the land, "per-forming rituals at a number of specified sites to which were brought the chil-dren who had been circumcised" (p. 115). The royal circumcision ceremony was quite spectacular and included an elaborate procession with members of the court and army (p. 127).

By what means do political aspirants succeed? In a word, surplus. To be more specific, it takes material capital to support rulers, their families, and their retinues and to sponsor public works and integrative events (e.g., Hayden 1995; Hayden and Gargett 1990; Trigger 2003:375). Consequently, adequate resources necessary to generate a surplus are a must, whatever the reasons for political change (Engels 1964 [1957]:274–275). While material factors have varying roles in the emergence of rulership, material resources undeniably are required to support the political economy. Promoters attract supporters and simultaneously create obligations that last beyond the time frame of rituals. This strategy results in long-term material benefits (e.g., debt relations). "A man possesses in order to give. But he also possesses by giving. A gift that is not returned can become a debt, a lasting obligation . . ." (Bourdieu 1990:126, 1977:191–195). These public events thus promote the production of surplus (Hayden 1995; Hayden and Gargett 1990) and enable political agents to acquire it.

As briefly mentioned, the first political agents likely come from founding family stock; their wealth, as descendants of first-comers of any given area and owners of prime land or other resources, allows them to sponsor community or small-scale public rites. These actions result in obligations whereby sponsors materially come out ahead. The scale on which rituals can be performed and the amount of surplus acquired vary in any given area.

The obligations created are not just unidirectional. With leadership come duties and responsibilities. Rulers now are obligated to take care of those who, at one level, pay for their services and protection (e.g., Leach 1970 [1954]:187). They are duty-bound to help clients or subjects in times of trouble and need. Failing to fulfill obligations or violating subjects' trust can result in the "contract" becoming null and void (Scott 1990:104). Finally, rulers' power may be limited or constrained to some degree because of the challenges of living up to the "idealized presentation of themselves to their subordinates" (p. 54). For example, regarding the relationship between serfs and their aristocratic masters in feudal Europe, James Scott (1990:104; emphasis in original) writes:

> . . . it would be important to understand how their claim to hereditary authority was based on providing physical protection in return for labor, grain, and military service. This "exchange" might be discursively affirmed in an emphasis on honor, noblesse oblige, bravery, expansive generosity, tournaments and contests of military prowess, the construction of fortifications, the regalia and ceremony of knighthood, sumptuary laws, the assembling of serfs before their lords, exemplary punishment for insubordination, oaths of fealty, and so forth. The feudal "contract" could be *discursively negated* by any conduct that violated these affirmations: for example, cowardice, petty bargaining, stinginess, runaway serfs, failures to physically protect serfs, refusals to be respectful or deferential by serfs, and so forth.

In this and other cases, problems can arise when nonelites buy into an elite or royal ideology more than elites or royals themselves do (p. 104).

In sum, while various ways of acquiring political power exist, the general processes of situating change typically do not; and a material foundation (namely, surplus goods and labor) is required. Ritual expansion occurs in tandem with political change, both of which are funded by surplus goods and services. Rit uals express and explain the changes occurring through familiar means. Ritual thus is not a source of political power in the same manner as the military, economy, and ideology but rather advances political agendas based on these intersecting sources of power. It allows people to redefine the worldviews and codes of social behavior that explain "why specific rights and obligations exist" (Earle 1997:8, 143–158; see Blanton et al. 1996; Wolf 1999:55). After all,

> . . . the same rite should seem to produce multiple effects while keeping the same components and structure. . . . Conversely, just as a single rite can serve several ends, several rites can be used interchangeably to bring about the same end. . . . What matters most is that individuals are assembled and that feelings in common are expressed through actions in common. But as to the specific nature of these feelings and actions, that is a relatively secondary and contingent matter. (Durkheim 1995 [1912]:390)

I have described how the politically ambitious use ritual to serve political ends. But how does this process occur?

Ritual and Political Change

Traditional power has on its side the force of habit; it does not have to justify itself at every moment, nor to prove continually that no opposition is strong enough to overthrow it. Moreover, it is almost invariably associated with religious or quasi-religious beliefs purporting to show that resistance is wicked.
RUSSELL (1938:38)

Rulers incorporate traditional beliefs and practices into more elaborate forums to situate political change using culturally familiar means. History has shown that the most successful rituals derive from the home (e.g., Bloch 1986). Needless to say, rituals sponsored and performed by rulers serve to integrate larger numbers of people than could ceremonies conducted in the home. However, rulers do not replace or restrict them. Consequently, public ceremony promotes solidarity, not to mention political agendas (Kertzer 1988; e.g., Joyce 2004). Ritual expansion occurs in tandem with growing political inequality. Rulers eventually link their rule with the continuance of vital elements of life such as fertility and rain (Rappaport 1999:281). They are looked to as munificent providers of plenty but are also blamed during periods without plenty (Lincoln 1994:207). The obvious, conspicuous displays of "wealth, material resources, mass approval or record-high productivity all tangibly testify to the fruitful fit between the particular social leadership and the ways things should be" (Bell 1997:129).

Pierre Bourdieu (e.g., 1977, 1990), Anthony Giddens (e.g., 1979, 1984), and others emphasize the importance of the dynamic relationship between structure (material and social) and practice. Structure provides choices and constraints or limits within which individuals practice or act but does not determine behavior. This flexible structure leaves the door open for variability and change. Hence, different but culturally acceptable behavior feeds back into the structure, transforming it. Consequently, the process of social change can be, and often is, incremental and typically comes from *within* a social group (Giddens 1979:223, 1984:247). As actions are imitated and reproduced, agents can affect change. Traditional rituals serve as an ideal forum for emerging rulers to insert and justify their own political agendas

> . . . just *because* of [their] conservative properties. New political systems borrow legitimacy from the old by nurturing the old ritual forms, redirected to new purposes. (Kertzer 1988:42; emphasis in original)

> Memories associated with . . . earlier ritual experiences color the experience of a new enactment of the rites. Rites thus have both a conservative bias and innovating potential. (Kertzer 1988:12)

Invoking ties to the past makes new ideas or change appear traditional (Bell 1997:149); they "contextualize and subordinate the current moment, thereby ordering the relations of the past and present and establishing a sense of continuity, security, and direction" (p. 168). Changes thus are "reconciled with tradition" (Pauketat 2000:123). These rituals are successful because they incorporate the same familiar traditional practices into more elaborate and larger settings to situate the growing political power of particular interest groups (cf. Bourdieu 1990:109–110; Flannery 1972; Weber 1958 [1930]:55). "[M]any of the originators of the changes in the ritual were conscious of the political implications of what they were doing, and that this motivated what they did" (Bloch 1986:162). For example, the Merina circumcision ritual basically remained unchanged (p. 122). There were some new elements, however, that identified it as a state ritual (e.g., a schedule and required fee/tax) (p. 115). A less successful alternative is abrupt or extreme change. Such actions are much less likely to succeed because new ideas, beliefs, and practices are too foreign and thus unacceptable. For example, the first emperor of China, Ch'in Shih Hwang Ti,

> . . . made an abrupt attempt to replace the prevailing Confucianist political philosophy, which emphasized moral precepts as the basis for social tranquility of the state, with a strongly pragmatic legalist doctrine backed by centrally administered, coercive force. . . . This attempt was an abject failure and

resulted in the destruction of the emperors' administration and dynasty after only 15 years. (Webster 1976:824)

Another well-known example comes from ancient Egypt. For a brief time in the late Eighteenth Dynastic period, a "heretic" king, Akhenaten, ruled Egypt (1353–1335 BC) (Kemp 1991:262–273). His claim to fame, or infamy, is that he implemented major religious reform by rejecting the human form of the sun cult (Amun or Amun-Ra) and replacing it with the sun disk, the Aten, a "disk from which many rays descended, each one ending in a little hand" (p. 262). Images of Amun, as well as other gods from the vast Egyptian pantheon, were defaced. Akhenaten established a novel temple format with open courtyards filled with altars; this contrasted with the traditional temple layout, where priests "wrapped the image of god in darkness and secrecy" (p. 262). Akhenaten also confiscated temple estates, where priests had become increasingly wealthy and powerful (White 1971 [1949]:246–248). Akhenaten and his court left the traditional religious capital of Thebes to build a new one, Akhetaten or "Horizon of the Aten" (known today as El-Amarna) (Kemp 1991:266–267). Akhenaten and his wife and consort, Nefertiti, were depicted as gods alongside the Aten as sole intermediaries, which further extended the pharaoh's power (Kemp 1991:265). However,

> . . . the Aten robbed Egyptians of a tradition of explaining the phenomena of the universe through an extraordinary rich imagery . . . which managed to contain the concept that a unity, a oneness, could be found in the multiplicity of divine forms and names. Akhenaten was telling the Egyptians something that they knew already, but in a way that made further speculation pointless. It is easy to understand why the Egyptians rejected the king's religion after his death. He had tried to kill intellectual life. (p. 264)

Soon after Akhenaten's death during his seventeenth year of rule, his successor, Tutankhamun, returned to "religious orthodoxy" and reestablished traditional temple cults and estates (e.g., Amun at Karnak) (Kemp 1991:267). Egyptians destroyed most of Akhenaten's monuments and basically erased much evidence of his rule from history; when he was referred to, he was "that enemy from Akhetaten" (p. 267). Within 100 years, Akhetaten was abandoned (p. 272).

In contrast, successful political leaders incorporate existing "principles of legitimation" (Earle 1989) but do not *expropriate* them. For example, T'ang (AD 618–906) imperial rites in China originated from earlier dynastic ones (e.g., Chou, 1121–220 BC) that themselves derived from earlier ancestral cults (McMullen 1987). These Confucian-sanctioned rites were central to the T'ang political system for both its origin and continuance, especially in the face of increasing royal control over critical resources (cereal and rice fields) and increasing taxation. Everyone, though, continued to conduct domestic ancestral rites privately. Imperial ancestral ceremonies, however, were conducted publicly on a much grander scale. Chinese emperors replicated and expanded household rites but did not restrict or replace them. All members of society conducted similar ancestral rites—from farmers and local bureaucrats to the emperor—with increasing grandeur and scale. Of course, they added new elements to traditional formats (e.g., the fact that they have the mandate of heaven), which were accepted because of the familiar format used.

The successful application of acceptable family or domestic rites increases the prestige of sponsors and legitimizes political authority, including rulers' monopolization of large amounts of land and their ability to acquire surplus from others (Bourdieu 1977:183–184, 1990:109–110; Cohen 1974:82; Giddens 1979: 1881–1895, 1984:257–261). Such rituals integrate larger numbers of people than the small-scale household or community rites from which they derive. For example, when Enga Big Men of precolonial Papua New Guinea became increasingly involved in external exchange networks, the growing wealth differences were situated within traditional ancestor and bachelor cult rituals (Wiessner and Tumu 1998:369).

When rulers sponsor public rites (e.g., feasts and ceremonies), they touch emotions (Bell 1997:73–74; Rappaport 1999:49, 226). Such feelings tend to dissipate afterward. Political actors thus use strategies that result in long-term benefits; key factors are content, repetition, and type of ceremony (Rappaport 1999:286), as well as the tangible symbols used (Helms 1998:166). Rulers typically associate themselves with rituals that revolve around vital elements of life such as rain, agricultural fertility, and ancestor veneration, conducted according to set schedules (ritual calendars) in special places (Cohen 1974:135). By directly associating themselves with natural forces of day-to-day life, rulers extend their influence beyond the duration of centripetal, integrative events.

Cross-culturally, rulership is associated with fertility, purification, and associated rites (Helms 1993:78–79). People believe rulers to have special powers (Ibn Khaldun 1967 [ca. 1382–1404]:319; Rappaport 1971, 1999:281; e.g., Geertz 1980:129–131); they are seen to have exclusive knowledge and skill and are viewed as closer to the supernatural realm (Friedman and Rowlands 1978; Helms 1998:74) or even as gods themselves. In time, they become directly involved in the continuity of natural forces (Frazer 1920 [1890]:51, 245–247). For example, after the 1905 revolution in Russia, Tsar Nicholas II discontinued many public ceremonies, including the annual blessing of the waters. The people "believed that the prayers purified the water. They blamed the outbreak of cholera occurring from 1908 to 1910 on the suspension of the ceremony" (Wortman 1985:

263). Similarly, in China the emperor played a major role in the regulation of the rivers; ". . . if the rivers broke the dikes, or if rain did not fall despite the sacrifices made, it was evidence—such was expressly taught—that the emperor did not have the charismatic qualities demanded by Heaven" (Weber 1964 [1951]:31).

Participation in public rites does not mean that people are automatons or that they are being hoodwinked; *"acceptance is not belief. . . . Acceptance . . . is not a private state, but a public act"* (Rappaport 1999:119–120; emphasis in original).

> Symbols, rituals, emblems, and names are powerful sources of social integration even if the members of a group do not attach the same meaning, motivation, or interpretation to them. Individuals are united in a community because they share signs and rituals, but they may share these things without sharing their meanings. (Lee 2000:151)

Public ceremony promotes solidarity and a sense of community, which is critical as part of evolving political relationships. How audiences respond to royal events can determine how successful they are (Inomata and Coben n.d.) and also create a situation where people contribute to their own subordination (e.g., Joyce 2000, 2004). "Performances communicate on multiple sensory levels, usually involving highly visual imagery, dramatic sounds . . . [resulting in a situation where] one is not being told or shown something so much as one is led to experience something" (Bell 1997:160). Rulers put on a show when they perform traditional rites. Commoners thus are not passive witnesses but active participants with a voice (e.g., Bell 1997:73; Houston and Taube 2000). Their goal is to reach gods and ancestors on behalf of the people to bring forth rain, bountiful crops, and so on. Thus, commoners benefit by attaining access to socially defined value-goods handed out at special events (food, objects, etc.) (Pauketat 2000). In addition, nonparticipation might be perceived as antisocial or noncompliance and result in social sanctions (e.g., ostracism, accusations of sorcery, and refused access to local resources).

> Religious nonconformity was an offence against the state; for if sacred tradition was tampered with the bases of society were undermined, and the favour of the gods was forfeited. But so long as the prescribed forms were duly observed, a man was recognised as truly pious, and no one asked how his religion was rooted in his heart or affected his reason. (Robertson Smith 1956 [1894]:21)

As illustrated by the T'ang rites mentioned above, however, domestic rituals never leave the home. Rulers replicate and expand them but do not replace or restrict them. People all participate in the larger-scale public ceremonies and their own small-scale private domestic rituals from which the former derived. Royal rites are superimposed on traditional ones (e.g., Godelier 1977:188), with new elements highlighting the special qualities of rulers (e.g., Chang 1983).

The fact that everyone, rich and poor, performs the same rites promotes solidarity and a sense of belonging (e.g., Bell 1997:123; Kertzer 1988:19). For example, in nineteenth-century Madagascar, all members of Merina society conducted new-year renewal ceremonies in which they called upon their ancestors to bless them (Bloch 1987). The same ritual bath was repeated in every household, from commoner to royal. These rituals, which took place at the beginning of the agricultural season, involved blessings from superior to junior, a feature that rulers expanded—from master to servant, ancestors to elders to children, father to son, to king to subjects. They not only served to legitimize authority but, more significantly, also provided a forum for advancing royal power, particularly after the often violent succession of a new king. In addition, gifts were presented from junior to senior, resulting in the king's receiving large amounts of tribute. Palace layout, cardinal directions, sacred places, and objects were also co-opted by Merina royals to emphasize their sanctified right to rule and common ties with their subjects (Kus and Raharijaona 1998, 2000).

Eventually, these series of events often result in the development of centralized systems where kinship ties are replaced with nonkin ties that take on the appearance of kinship relations and are later replaced by nonkin ties where pretense no longer is required (Cohen 1974:24; Earle 1997:4−6; Godelier 1977: 123), though patrimonial rhetoric can still be used (Blanton et al. 1996). Additionally, once they have a certain degree of power, rulers can create completely new and different rituals without ties to the past for public as well as private or restricted consumption. For example, early Frankish kings in the Middle Ages were anointed with the same oil used to baptize the first Christian Frank, St. Clovis (Giesey 1985). The king's first entrée into Paris was celebrated by enactments of the baptism of Clovis along his route. After 1550, however, the content of celebrations in Paris shifted to the king himself from earlier religious and historical themes. By the eighteenth century the entrée into Paris was dropped altogether, replaced by another set of rites revolving around the "cult of the Sun King." In this case, traditional rites were initially replicated, then expanded, and later transformed. When French kings acquired enough power (e.g., a standing army), they could replace earlier rites with both public and private/restricted ones: "*When a dynasty is firmly established, it can dispense with group feeling*" (Ibn Khaldun 1967 [ca. 1382−1404]:314; emphasis in original). However, the French continued to conduct traditional Catholic rites in their homes and local churches.

What factors set in motion monarchs' loss of power? Since the foundation of political power is surplus, long-term interference with surplus production and appropriation can and does bring down the political house of cards. Political elites lose their power because their rituals fail to reach the gods. Before addressing this question further, I define political collapse.

Demise of Political Power

Dynasties have a natural life span like individuals.

IBN KHALDUN (1967 [CA. 1382–1404]:343; EMPHASIS IN ORIGINAL)

George Cowgill (1988) has defined various types of collapse. In most cases, it involves "political fragmentation" whereby politically unified systems break down into their constituent parts (e.g., Mesopotamia, India, Egypt, and the Roman Empire). Great traditions, however, typically persist, as they did for long periods in Roman territories, Egypt, and Mesopotamia. Replacement also occurs, whereby new governments replace previous ones for various reasons, as was the case in Mesopotamia, Egypt, and France. In rare cases people abandon a region, as in some areas of the southern Maya lowlands and likely parts of southern Mesopotamia (Cowgill 1988; Tainter 1988:191). It is also rare when a political vacuum remains empty, which was the case in the southern Maya lowlands in the Terminal Classic period.

Norman Yoffee (1988) calls for a distinction between the collapse of "states" and the disappearance of "civilizations." In the former case, the political economy fails, resulting in a reversion to prestate organization or the replacement of one political hierarchy by another. For example, while centralized political systems of Egypt have changed hands for millennia, their subsistence base (the Nile and alluvium) has remained stable through present times (Kemp 1991:10–13). In the latter case, it is the disappearance of "great traditions," including writing systems and elite and royal symbols and monumental architecture. For example, Yoffee (1988; Baines and Yoffee 1998) details how variously sized political fortunes changed hands several times during the millennia but shows that the Mesopotamian "great tradition" persisted long after Mesopotamian political systems were replaced by foreigners in ca. 539 BC (Cyrus of Persia) until at least ca. AD 75.

Joseph Tainter (1988) also notes that collapse is not necessarily catastrophic, especially for the majority of people; usually only people in the upper political echelons and administrators are affected by political disintegration. Furthermore, collapse can be an adaptive mechanism when, for whatever reasons, the current system no longer works (p. 198). It is typically political histories that change or disintegrate, rather than traditions; the majority of people are rarely put out since, as mentioned above, political systems are superimposed on existing social and economic institutions, which typically long survive political systems. For example, based on their work at the Zapotec regional center of Río Viejo, Oaxaca, Mexico, Arthur Joyce et al. (2001) posit that nonelite farmers, if they did not have a direct role in the demise of the political elite, definitely made their feelings known after rulers fell from grace at the end of the Classic period. They reused royal monuments as building materials and subsistence tools (e.g., metates) and built their homes on the former royal acropolis.

For purposes of this study, a collapsed society can be defined as one that is "suddenly smaller, less differentiated and heterogeneous, and characterized by fewer specialized parts; it displays less social differentiation; and it is able to *exercise less control over the behavior of its members*" (Tainter 1988:38; emphasis added). The latter part of this statement is particularly significant—losing access to the labor of others, the reasons for which become apparent throughout this work.

Climate, Resources, and Political Histories

. . . a Prince who rests wholly on Fortune is ruined when she changes.
MACHIAVELLI (1994 [1514]:81)

In a fascinating series of studies, Carole Crumley (1993, 1994, 1995a, 2001) convincingly argues that the height of Roman power in Europe was facilitated by a stable climate pattern that favored an urban-rural lifestyle. This climatic period (ca. 300 BC–AD 250), called the Mediterranean climatic regime, consisted of hot and dry summers and rainy winters. Climate prior to this period was cooler and more seasonally unpredictable. Crumley suggests that the unstable climate episodes required more flexible subsistence, social, and political strategies, like those found before 300 BC in Celtic Europe. The Celts practiced agropastoralism, were somewhat mobile, and had a loose social structure. During Roman hegemony, also known as the Roman Climatic Optimum (300 BC–AD 250), the stable climate "facilitated urbanization [and] the homogenization of the landscape through the commoditization of rural produce . . ." (Crumley 1994:198) and sustained relatively "inflexible forms of governance" (p. 192), resulting in what Crumley (1995a:26) refers to as an "ecology of conquest." Climate change, when more unpredictable and cooler seasons predominated beginning in the late second century AD, resulted in consistent crop failures, hailstorm damage, and blight (Crumley 2001). The Roman Empire depended on agricultural surplus to feed the people of Rome and to fund the political economy. The loss of surplus resulted in the rug being pulled out from under Roman hegemony, a process exacerbated by other events of the time (e.g., foreign invasions). Finally, Celtic peoples, now free from Roman demands, did not and could not revert to the life they had led before 300 BC; different circumstances existed, much history had passed, and much knowledge about the natural landscape had disappeared, setting the stage for serfdom (Crumley 2003).

The period after the fall of the western Roman Empire became known as the Dark Ages (AD 400–900) (Gunn 1994), which really meant that there were not many written records, since the recording of dynasties, royal events, tribute lists, and so forth was unnecessary. The Dark Ages were followed by another favorable climatic regime (favorable for surplus production and appropriation, anyway), known as the High Middle Ages (AD 90–1250). Population "plummeted" in the Late Middle Ages (AD 1250–1450) with the "return of cool and moist summers" (Gunn 1994:94). Interestingly, Joel Gunn (1994:95) notes that when "Europe is blossoming, the Mayas retire to subsistence agriculture"—at least in the southern lowlands.

While the scenario in Europe might appear to hark back to formulaic cultural ecology (warmer, stable climate = inflexible political systems; and cooler, variable climate = flexible political systems), it does make sense in light of the available evidence, especially when taking into account historical and social factors. For example, community organizations, with flexible sociopolitical organization and plentiful resources, could more easily adapt in the face of climatic change. The same could not be said for centralized and integrative polities, which are less politically flexible. Local polities fall somewhere in between; consequently, specific historical circumstances largely determine their fate. In other words, different trajectories are set in motion by changing climate (e.g., Fagan 2004). The more powerful and inflexible they are, the harder they fall in the face of long climatic perturbations. While political systems may fail, fragment, or be replaced, average commoners are working to adapt their subsistence and settlement practices to changing conditions, a strategy that has been in place since the dawn of humanity.

Climate change also exacerbates other existing problems. For example,

> . . . the Sumerian, Akkadian, and subsequent civilizations in the Tigris and Euphrates River Basin in present-day Syria, Iraq, and western Iran, and the Indus, or Harappan, civilization in the Indus River Basin in present-day Pakistan and western India were all negatively impacted by deforestation, overgrazing, and salinity built up from long-term irrigation. (Hardesty and Fowler 2001:79)

These factors affect surplus production and hence political systems. Farmers in ancient Egypt did not have to face the problem of salinity, because "after the harvest in summer, the ground dried and cracked, enabling aeration to take place, which prevented water logging and the excessive accumulation of salt" (Kemp 1991:10). Since their political foundation was based on surplus fruits born of the Nile, however, inadequate flooding during dry years spelled trouble for pharaohs when famine and plagues spread throughout the land. Fekri Hassan (1994) plots the relationship between climate and political history and notes that periods of political instability largely resulted from low floods and drought. Dynasties weakened or failed altogether. Egyptologists refer to these times as intermediate periods.

A well-known biblical story emerged during one such period: the story of Joseph in the Book of Genesis (41–47). Several scholars place the story in the early part of the Second Intermediate period (1640–1540 BC), when Hyksos ruled Egypt for a time (Bright 1981:87). In the story Joseph, originally brought into Egypt as a slave, successfully interprets the pharaoh's dream signifying seven years of plenty followed by seven years of famine. Forewarning allowed the pharaoh to stockpile grain and thus be prepared when annual floods were inadequate and famine eventually spread throughout the land. In the first year of famine, people gave "money" and livestock in exchange for food. In the second and following years, when people's money and livestock were depleted, the people handed over their land and offered their labor in exchange for food and access to land they formerly owned. They still farmed the land they once owned but now owed a fifth of the crop to the pharaoh. I am sure that if the famine had lasted longer, eventually even the pharaoh's stockpile would have dissipated. They might have been able to feed their people with food acquired via trade, but eventually the surplus they needed for exchange would be depleted, as would their political power. Clearly, while climate change can result in political instability, it can also benefit the political savvy under certain conditions.

These examples clearly illustrate the critical role that climate patterns and change played in subsistence and political systems. How do these factors affect different political systems?

Communities and local polities are typically more stable and durable than centralized and integrative polities because they rely less on large-scale subsistence technology and rulers' capital and food stores and make fewer demands on resources. Nonetheless, in all situations there are circumstances that are beyond their control. The more flexible their social and political system, however, the better people can deal with, for example, changing climate or other drastic changes.

When noticeable change does occur, for whatever reason, it can affect political systems in various ways—they can fragment into their constituent parts, or governments can be replaced from within or with external forces (Cowgill 1988).[1]

Ritual and Political Collapse

Rituals are performed in all societies, whatever the political system. As Arthur Hocart (1970 [1936]:35) aptly notes, rituals existed long before governments. In community organizations elites sponsor feasts, performances, and religious rites and organize small-scale projects (e.g., building religious structures, terraces, and canals) to promote solidarity in the face of wealth differences. Household rites involve ancestors and fertility, both critical to their survival. In local polities, chiefs perform rituals in public arenas that involve chiefly ancestors as descendants of gods, as well as agricultural fertility, rain, and war gods. All members conduct similar rites in the home and community. In centralized and integrative polities, royal rites revolve around royal ancestors and the fact that they have the "mandate of heaven." Rulers conduct elaborate ceremonies and feasts in monumental settings including temples, stadiums, and arenas to attract and keep followers. Ceremonies also acknowledge the importance of other gods, especially those in the upper echelons of the supernatural hierarchy. Household and community rites continue to revolve around ancestors and traditional deities concerned with rain and crops. They are still quite important, especially since farmers are relatively economically self-sufficient and thus must rely more on their own ceremonies. Rulers, however, are the major players in reaching the supernatural world and highlight the perception that the continuance of their rule results in prosperity for them all.

In all political systems, ritual never leaves the home; and when rulers disappear or political dynasties are replaced, people continue to conduct the same rites in the same places they had since before the emergence of political leaders. Nor is there any doubt that ritual is critical for political power and survival. Rulers who associate their rule with the supernatural are successful in times of plenty. When food and/or water supplies diminish to the point where people are materially affected, however, rulers are the first to be blamed when their ceremonies fail. Clearly the gods no longer support rulers (Frazer 1920 [1890]:352; e.g., Helms 1998:168; Kaufman 1988). This failure might result in last-ditch efforts to reach the gods through even more elaborate rituals, which might actually hurt the system even more if surplus is being used to fund ceremonies rather than feed people.

Political power thus lasts as long as rulers demonstrate that their ceremonies successfully propitiate supernatural entities (Hocart 1970 [1936]:142–155). When they cannot, there is no longer any reason for farmers to contribute to political coffers:

> . . . beliefs vindicating the power of rulers also became limits on their power. If they ruled because they enjoyed the approval of forces greater than they, or

because they were wiser or more virtuous than their fellows, it followed that evidence of supernatural disapproval, or of folly or vice, vitiated their claims to general obedience. Gradually, the doctrines that conferred on them the ability to elicit obedience came in some cases to justify insubordination and even rebellion. Indeed, in time, the doctrines not only *permitted* such resistance to undeserving rulers; they were sometimes held . . . to *mandate* it. The security and power of the inner governing circles were thus weakened by the very principles that had once blocked challenges to their ascendancy. (Kaufman 1988: 226–227; emphasis in original)

For example, in China there is evidence as early as the Chou dynasty (1100–256 BC) of a "heaven's mandate" that related to whether or not kings were successful (Chang 1983:34). "[P]olitical dynasties fell because the king misbehaved and no longer deserved to rule. . . . The dynastic cycles . . . have nothing to do with the rise and fall of the civilization; it merely signifies the shifting political fortunes of specific social groups whose rulers gain or lose their claim to the moral authority to rule" (Chang 1983:35). A similar situation existed in Bali; J. Stephen Lansing (1991:109) discusses how temple priests and princes could lose the mandate of heaven if they were unable to amass the necessary labor and goods to sponsor large-scale rituals, which they could not do when water supplies were low.

The point is this: the power of rulers is closely tied to divine support, a relationship maintained through ritual and funded through surplus. When support is removed, so is their power.

In the next section I present a possible scenario as to the process of how political rulers emerge, how the majority of people participate in the creation of political obligations, and how political power is lost. The following scenario can (and does) occur at any time and place and serves as the framework for the present study.

A Scenario

History repeats itself.

In cases where farmers migrate to previously uninhabited areas (versus the autochthonous emergence of a farming lifestyle), first founders eventually distinguish themselves from newcomers by building larger houses and acquiring exotics. Everyone performs the same rites; elites, however, use more expensive items as offerings—they can afford to relinquish them forever. Elites compensate workers with prestige items, food, and/or access to resources. Workers must be well paid since they could choose to work for other elite families. Patrons sponsor ceremonies and feasts for workers, their families, and the entire community to show their gratitude and to attract more clients. These events provide a break from work, a time to socialize, and opportunities to exchange information and goods. Public ceremonies and feasts also provide elites a chance to increase their prestige in the eyes of farmers and other elites who compete for labor and prestige. Finally, these events allay conflict in the face of socioeconomic differences.

This story has been repeated again and again throughout time and space. The question becomes, when and how does equal compensation (choice) transform into tribute extraction (little or no choice)? That is, when do wealthy individuals or elites become rulers? When and how do patron-clients become ruler-subjects? Where necessary material conditions do not exist, of course, these questions are moot. But when they do, and historical circumstances are just so . . .

Initially, extensive farming provides enough food for everyone. Later, as more and more people move into any given area and population grows, farmers start to invest more effort and time in intensive strategies to produce greater yields. Kinship groups no longer can resolve disputes over land and water allocation since they often involve nonkin interactions. Nor can farmers protect themselves from outsiders without organized assistance. A greater reliance on domesticates makes farmers more vulnerable and dependent on rainfall, especially in the face of seasonal flood damage and drought. Elites with larger landholdings typically have more stored foods, which they dole out in times of need. Emerging leaders do not provide these services for free. Ambitious people realize that they can demand payment for use of their services, above and beyond what could be defined as equal compensation. Some acquire large landholdings—corporate or otherwise—from hungry or thirsty people who then become tenant farmers. They have to be careful, however, not to demand too much, or farmers could flee; in other words, farmers do have some leverage.

Leaders' chances are enhanced in areas with noticeable seasonal issues or problems. The story of Joseph in the book of Genesis illustrates this point quite well; after the seven-year famine, the pharaoh owned many means of production—in this case, fertile land. And this story is repeated again and again throughout history. When circumstances become favorable again, it is clearly due to rulers' successful supplication of gods and ancestors, which they do in increasingly grand forums by performing traditional rites and funding grand ceremonies and feasts ("bread and circuses"). These events provide a break from the hardships of daily survival and opportunities for leaders to illustrate their success in the eyes of their clients and fellow patrons. If famine lasts too long and food stores run out, however, people no longer can rely on rulers' ability to reach the gods.

A leader's success keeps people paying and keeps attracting others, including people who are persuaded to leave rival factions. To further increase the number of tax-paying members, political leaders use surplus acquired from others to support military incursions into neighboring polities; the goal is to conquer for access to more land and labor, not to kill people per se (other than enemy leaders, of course). More people require more food and water, and consequently they further rely on intensive agricultural regimes. While leaders may not own such systems or organize their actual construction, they do provide capital to rebuild them after damage caused by, for example, flooding. During famine, they also open their storage facilities, filled to the brim with food from their fields or from trade. Again, these services are not provided for free. Leaders continue to sponsor integrative events in large arenas to promote solidarity and a sense of belonging. Traditional rites writ large include new elements that highlight ruler's ability to reach the gods. Leaders also perform new rites that revolve around royal families for both public and private viewing.

Eventually, one powerful ruler arises above others in an area where seasonal fluctuations in water and food supplies exist and where people rely heavily on large-scale water/agricultural systems—as well as the plentiful agricultural land that supports their lifestyle and subjects. Farmers by this time do not have many options but to pay taxes. Avoidance and resistance are met with force. Blatant coercion, however, is unstable and potentially politically dangerous. Rulers must offset any negative feelings about their power over others by providing protection, food, and capital and sponsoring grand events. But commoners have to get something in return for their tribute (e.g., protection, capital, acknowledgement of social membership, or food and water in times of need). Maintaining a balance is the challenge. If demands are too much, farmers flee to a rival kingdom or, if possible, flee political demands altogether and live in more marginal areas. If demands are inadequate, rulers cannot fund the political economy.

Rulers distinguish themselves from others not only through living in palaces and owning a plethora of wealth items but also through having skilled artisans copy their likenesses onto public and private media—from rollout stamps and coins to massive and grandiose sculptures and buildings. Often kings make sure they are depicted alongside gods as if they, too, are divine. Everyone participates in ceremonies that revolve around the royal family to celebrate their divine or special status. Such rites are superimposed on traditional ones that everyone continues to perform, royal or not. They also integrate a large enough number of followers to require a recording system to keep track. If writing does not develop for economic matters (trade and taxes), it emerges to rewrite history to place rulers and their families in a better light than reality *post hoc facto*—that is, they successfully outcompete other elite families, who then become enemies, administrators, and/or local representatives.

All good things come to an end, however—the more monarchs depend on surplus provided by others for their bread and butter, especially in the face of seasonal vagaries, the more vulnerable they are to changing material conditions. As Crumley demonstrates, inflexible political and subsistence systems are less able to adapt to changing conditions. Rituals no longer work, and rulers fail in their supplications to supernatural entities. Close ties to the otherworld have pros and cons; pro when rain and food are plentiful, and con when they are not. Of course, farmers blame the ruler. After a king falls from grace, elite and non-elite farmers continue to conduct the same rites they always had before and during the appearance of rulers, which remained geared to surviving in a changing world.

Concluding Remarks

The approach taken in this work bridges the gap between studies on the emergence and demise of rulership by focusing on two factors—water and ritual. I attempt to show how emerging Maya rulers expanded family-scale rites (especially dedication, ancestor veneration, and termination rituals) into larger communal ceremonies as part of the process that drew seasonal labor from farmsteads to centers. This system worked for nearly a millennium. What happened to cause farmers to abandon their rulers? Why did rulers eventually fail to convince farmers to pay homage in the form of surplus goods and labor? The remainder of this book seeks to address these questions.

CHAPTER 2

Classic Maya Political Histories

No one questions the existence of powerful Classic Maya rulers in the south-ern Maya lowlands of present-day Central America (northeastern Chiapas, eastern Tabasco, southern Campeche and Yucatán of Mexico, north and cen-tral Guatemala, Belize, and western Honduras) (Figure 2.1). To appreciate their accomplishments, we need to understand the variety of political systems as well as the people who supported rulership via surplus goods and labor—common-ers. Farmers provided rulers' foods, goods, and the labor to work in their fields and to build their palaces, temples, and ball courts. Evidence for surplus above and beyond household and community needs is quite apparent in the archae-ological record—monumental buildings (temples, palaces, and ball courts), large-scale water systems (e.g., reservoirs), skillfully manufactured and labor-intensive wealth objects and inscribed and carved monuments, and the pres-ence of nonsubsistence producers (e.g., artisans and rulers and their families, retinues, and underlings). Maya kings could not have funded these activities without the support (surplus) of many others. While it is not possible at pres-ent to determine exactly how surplus was organized (equal compensation, cor-vée labor, or combinations of both), there can be little doubt that surplus labor was available and that kings were able to access it.

How did Maya rulers acquire surplus from others? What say did commoner farmers have? These questions are crucial in view of how the Maya lived on a day-to-day basis and what this meant for rulers who wanted, and needed, to in-teract and communicate with farmers to be able to appropriate surplus labor and goods. They also relate to how powerful Maya rulers became. Simply put, the most complex and powerful polities emerged in areas with the most notice-able seasonal rainfall concerns—not enough or too much—and large amounts of fertile land. Before focusing on the varied Late Classic Maya political sys-tems and histories at minor, secondary, and regional centers in Chapters 4, 5,

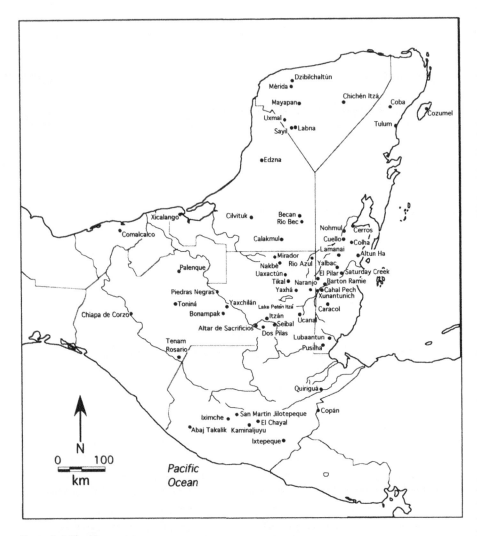

Figure 2.1. The Maya area

and 6, I briefly describe Maya subsistence and settlement, a history of Maya rulership, and characteristics that distinguish different centers.

Ancient Maya Living

Among the ancient Maya, as in other agricultural societies, the distribution of resources and people across the landscape affected the ability of rulers to interact with and integrate people and expand the political economy. Farmers used varied agricultural techniques to grow maize, beans, and squash, including house gardens, short-fallow infields, and long-fallow outfields, or combinations thereof (Flannery 1982; Harrison and Turner 1978; Killion 1990). Maya agriculture was rainfall-dependent, and farmers used various water or agricultural systems including *aguadas*, artificial reservoirs, raised fields, dams, canals, and terraces (Dunning et al. 1997). The majority of farmers lived in farmsteads (one to five structures facing an open area or patio) dispersed throughout the hinterland, as well as near or in centers, mirroring scattered pockets of fertile land (Dunning et al. 1998; Fedick and Ford 1990; Ford 1986; Rice 1993; Sanders 1977). Many farmers also seasonably inhabited field houses away from their homes (e.g., Lucero 2001:35–38; Webster et al. 1992). In addition, farmers searched for new land in the face of population growth and competition over land (Ford 1991a; Tourtellot 1993). Finally, it appears that scattered hinterland settlements were largely economically self-sufficient (Lucero 2001). Something then had to bring farmers and other subsistence producers to centers and get them to pay taxes, so to speak. It was not stored food, since centralized or large-scale storage facilities are unknown in the southern Maya lowlands (Lucero n.d.a). The average farmer probably did what the Lacandon of highland Chiapas do at present; farmers collect corn every few days from their fields as needed (McGee 1990:36). They turn the ears of corn downward to prevent damage from rain and pests (e.g., birds).

Maya political agents were faced with integrating a dispersed, relatively self-sufficient populace, and one that may have been somewhat seasonally mobile. Traditionally, Maya move their families around for several reasons. For example, during the agricultural season in San José, Lake Petén Itzá, Guatemala, many farmers live in their field houses away from their village homes; the size and distance of milpa fields determine whether they stay just during the week (49%, *n* = 39) or move their entire families to the field for the duration of the growing season (11%, *n* = 9) (Reina 1967). This strategy is often necessary due to the demands of agriculture; for example, in the Lake Petén Itzá area, fields are first cleared (cutting can be easier during the rainy season when vegetation is green; Faust 1998:153) and then burned at the end of the dry season. The Maya plant seeds at the beginning of the rainy season, after which the most intensive labor is required for daily maintenance (e.g., weeding) when crops are growing (Reina 1967; see also Atran 1993).

Ruben Reina (1967) also notes that farmers abandon field houses every three to four years when crop productivity decreases in search of more fertile land. Betty Faust (1998:56–57) describes a similar pattern for the Maya in Pich, in the southeastern Yucatán; each family group has rights to two or three *rancherías* (field houses). Each field is planted for about two years and left fallow for fifteen to twenty years. Consequently, each household could conceivably build at least three field houses, if not more, during the course of a generation. Faust (1998:82) also found that people migrated in search of water:

> ... oral histories collected from 1985–1992 indicate that normal yearly fluc-
> tuations just result in temporary migration to relatives in neighboring villages
> that have more reliable wells. . . . These same oral histories refer to processes
> of village fission, where groups of young people leave to look for existing
> ponds (which possibly were abandoned reservoirs of former occupied settle-
> ments) near good soil, where they can begin new hamlets.

Seasonal and residential mobility occurred during the Colonial period too (e.g., Farriss 1984:199–223; Graham 1994:325; Tozzer 1941:90). Social and political factors also can result in migration; for example, migration was an effective strategy to escape Spanish demands in colonial Mexico (Fox and Cook 1996). The point of this brief presentation of historic and ethnographic cases of seasonal and residential mobility is to highlight the fact that these processes also likely took place in the more distant past—especially to meet dry-season water needs. Thus, even if the majority of prehispanic Maya farmers were involved in intensive agricultural and permanently settled in hinterland areas, the need for water may have drawn them into centers.

Nearly everything in Maya life was rainfall-dependent (e.g., Scarborough 2003). The annual dry season, up to six months long, had to be a concern, especially in areas without surface water. While the dry season was an agricultural down-time for the most part (usually January through May or June), people still required water for daily drinking needs, not to mention for cooking maize and other food preparation, making plaster and ceramics, bathing, and other activities. When the southern Maya lowlands became a green desert each year, water was vital and became a key factor in the emergence of political power in many, if not most, areas (Lucero 1999b). People relied on artificial reservoirs (e.g., Ford 1996). For example, Vernon Scarborough (2003:51; Scarborough and Gallopin 1991) shows that the water catchment system at Tikal could collect more than 900,000 m^3 of water (based on 150 cm of annual rainfall). The central precinct reservoirs (six) alone could hold from 100,000 to 250,000 m^3 of water. Using the estimate suggested by Patricia McAnany (1990) that each person needs 4.8 liters of water daily (which includes water for drinking, washing, making ceramics, cooking, and other daily requirements), we can estimate how many people Tikal's reservoirs potentially serviced. There are several estimates for Tikal's population, including the periphery; William Haviland (2003) suggests about 45,000 people, while T. Patrick Culbert et al. (1990) suggest up to 62,000. Given that 1 m^3 is equal to 1,000 liters, 45,000 to 62,000 people would require, for a period of six months, from 38,880,000 to 53,568,000 liters or

38,880 to 53,568 m^3 of water. These figures do not take into account other types of reservoirs at Tikal (residential and *bajo*-margin reservoirs and *aguadas*) (Scarborough and Gallopin 1991) or other types of activities that require water (e.g., agricultural activities and building projects). However, this brief exercise does illustrate the potential number of people who could have used royal reservoirs at Tikal (and other centers).

Hinterland farmers may have had another option than relying on royal reservoirs: spring wells. Kevin Johnston (2004b) suggests that some Maya in the Petén dug wells at fault springs, which he found to be the case at Itzán (which is less than a kilometer from Laguna Itzán), Uaxactún, and Quiriguá. None of these sites, however, are regional centers. Adequate dry-season water supplies meant that rulers did not have the means to acquire much power. And in contrast to parts of the northern lowlands, the water table is too low to access water via wells in the southern Maya lowlands (McAnany 1990), except in a few instances (e.g., Quiriguá) (Ashmore 1984).

The wet season also brought its own suite of problems, especially flooding and hurricanes. While the prehispanic Maya did not settle directly in areas that flooded annually on the coast or the lower river terraces, tropical storms caused heavy damage to crops and water/agricultural systems everywhere, as they do at present (e.g., Hurricane Katrina). Farmers repaired small-scale systems on their own. Large-scale ones, however, required organization and capital to repair, something that Maya kings provided (Lucero n.d.b).

A final seasonal issue that had an impact on farming schedules is when the rainy season actually began. In any given area in the lowlands, the beginning of the rainy season could vary by up to five months, and the annual rainfall also varied (Gunn et al. 2002). If the rains came later than expected, planted seeds rotted. If they began earlier than usual, seeds did not germinate. And there was always the risk that farmers might not burn their milpa fields early enough before the rains began; wet brush does not burn easily, if at all.

I contend that Maya kings provided water during annual drought through maintaining water systems and/or provided capital when water/agricultural systems and crops were lost to storm gods. Rulers brought people together by sponsoring public events that derived from household, agricultural, and water rituals that highlighted their special abilities in reaching gods and ancestors. As a result of this strategy, common farmers participated in creating their own subordination, not to mention debt relations.

History of Maya Rulership

The Preclassic (ca. 1200 BC–AD 250)

The Middle Preclassic (ca. 1200–250 BC) is characterized by the migration of Maya peoples into formally unoccupied inland areas (e.g., the Petén) from riverine or coastal areas (Ford 1986:59, 80–82).[1] Tikal and its core area, located in the deep interior of the Petén, were one of the last regions settled. This area has some of the richest agricultural soils in the tropical world but has limited water sources; some scholars suggest that some *bajos* (seasonally inundated swamps) at one time may have been perennial wetlands or even lakes, which may have silted up due to erosion by the beginning of the Classic period (e.g., Culbert 1997; Dunning et al. 1998, 2003, n.d.; Hansen et al. 2002; Pope and Dahlin 1989). Either way, as populations grew, water became a concern.

The earliest southern lowland Maya elites or wealthy families emerged in the Middle Preclassic (ca. 900 BC) as first founders. We also see the first appearance of Olmec iconography, which has implications for rulership later on. Everyone, rich and poor, conducted domestic rites (e.g., at Cuello; Hammond and Gerhardt 1991; Hammond et al. 1991). And the first lithic "eccentrics" appear during this period (McAnany 1995:46). Eventually elites organized the building of monumental architecture, including small temples, often with masks flanking staircases (e.g., Cerros), ball courts (e.g., Nakbé), and platforms (e.g., Cerros, Nakbé, Cuello, Lamanai, El Mirador) (Freidel and Schele 1988; Hammond et al. 1991; Hansen 1998; Marcus 2003; Matheny 1987; Pendergast 1998).

The Maya, however, built water/agricultural systems even before they constructed monumental architecture (Scarborough 1993). The earliest known water systems in the southern Maya lowlands (ca. 1000 BC) are found in northern Belize and consist of "shallow ditches draining the margin of swamps" (Evans and Webster 2001:354; Scarborough 2003:50). Their construction accelerates after 1000 BC, when Maya began to migrate into inland areas lacking permanent water sources. Water systems include wetland reclamation (e.g., Cerros) and "passive" or concave micro-watershed systems where the Maya took advantage of the natural landscape, particularly depressions (e.g., El Mirador, Petén) (Scarborough 1993). Water symbolism also appears in the Preclassic and is associated with early public monumental architecture (Scarborough 1998).

In the Late Preclassic period (ca. 250 BC–AD 250), high-ranking lineages were transformed into royal ones, when rulers may have assumed shamanistic characteristics to mediate between people, ancestors, and gods and became ritual specialists par excellence (Freidel et al. 1993; cf. Stuart 1995:188). Virginia Fields (1989:6) has demonstrated that "the thematic content of the primary symbols of Maya rulership (i.e., royal regalia and titles), whose imagery was rooted in the natural world, reveals a continuity with more ancient Mesoamerican culture [i.e., Olmec]." These include "the depiction of rulers as seated (also embodied in the 'seating' glyphic expression for accession), the use of jaguarian imagery to express rulership . . . and the 'maize headband,' which, as the Jester God, becomes a primary icon of rulership among the lowland Maya" (p. 98). The use of the headband suggests to Karl Taube (1995) that Maya kings performed agricultural and rain-making rites.

Centers like El Mirador and Nakbé arose during this time, only to be abandoned by the end of the Preclassic, perhaps because of failed water-management systems as a result of silting-up (Hansen et al. 2002; Scarborough 1993), drought (Gill 2000), or subjugation by more powerful polities (Marcus 2003). If there were perennial wetlands and/or lakes, they also silted up as a result of erosion (e.g., Hansen et al. 2002). Monumental architecture became more standardized (Hansen 1998). For example, the E-Group assemblage makes its debut (Chase and Chase 1995). The first elite tombs also appear in the Late Preclassic (Krejci and Culbert 1995). Inscriptions focused on ceremonial events (e.g., accession), which were carved or painted on portable objects rather than on public monuments (Mathews 1985; Schele and Miller 1986:109). Individuals were not yet depicted, though the term *ahaw* (lord, ruler) appeared by the first century BC. The first recorded royal dynasties were founded in the first century AD, at least retrospectively (Grube and Martin 2001).

The Early Classic (ca. AD 250–550)

The Early Classic is characterized by increasing population shifts (e.g., to centers in some areas and abandonment of others) and growth (Adams 1995; Rice 1996). Bruce Dahlin (1983) notes the appearance of defensive works, especially in the northeastern lowlands (e.g., Becan; Webster 1977).

Water storage, especially artificial reservoirs, became particularly important in the Early Classic (ca. AD 250–550), when Maya farmers continued to move into upland areas with fertile land but with few, if any, permanent water sources (e.g., Tikal). Even people living close to rivers such as Río Copán and Río Azul began to build reservoirs and other water systems (Fash and Davis-Salazar n.d.; Harrison 1993).

This period witnessed full-blown Maya rulership. Inscriptions shifted from a focus on ceremonial bloodletting to individual rulers (Mathews 1985; Pohl and Pohl 1994). Genealogical succession and the role of *ahaw* were firmly established. This fact is ornately portrayed on free-standing public monumental sculpture (stelae and altars), including the first appearance of rulers holding the manikin scepter, a staff symbolizing rulership (Freidel and Schele 1988; Stuart

1996). The Maya built the first royal architectural features (e.g., hieroglyphic stairways and palace complexes) at regional centers, including Copán (Fash 1998), Tikal (Jones 1991), and Palenque (Barnhart 2001). This period "was characterized by states with palaces, standardized two-room temples arranged on platforms in groups of three, royal tombs, and a four-tiered settlement hierarchy . . ." (Marcus 1998:61).

The earliest rulers arose at regional centers such as Calakmul and Tikal (Marcus 1993) and later at secondary centers. Kings conflated the traditional practice of ancestor veneration with rulership (Gillespie 2000b; McAnany 1995:227). Early Classic deposits became much more diverse in terms of quality, form, and quantity in elite and royal contexts but remained largely the same for nonelite deposits. Rulers emphasized the importance of royal ancestors in the lives of everyone and their close ties to important deities (rain, maize). They conducted ceremonies on palace platforms and the top of tall, multitiered temples overlooking audiences in large plazas. Rulers resolved the increasing numbers of disputes arising over land and water allotment. Corporate kinship relations were no longer adequate to adjudicate disputes involving resources. Kings (for example, at Tikal and Copán) also incorporated foreign themes such as the central Mexican non-Maya rain god, Tlaloc, and other elements from Teotihuacan (Fash 1998; Schele and Miller 1986:213) that demonstrated their esoteric ties and knowledge. Inscriptions tell of monumental building dedications (Schele and Freidel 1990). They also mention conquests and the capture of royal persons, royal visitations, heir accession, bloodletting, and period-ending rites (e.g., *katun* or twenty years at Tikal, Copán, Yaxchilán, Altar de Sacrificios, and Piedras Negras). Competition between centers became more obvious, as reflected in the iconography, where military themes start to appear (Mathews 1985; Stuart 1993, 1995:133).

"A political breakdown (known as 'the hiatus') characterized some, but not all, Petén sites during the Middle Classic, AD 534−593 . . ." (Marcus 1998:61; Pohl and Pohl 1994), which likely indicates fluctuating political histories, not to mention shifting labor pools (Lucero 1999b). Throughout the Early Classic, competition between centers increased for control over labor, exemplified by the increasingly hostile relations of Tikal, Calakmul, Caracol, and other centers (Chase and Chase 1989).

The Late Classic (ca. AD 550–850)

The Late Classic is characterized by increasing population (Rice 1996), competition, and warfare. Inscriptions leave little doubt as to the prevalence of warfare throughout the Late Classic (Stuart 1995:133, 304), at least in the written records. Victorious Maya kings won over the labor pools of vanquished rulers because of their success on the battlefield.

Water management reached its height in sophistication and scale in this period, epitomized in convex macro-watershed systems where reservoirs, dams, and channels were designed to capture and store water (e.g., Tikal, Caracol) (Scarborough 1993, 2003:50–51; Scarborough and Gallopin 1991). This pattern is mirrored in other water/agricultural systems as well (e.g., Harrison and Turner 1978).

This period witnessed the florescence of political power and royal public rituals, not to mention the continuation of traditional rites in the home. Inscriptions include the elevated status *k'ul ahaw* (divine or holy lord) (Houston and Stuart 1996; Stuart 1995:189). Inscriptions and iconography also amply illustrate that Classic Maya rulers had close connections to important Maya deities (e.g., lightning's power, ancestral spirits) and to the otherworld (e.g., Marcus 1978; Peniche Rivero 1990; Schele and Freidel 1990). Rulers often impersonated gods (Houston and Stuart 1996), and their names embodied some of their qualities—for example, K'inich (Sun god) Balam (Jaguar) of Palenque. Other inscriptions tell of "house censing" or "house burning" (Stuart 1998) and illustrate the proliferation of royal or nondomestic rites, in addition to pan-Maya ones, that included ball games, royal marriages, period-ending rites, royal anniversaries, royal visitations, heir accession, sacrifice of royal captives, bloodletting, and other rites not yet understood (fish-in-hand, flapstaff) (Gossen and Leventhal 1993; Schele and Freidel 1990; Schele and Miller 1986). Late Classic ritual deposits demonstrate great diversity in terms of form, quality, and quantity—at elite and royal structures at least. The most powerful kings were entombed in funerary temples facing large plazas that could hold thousands of people (McAnany 1995:51).

Scenes on Late Classic polychrome vessels depict royal rites and ritual dances taking place "on the spacious stairs and upper terraces of the palace complex" (Reents-Budet 2001:202). These buildings faced plazas where large numbers of people could watch and participate in ceremonial events. Scenes on vessels and other iconography also depict feasts, banquets (Reents-Budet 2001), and tribute payments to rulers (Stuart 1995:365). Such payments are "often represented by *Spondylus* shells attached to heaped mantles" and "quantities of cacao beans" as well as "heaps of tamales and bowls of pulque" (Houston and Stuart 2001:69). Rulers were also depicted alongside gods, indicating their near-divine status: "These symbols of supernatural identity strongly suggest that rulers had significant priestly functions in the making and celebrating of stations of the calendar, a function that was central in defining their ritual responsibilities . . ." (Stuart 1995:199).

The Terminal Classic (ca. AD 850–950)
and Early Postclassic (ca. AD 950–1200)

The Terminal Classic is characterized by "disintegration," whereby the Maya abandoned most centers (see Demarest et al. 2004b). At an early stage, however, smaller centers started to build monuments on their own or, more specifically, independent of major centers (Marcus 1976; Pohl and Pohl 1994). For example, rulers of the small centers of Ixlú and Jimbal, formerly subordinate to Tikal, both proclaimed themselves K'ul Mutal Ahaw (in AD 879 and AD 889, respectively), a title once only used by Tikal's rulers (Valdés and Fahsen 2004). Farmers left centers—more specifically rulers—or migrated out of the southern Maya lowlands altogether. In addition, architectural evidence from the Petén lakes region suggests a different type of sociopolitical organization or reorganization (Rice 1986). Access to private royal palaces was no longer restricted; there were no large funerary monuments. The majority of the last-dated monumental construction also occurred at this time (e.g., Tikal, AD 869; Piedras Negras, AD 810; Bonampak, AD 790; Yaxchilán, ca. AD 810). And the last known inscriptions at many centers (e.g., Yaxchilán, Palenque, Piedras Negras, etc.) all involve military themes. "At the very moment that cities like Tikal were collapsing, others in Belize (such as Lamanai) and in the Puuc region of the Yucatán Peninsula were ascending to their greatest heights. . . . And when some cities in Belize and in the Puuc began to decline, there was a new surge in state formation and expansion, particularly in northern Yucatán . . ." (Marcus 1998: 62; e.g., Carmean and Sabloff 1996). Many Terminal Classic inscriptions no longer incorporated individual rulers or dynasties but instead emphasized deities (e.g., Chichén Itzá) (Wren and Schmidt 1991).

In addition to what was happening internally, Terminal Classic ceramics, stelae, and architectural evidence indicate that there was also an intrusion of some sort by non-Petén Maya (e.g., perhaps the Chontal Maya), for example, in the Petén lakes region (Rice 1986). Foreign or new/different elements, perhaps from Ucanal in the northeast (Tourtellot and Sabloff 2004), also start to appear in the iconography and architecture at Altar de Sacrificios and Seibal, especially the latter; they include "non-Classic Maya figures, long hair, strange costumes and regalia. . . . phallic 'Atlantean' dwarfs, a 'Toltec' prowling jaguar, a circular pyramid, ball courts, radial temples, causeways, a remote stela platform . . ." (Tourtellot and González 2004:61). David Stuart (1993) suggests, however, that they may represent a new social order where for the first time nonroyal personages were incorporated into monumental or public art, a further sign of changing times. The appearance of nonroyal personages in the iconography also occurred at centers not affected by foreign influences, such as Copán (Fash et al. 2004; Fash and Stuart 1991), which likely was related to the erosion of both resources and political power. However, there were definitely outside influences coming into the Maya lowlands that reflected a political system more susceptible to external penetration due to the increasing sociopolitical disintegration. Whatever the causes, it should be noted that centers that show "foreign" influences, such as Seibal (e.g., last dated monument—AD 889), Altar de Sacrificios (last date AD 849), and other southern centers, went through a period of florescence (albeit brief) when other areas in the interior Petén were crumbling (Culbert 1988; Sabloff 1992; Willey and Shimkin 1973).

In sum, the Terminal Classic period can be described as one where the seams of the political system were coming apart. This system, once supported by a large labor pool, collapsed without the support of people who now were migrating out to other areas or dispersing permanently into the hinterlands. A different story unfolds in the northern lowlands, which experienced a florescence from ca. AD 750 to 1000 (e.g., Carmean et al. 2004; Demarest et al. 2004a).

The Early Postclassic period in the southern Maya lowlands is characterized by smaller settlements; many, if not most, of them are found near permanent water sources. For example, the Maya continued to live in the Belize River valley, although not necessarily in centers (e.g., Ashmore et al. 2004; Lucero et al. 2004; Willey et al. 1965:292), other Belize valleys (e.g., McAnany et al. 2004), wetland areas in northern Belize (e.g., Andres and Pyburn 2004; Masson and Mock 2004; Mock 2004), and near lakes and rivers in the Petén (e.g., Laporte 2004; Rice and Rice 2004) and elsewhere (e.g., Fash et al. 2004; Johnston et al. 2001). For example, population shifted north to Chichén Itzá (Cobos 2004), likely attracted by better opportunities (e.g., trade) and a new ideology originally from central Mexico centered around Kukulcan, the feathered serpent. Trade became more focused on maritime routes involving both subsistence and exotic or prestige goods (e.g., salt production) (McKillop 1995, 1996).

The disintegration of the southern lowland Maya polities, embedded in ritual, water, and resources, also was expressed in the changing focus of public iconography, which is now largely found in the northern lowlands. During the Classic period, there were a number of gods particularly associated with the ruling elite, especially K'awil and God D (Itzamna) (Miller and Taube 1993:99; Taube 1992:31–42, 78; Thompson 1970:200–233). The main focus on Itzamna dramatically lessened with the political collapse, not surprisingly, since this was a god associated with divination, esoteric knowledge, and writing (Taube 1992: 31–40). This deity was also connected to the sun, rain, and maize gods (Thompson 1970:210) and, significantly, also had an evil side having to do with the destruction of crops. Thus, what we see in the Early Postclassic period is a different type of religious focus than the one found in the Classic period, which mirrored the political system it formerly legitimized—that is, semidivine rulers versus group rulership (*popol na* or council house) (Pohl and Pohl 1994).

To summarize the major points in Maya prehistory, notable trends include population growth (steady growth over a millennium; Deevey et al. 1979; Rice 1996) and shifts, changing political histories and competition, and the presence of ornate royal paraphernalia. At the household level, however, things pretty much remained the same, and domestic rites never left the home (e.g., Andres and Pyburn 2004). Political demands and royal rites had been superimposed onto existing systems that in some degree continue to this day. So for the common farmer what changed was the lifting, for a time, of the burden of paying tribute.

Water and Late Classic Maya Political Systems

The scale and degree to which Maya rulers and elites could expand rituals and political power at minor, secondary, and regional centers were largely conditioned by the amount and distribution of agricultural land, seasonal water vagaries, scale of water/agricultural systems, and settlement patterns (Lucero 1999b, 2002a, 2003). In general, kings acquired and maintained varying degrees of political power through their ability to provide water during the annual dry season and capital during the rainy season and to integrate farmers through ritual, especially dedication, ancestor veneration, termination, water, and other traditional rites.

Each center type can be viewed as part of a continuum. The model is a heuristic device to assess political histories at different Maya centers. The types are not static and impermeable; they are fluid and are only an attempt to separate the constituent parts of complex and dynamic systems. Each center has its own specific history; even though this is the case, all Maya, elite or not, lived in a tropical setting that had an impact on their social, economic, political, and religious lives. Structurally, center types are similar to those briefly presented in Chapter 1. The major difference is that in the Maya case we are dealing with one society in one major period. In many cases, centers can be viewed as nested hierarchies, though clearly the histories of how they relate to one another vary by type and particular circumstances. Consequently, some centers were independent entities and others were subsumed under larger polities. This being said, minor centers have features similar to those of community organizations, though typically larger-scale; secondary centers are the same as local polities, regional river centers the same as centralized polities, and regional nonriver centers the same as integrative polities. The factors used to define types (which are detailed in Chapters 4, 5, and 6) are similar to those in Chapter 1 and include resource distribution, elevation, annual rainfall, seasonal water issues, the presence of water or agricultural systems, settlement patterns and density, internal differentiation, leadership, resource access, territorial extent, external relations, political economy, conflict, interaction sphere, type and scale of monumental architecture, scale of integrative events, public iconography, the presence of writing and emblem glyphs, duration, and Terminal Classic events (Table 2.1). While I discuss some factors more than others, I include them all here to provide a more complete backdrop.

RESOURCE DISTRIBUTION: The location of centers with regard to water supply and concentrated, dispersed, or extensive agricultural land bears on population size and density, as well as whether or not resources could produce enough surplus to fund the political economy. Agricultural potential of soil is based on soil fertility, soil parent material, workability, root zone, drainage, slope, and erosion (Fedick 1996).

ELEVATION: This factor relates to precipitation, terrain, temperature, and agricultural soil type (Fedick 1996). It may also relate to whether or not wetlands were perennial or seasonal; for example, Kevin Pope and Bruce Dahlin (1989) note that perennial wetlands are more common in elevations below 80 m asl (above sea level).

ANNUAL RAINFALL: The amount and timing of seasonal rainfall affected agricultural schedules and settlement practices, factors that were critical since the Maya were rainfall-dependent.[2]

SEASONAL WATER ISSUES: Water shortages during annual drought were particularly problematic, which the political elite used to their advantage. Flooding, hurricanes, and other rain damage also affected settlement decisions, agricultural practices, and political power. The lack of obvious large-scale storage facilities indicates that Maya kings did not provide food during times of need, as was the case for other complex societies (D'Altroy and Earle 1985; Lucero n.d.a).

WATER OR AGRICULTURAL SYSTEMS. Artificial reservoirs, check dams, canals, terraces, *aguadas,* aqueducts, and ditches reflect local adaptive strategies, as well as the number of people they serviced. Their location (concentrated or dispersed) and scale (small or large) also reflect their role in politics. Small-scale systems are built and maintained at the household and/or community level; large-scale systems are funded or built, or at least maintained, by Maya rulers.

Table 2.1. Late Classic Maya political systems (ca. AD 550–850)

Scale	Community Organization: Minor Centers	Local Polities: Secondary Centers[a]	Centralized Polity: River Regional Center	Integrative Polity: Nonriver Regional Center
Resource Distribution	River, extensive alluvium	River, uplands with dispersed or limited agricultural soils	River, concentrated alluvium	No rivers, uplands with large tracts of dispersed agricultural land and artificial reservoirs
Elevation (m asl)	20–40	70–175[b]	Copán—550 Palenque—200	245–500
Annual Rainfall (cm)[c]	216	200–285	Copán—130 Palenque—370	167–210
Seasonal Water Issues	Annual inundation and recession; no known storage facilities; water plentiful year-round	Varies; seasonal vagaries—high and low; small-scale storage	Noticeable; small-scale storage	Noticeable; small-scale storage
Water/Agricultural Systems	None	Small-scale	Large-scale; responsibility of communities except reservoirs	Large-scale; responsibility of communities except reservoirs
Settlement Patterns and Density	Relatively dispersed and low settlement density; 100–150[d] str/km²	Slightly higher center density than hinterlands; 275[e] vs. up to 145 str/km²	High center density vs. hinterlands; 643–1,449[f] vs. 28–99 str/km²	High center and hinterlands density; 235–557[g] vs. 39–313 str/km²
Internal Differentiation	Household wealth differences	Household wealth differences and some political surplus	Household wealth differences and political surplus	Household wealth differences and political surplus
Leadership	Patrons, first founders	Secondary ruler	Primary ruler	Primary ruler

Resource Access	Elite landowners (but did not control means of production)	Provide capital when possible, domination of long-distance exchange	Capital/repair of large-scale water/agricultural systems; access to concentrated alluvium	Capital/repair of large-scale water systems
Territorial Extent	Community landholdings/usage—corporate?	Center and immediate hinterlands	Center, immediate hinterlands, and secondary and minor centers	Center, immediate hinterlands, and secondary and minor centers
External Relations	May or may not be subsumed under regional system	Hierarchical relations with larger polities, equal ones with other secondary centers	Equal and unequal inter-polity relations	Equal and unequal inter-polity relations
Political Economy	No tribute; labor compensated	Some tribute, compensation	Tribute	Tribute
Conflict	None—local feuding	Opportunistic conquest, elite warriors	Conquest for labor through alliance/royal battles; for prestige	Conquest for labor through alliance/royal battles; for prestige
Interaction Sphere	Local and nonlocal trade for utilitarian goods without elite interference; elite interaction: prestige-goods exchange	Elite and royal interaction (secondary): prestige-goods exchange, intercenter alliances, marriages, and warfare, and royal dynasties and rites; local and nonlocal trade for utilitarian goods without elite interference	Elite and royal interaction (primary): prestige-goods exchange, intercenter alliances, marriages, and warfare, and royal dynasties and rites; local and nonlocal trade for utilitarian goods without elite interference	Elite and royal interaction (primary): prestige-goods exchange, intercenter alliances, marriages, and warfare, and royal dynasties and rites; local and nonlocal trade for utilitarian goods without elite interference
Type and Scale of Monumental Architecture	Small temples and ball courts	Large ball courts, palaces, temples, some funerary temples	Large ball courts, private and administrative palaces, temples, funerary temples	Large ball courts, private and administrative palaces, temples, funerary temples

(continued)

Table 2.1. (*continued*)

Scale	Community Organization: Minor Centers	Local Polities: Secondary Centers[a]	Centralized Polity: River Regional Center	Integrative Polity: Nonriver Regional Center
Scale of Integrative Events	Household rites, community events (ceremonies, public works); small public areas	Household rites, community events, royal rites; large public areas	Household rites, community events, large-scale royal political/ceremonial events; largest public areas	Household rites, community events, large-scale royal political/ceremonial events; largest public areas
Public Iconography	No political iconography	Rulers and water imagery[h]	Rulers, supernatural world, and water imagery	Rulers, supernatural world, and water imagery
Writing and Emblem Glyphs	None	Highlights ties to regional centers; many have emblem glyphs[h]	Highlights royal events; all have emblem glyphs	Highlights royal events; all have emblem glyphs
Duration	Stable, long-lasting	Political system tied to external ties; subsistence system relatively stable	Political and subsistence systems stable as long as resources are stable	Required continual maintenance (integrative strategies); affected by fluctuations; subsistence system relatively stable

Terminal Classic Events	Not abandoned	Varies—relates to political ties and/or local resources; center abandoned, hinterlands not, or neither center nor hinterlands abandoned, or center briefly prospered; last inscribed dates: AD 761–909	Centers abruptly abandoned, gradual abandonment of hinterlands as resources diminish; last inscribed dates: AD 822–799	Centers abruptly abandoned, gradual abandonment of hinterlands as resources diminish; last inscribed dates: AD 810–869
Examples	Saturday Creek, Barton Ramie	Lamanai, Altar de Sacrificios, Yalbac, Piedras Negras, Quiriguá, Seibal, Yaxchilán, Xunantunich, Dos Pilas, Bonampak, Cuello, El Pilar, Toniná, Río Azul	Copán, Palenque	Tikal, Caracol, Calakmul[i]

[a]Some secondary centers may very likely turn out to be regional centers, particularly Yaxchilán and Piedras Negras. Numerous other centers fit into this category; the table lists only sites discussed in text.

[b]The elevation of Lamanai differs dramatically—15 m asl. It also has a unique history as it was occupied through colonial times until the seventeenth century.

[c]Most rainfall data are from Neiman (1997:Table 15.1).

[d]Lucero et al. 2004; Rice and Culbert 1990:Table 1.1.

[e]Ashmore 1990; Loten 1985; Rice and Culbert 1990:Table 1.1; Tourtellot 1990.

[f]Barnhart 2001:Table 3.1; Rice and Culbert 1990:Table 1.1; Webster and Freter 1990.

[g]Culbert et al. 1990; Folan et al. 1995. *Bajo* settlement typically accounts for lower densities.

[h]The presence of writing and rulers in public iconography at secondary centers differs from local polities as defined in Chapter 1. However, since I am dealing with the same society rather than different ones, this is not a concern.

[i]While I do not discuss Naranjo, it definitely would fall into this category; other nonriver centers where primary rulers did not emerge due to various historical (political) and material (less agricultural land) circumstances include, for example, La Milpa, Uaxactún, and so on.

SETTLEMENT PATTERNS AND DENSITY: How many people there were and in what manner they were distributed across the landscape affected the ability of leaders to incorporate and communicate with people, not to mention their ability to tap the surplus of others. Estimating population size in the southern Maya lowlands is a relatively contentious topic (see Lucero 1999a). For example, due to the high Late Classic population estimates proposed by some (e.g., Culbert and Rice 1990), Scarborough et al. (2003:xvi) "suggest that absolute village autonomy during the Classic period was not an option." However, as I have written and summarized elsewhere (Lucero 1999a), evaluating population size is difficult at best. The lack of refined chronologies (e.g., less than fifty years) does not help matters. Further, we need to take into account the movement of people through the landscape (e.g., seasonal mobility, migration) and structure function (e.g., percentage of specialized structures vs. domiciles such as workshops, religious structures, sweat houses, field houses, storages structures, kitchens, and administrative buildings). In addition, there are "invisible mounds," which are difficult to identify in the archaeological record (Johnston 2004b; Pyburn 1997). For present purposes, I use structure densities, a relative measure that is easier to compare among sites. Whatever the population size, there is no doubt that the highest population numbers and densities occurred in the Late Classic period (Rice and Culbert 1990).

INTERNAL DIFFERENTIATION: This factor distinguishes surplus resulting in wealth differences where elites compensated laborers for services rendered from surplus politically extracted without equal compensation.

LEADERSHIP: The more surplus one appropriated without equal compensation, the more powerful one was.

RESOURCE ACCESS: Monopolizing resources provided the necessary wealth to sponsor ceremonies and feasts and create obligatory relations through gift-giving (e.g., debt). Rulers also provided capital to repair public works damaged by the vagaries of weather gods (e.g., flooding and hurricanes).

TERRITORIAL EXTENT: How many people Maya kings politically incorporated from surrounding hinterlands and smaller centers illustrated the extent of their power, as well as providing an idea as to how much tribute they acquired (e.g., de Montmollin 1989:103).

EXTERNAL RELATIONS: This factor relates to the nature of ties with other rulers, whether or not center polities were autonomous (peer/equal or unequal) (e.g., Freidel 1986; Sabloff 1986). While not all relations are political in nature, the more frequent and widespread emblem glyphs and rulers' names were in the inscriptions, presumably the more powerful they were (Marcus 1976; Martin 2001).

POLITICAL ECONOMY: The amount of surplus that was extracted via taxation corresponds with political power.

CONFLICT: Incorporating more people resulted in more tribute and hence more political power. The scale and motives of Classic Maya warfare are also contentious topics in Maya studies (Webster 1998, 2000). Conditions in the southern Maya lowlands jungle—wet and dry seasons, lack of roads, no beasts of burden, no metal armaments, and travel issues—make it difficult to assess the nature of warfare (Webster 2002:223–228). Nor is there an obvious war god, though some gods appear to be associated with violent death and sacrifice (Taube 1992:148–149). However, Stuart (1995:361) notes the clear association of warfare and tribute in the hieroglyphic record. Some battles may have resulted in territorial gain (Culbert 1991; Marcus 2003), especially those fought between centers in close proximity to one another (e.g., in the Petexbatún area; Demarest 1997), but most likely consisted of struggles among elites to gain prestige in the eyes of their supporters (Webster 1998). Maya rulers could not provide much protection per se; commoners protected themselves by escaping to other areas or into the bush.

INTERACTION SPHERE: Elite interaction is expressed through prestige-goods exchange, whereas royal interaction is expressed through prestige-goods exchange plus intercenter alliances and marriages and royal dynastic rites. The way in which and degree to which elites and royals distinguished themselves reflect wealth and power. Interaction also included the exchange of goods between commoners in different communities or centers, typically free from elite interference.

TYPE AND SCALE OF MONUMENTAL ARCHITECTURE: This includes private and administrative palaces, temples (built in several stages over time), funerary temples (built in one major construction event as a tomb for a single ruler), and ball courts. The type and scale of monumental architecture reflects labor organization and control (compensation versus tribute); restricted (royal) versus public activities; and the number of participants.

SCALE OF INTEGRATIVE EVENTS: The scale of ritual activities corresponds to the number of people participating and includes household rites, community small-scale ceremonies, and large-scale public ceremonial and political events. Public events require open areas (plazas). Successfully propitiating supernatural entities guaranteed material rewards for both intermediaries and participants.

PUBLIC ICONOGRAPHY: The predominance of rulers and their ancestors and water symbolism (e.g., Cauac or Witz Monster, Water Lily Monster, fish, crocodiles, water lilies, and turtles) in the iconography clearly signifies their importance in political, social, and religious life.

WRITING AND EMBLEM GLYPHS: Literacy and access to scribes were largely royal prerogatives for the recording of royal events and dynastic histories. The use of emblem glyphs, insignia representing a ruler's domain (Stuart and Houston 1994), has territorial and political implications.

DURATION: This factor highlights differences between political and occupation histories. Since political demands were superimposed onto existing social and economic systems, they had varied responses to changing political histories. In other words, changing political fortunes may or may not have caused commoner farmers to leave their homes and lands, depending on the circumstances.

TERMINAL CLASSIC EVENTS (CA. AD 850 – 950):   Here I focus on the varied political and social (settlement decisions) responses at different centers to changing climate (see Chapter 7).

In brief, kings of regional polities acquired and maintained political power through their access to concentrated resources and large-scale water/agricultural systems and their ability to integrate densely settled and/or scattered farmers through ritual. Kings at secondary centers acquired power by dominating prestige-goods exchange and nearby agricultural land, but to a lesser extent than regional kings, because they were unable to access all the dispersed pockets of agricultural land, small-scale water/agricultural systems, and scattered farmers. Elites at minor centers could not obtain tribute but relied on their wealth as landowners to procure prestige goods and organize local ceremonies. They did not have much or any political power, because agricultural land was extensive and plentiful, and elites could only integrate farmers in the immediate vicinity. Nor did farmers rely on water/agricultural systems, since water was plentiful year-round; instead they relied on the annual flooding and receding of the river for agriculture. Whether or not they were beholden to rulers at major centers, as members of a larger society, Maya at minor centers interacted and exchanged information and goods with Maya from other areas.

The Classic Maya were similar to other ancient civilizations where water and seasonal issues played a major role in the underwriting of political power and where subjects perceived rulers as protectors and providers. When conditions changed and rainfall decreased, rulers were the first ones blamed. This resulted in their loss of rights over the surplus of others and their primary means of support and, ultimately, in their loss of power. In the next chapter, I set the stage to explain how Maya rulers acquired and maintained the right to exact tribute—through ritual.

CHAPTER 3

Maya Rituals: Past and Present

God,
  My Lord,
  See here, my Father,
    See here, my Lord.
May I pass before Thy glorious eyes . . .
For this, my lowly mouth departs,
  For this my humble lips depart,
For this, my lowly chunk of incense,
  For this, my humble cloud of smoke,
For this, my three lowly torches,
  For this, my three humble candles.
I go to beg holy pardon,
  I go to beg divine forgiveness . . .
A TRADITIONAL ZINACANTAN HOUSE
DEDICATION PRAYER, VOGT (1993:54)

The goal in this chapter is to illustrate the continuity of traditional Maya rituals from past to present to demonstrate how the present can inform the past and vice versa. Before discussing the Maya, however, I define ritual—what it is and what it is not, and how to identify ritual in the archaeological record. In the final section I discuss Maya rituals and present expectations regarding the relationship between traditional rites and the emergence of Maya rulership.

The definition of ritual is not agreed upon in anthropology (Richards and Thomas 1984), not to mention elsewhere. For example, in the 1993 unabridged Random House dictionary, the word "ritual" has twelve definitions. Interestingly, but not surprisingly, most definitions have religious connotations (Random House 1993:1661; emphasis in original):

1. an established or prescribed procedure for a religious or other rite. 2. a system or collection of religious or other rites. 3. observance of set forms in public worship. 4. a book of rites or ceremonies. 5. a book containing the offices to be used by priests in administering the sacraments and for visitation of the sick, burial of the dead, etc. 6. a prescribed or established rite, ceremony, proceeding, or service: *the ritual of the dead.* 7. prescribed, established, or ceremonial acts or features collectively, as in religious services. 8. any practice or pattern of behavior regularly performed in a set manner. 9. a prescribed code of behavior regulating social conduct, as that exemplified by the raising of one's hat or the shaking of hands in greeting. 10. *Psychiatry.* a specific act, as hand-washing, performed repetitively to a psychological degree, occurring as a common symptom of obsessive-compulsive neurosis.—adj. 11. of the nature of or practiced as a rite or ritual: *a ritual dance.* 12. of or pertaining to rites or rituals: *ritual laws.*

While definitions of ritual vary, anthropologists at least agree that ritual pervades all aspects of life (Leach 1966), including religious, political, and economic realms, all of which intersect. Because ritual expression typically involves the use of symbols, dancing, singing, oral stories, ceremonies, and feasting, many of these acts leave telling material evidence due to their "structured nature," representing repetitive behaviors (Richards and Thomas 1984:191; cf. Kertzer 1988:9). "All acts of ancient worship have a material embodiment, which is not left to the choice of the worshipers but is limited by fixed roles" (Robertson Smith 1956 [1894]:84).

The material qualities of ritual make it possible: (1) to identify ritual in the archaeological record; (2) to illustrate the type and continuity of material expression or ritual through ethnographic research and analogy; and (3) by doing so, to contribute to bringing ancient rites back to life. I wish to expand briefly on this last point. Archaeologists indeed can reveal ancient ritual activities. With the aid of ethnographic analogy, we can also perhaps identify the type of ritual. But we cannot illuminate the beliefs behind the rituals. For example, I have excavated several prehispanic Maya burials in the floors of houses in central Belize. Based on ethnographic, ethnohistorical, and epigraphic data, I would be comfortable, as are others, in suggesting that burials, based on their location and grave goods, reflect ancestor veneration. However, it is not sound scholarship to attempt to discuss the beliefs behind ancestor veneration, other than stating that ancestors were clearly important to the ancient Maya, as they are at present. Time and history have passed to the degree that it is not possible to equate recent beliefs with ancient ones. In addition (and as I illustrate below), different people often believe different things while participating in the same rite.

Ritual Is Action, Not Beliefs

Religious phenomena fall into two basic categories: beliefs and rites. The first are states of opinion and consist of representations; the second are particular modes of action. Between these two categories of phenomena lies all that separates thinking from doing.

DURKHEIM (1995 [1912]:34)

Scholars tend to conflate ritual and religion, and hence beliefs, because they focus on the religious aspects of ritual rather than on the ritual aspects of religion. And since religious beliefs are "beyond the realms of archaeological inference . . ." (Richards and Thomas 1984:189), presumably so is ritual. Ritual, however, is not epiphenomenal. "Labeling ritual as ideology universally masks the material qualities of ritual action . . ." (Walker 2002:162), and we cannot reduce "actions to beliefs" (Walker 1995:67). Of course, most rituals involve religion.

> That some of these relationships are with beings, forces, or powers having no "rational" or "practical" standing is irrelevant to the study of the manipulation of material culture engendered by those relationships. For archaeology, deposits and sequences of deposits resulting from such relationships become tangible evidence of prehistoric religion. (Walker 2002:161)

Ancient ritual activities are being revealed worldwide, especially religious and political ones—and secondarily economic rites (e.g., Bradley 1990; Walker 1998, 2002). For example, William Walker (1998), using ethnographic data, artifact context, and depositional histories, argues that the ritual killing of witches explains the obvious evidence for violent death in the prehistoric U.S. Southwest, rather than just cannibalism and warfare. In another case, Walker (2002) again uses artifact context and depositional histories to illustrate that Casas Grandes in Chihuahua, Mexico, was ritually dismantled and abandoned and not destroyed during a catastrophic battle as others have claimed.

The archaeological record, however, cannot reveal beliefs. Rituals can be observed; beliefs cannot. As a matter of fact, participation in the same rituals does not entail participants having the same beliefs (Kertzer 1988; Rappaport 1999: 119–120; Robertson Smith 1956 [1894]:16). For example, sociologist Daniel B. Lee has studied religious practices of the Weaverland Conference Old World Mennonites of New York and Pennsylvania and shows that they did not have to share common beliefs. "Ritual is socially meaningful as a source of social solidarity because it transcends the personal beliefs of individuals" (Lee 2000:1). To illustrate this, Lee (pp. 4–5) discusses the "kiss of peace"; people are supposed to say certain things in greeting (which actually varies). As to the significance of the kiss of peace, when asked, each person has a different response—for example: "Our ancestors brought the kiss with him or her from Germany and Switzerland. We want to hold on to those traditions," or "The kiss was established by the early leaders of the church," or "It's from the Bible. The disciples did it," or "I don't know why we do it" (p. 5). According to Lee, the important point is to "make it look right" (p. 5). "[A]s long as members follow the rules of the church, their personal reasons for doing so are of little social consequence" (p. 143).

William Robertson Smith (1956 [1894]:17) noted this fact over a century ago in his treatise on the origins of Semitic religions. As Lee demonstrates, rituals serve to promote solidarity and a sense of belonging (see Kertzer 1988:11, 62). David Kertzer (1988:67) labels these integrative events "solidarity without consensus." In other words, different people often explain the same ritual in different ways, as the Mennonites do. Rituals (and symbols) can and do have multiple meanings (Cohen 1974:29, 36; Durkheim 1995 [1912]:390). Solidarity, however, is created by people participating together (Kertzer 1988:72), "not by people thinking together" (p. 76; Lee 2000:142). Ritual clearly is an efficient means to communicate ideas, worldviews, status, economic, and political differences with the purpose of integrating people (Kertzer 1988:30). "Rituals bring people together, identifying a common allegiance through these symbols and making them feel as one" (p. 64). For example, among the Merina of Madagascar, Bloch (1986:122) notes that the circumcision ritual has basically remained unchanged from its first known recording in 1800 to a recent recording in 1971, though social, economic, and political histories have changed dramatically.

Because of these features of ritual, it can serve as a powerful medium of change. "Ritual becomes a mechanism of social and material reproduction, in that it sanctions the redefinition of people and things" (Richards and Thomas 1984:190). While we cannot elucidate the multiple meanings or beliefs of rituals and their symbols, we can reveal the rituals themselves and their settings (private, restricted, or public) and scale (small or large).

Identifying Ancient Ritual

As I detail elsewhere (Lucero 2003) and note again, the most promising archaeological evidence of the relationship between ritual and politics is the *variability* resulting from the dynamic relationship between structure and practice and the way in which political aspirants expanded upon that variability (Walker and Lucero 2000). Variability and expansion leave telling evidence in the archaeological record (Schiffer 1976:7), especially ritual, since it has both conservative and innovative properties. For example, Kent Flannery (1976) proposes that during the more egalitarian period in Oaxaca all members of society practiced bloodletting, using stingray spines. By the Middle Formative, however, "chiefly" individuals appear to have used jade spines, community leaders stingray spines, and the rest imitation spines made from mammal bones. Chiefs conducted bloodletting rites in public arenas. The temporal variability in artifacts and location may indicate the expansion of traditional rituals for larger-scale religious and presumably political activities. A similar scenario took place in Western Europe from the Neolithic through the Iron Age. The aquatic location of ritual offerings does not change through the millennia. The types of materials used and the quality of manufactured goods increased, however, and the focus changed ". . . so that what started as an informal transaction between the living and the gods was transformed into one of the central political activities in prehistoric society" (Bradley 1990:202).

The material aspects of rituals, including how they are replicated and expanded, leave traces in the archaeological record and include ceremonial and religious structures, temples, caches of ritual objects, and burials (e.g., Bradley 1990:10–14; DeMarrais et al. 1996). For example, because the Maya performed rituals for nearly every construction phase during the building and rebuilding of houses, palaces, and temples, the life histories of structures reflect such events and result in the creation of interconnected sequential deposits, including fill, artifacts in fill, floor features, and artifacts on floors (Walker and Lucero 2000). Ceramic vessels smashed and burned on floors differ ritually from whole vessels found in fill under floors. The pots themselves became part of the life history of the structure (e.g., Gillespie 2001) as their life history changed from a domestic vessel to a ritually deposited item, whole or broken (see Thomas 1991:57, 63; e.g., Kunen et al. 2002). "It is common in the archaeology literature for the term 'ritual' to be used as a catch-all designation for anything which defies a crudely utilitarian explanation" (Richards and Thomas 1984:189). "Utilitarian" versus "nonutilitarian" designations are thus a false dichotomy (Walker 1998, 2002). It has to be eradicated if our goal is to recognize "structured deposits" (Richards and Thomas 1984), created by repetitive, formalized actions or "purposeful deposition" of items, whether they be pig bones or gold diadems.

Repetitive behaviors result in specific sequences in the archaeological record that reflect ritual actions. Consequently, the contexts of artifacts are key for identifying ritual activities (Walker 1995). Domestic objects such as cooking pots can become ritual items if they are taken out of a kitchen and used in a ceremony or, in the case of the ancient Maya, if a serving dish is taken from a house, rendered useless by ceremonially "killing" it, and then offered as a dedicatory cache. Rather than just evaluating strata in terms of chronology, we can view them as reflecting sequences of (ritual) behaviors—more specifically, ritual replication and expansion—where similar formal ritual activities took place in a variety of architectural contexts, from houses to palaces and temples. While the quality and quantity of goods may have changed from commoner house to elite compound to palace and temple (e.g., from one or two plain vessels to numerous labor-intensive polychrome vessels), their context (under or on top of surfaces) and ritual significance (e.g., dedication cache or termination deposit) are the same. This behavior resulted in functionally and structurally similar ritual deposits in houses, palaces, and temples.

For example, the content of Zapotec rituals between 1500–500 BC included ancestral spirits and *pèe*, "the vital force within powerful natural forces of the cosmos" (Marcus 1996:286). Figurines dating to ca. 1500–850 BC associated with ancestor rites were recovered from residences but not from public areas. Beginning ca. 1150 BC, figurines became more diverse in form and context, signifying increasing status and wealth differences. By 500 BC, however, figurines seem to disappear from domestic contexts. Marcus suggests that the focus shifted out of domestic contexts to standardized temples where ritual specialists performed rites to ancestors of elites and royals. This practice expanded; and by Monte Albán II (ca. 100 BC–AD 200), Joyce Marcus and Kent Flannery (1996:182) suggest that full-time priests "took a great deal of ritual out of the hands of Zapotec laymen." But they also note that not many commoner houses have been excavated. Eventually, however, at least in Monte Albán proper, commoners apparently were increasingly excluded from state rites altogether (Joyce et al. 2001).

In another example, excavated residences outside of the Aztec capital of Tenochtitlan (e.g., at Chiconautla, Nonoalco, and Cuexcomate) yielded evidence for domestic new-fire ceremonies, including ritual dumps of ash and large sherds from vessels of all kinds—utilitarian, incensarios, and figurine fragments (Elson and Smith 2001). The Mexica adopted the new-fire ceremony during the Postclassic period, a rite conducted every fifty-two years that was widespread in northern Mesoamerica. Aztec emperors, however, instituted new practices whereby all fires had to be lit by imperial runners once a new fire was lit during the imperial ceremony on Mount Huixachtlan, a sacred mountain near Tenochtitlan.

These few examples illustrate the material reality of ritual actions. In the following section, I detail the long history of Maya rituals. Ethnographic and ethnohistoric cases provide the backdrop to examine the role of prehispanic Maya rituals in the rise of rulers.

Maya Household Dedication, Ancestor Veneration, and Termination Rituals

The significance and prevalence of Maya rituals are illustrated in the ethnographic and ethnohistoric records, including feasts and cave, rain, renewal, household, agricultural, and water ceremonies. I focus on household dedication, ancestor veneration, and termination rites because they have a long tradition and leave clear evidence in the archaeological record. These rites always remained in the home and were expanded for community solidarity and later for political purposes. Domestic rituals revolved around life, death, and renewal, aspects that concerned everyone in Maya society. Therefore, they are ideal for political appropriation. My intent is not to deemphasize the significance of other rituals; this work is only an exercise to illustrate ritual replication and expansion. It does not take away from the significance of other public ceremonies, such as those conducted at the community level. Community rites took place in open areas near water sources, small plazas, and ball courts and leave less obvious evidence; further, archaeologists seldom excavate these areas (e.g., Davis-Salazar 2003; Fox 1996; LeCount 1996; Robin 2002). Evidence for dedication, ancestor veneration, and termination rites, however, abounds. And if it can be shown that these rites were replicated and expanded, it follows that other traditional rituals also were, especially water ceremonies.

The Ethnographic Record: Syncretism

The material expression of Maya rituals has continued from prehispanic times to the present (Deal 1988). Beliefs have not. There have been dramatic changes in the last millennium, including the abandonment of Maya centers and parts of the southern Maya lowlands in the AD 900s, Spanish conquest in the 1500s, forced settlement nucleation, conversion to Christianity, and depopulation due to foreign diseases. Today we at least can record people's beliefs revolving around present rites even though they themselves can vary, as Lee (1998, 2000) illustrates in the Mennonite case. For example, in the Lacandon village of Najá in southeastern Chiapas, Mexico, the Maya are still largely non-Christian and practice the "old" ways (McGee 1990:6–7); however, on their list of principal deities (1990:Table 6.1) is at least one new god, Akyantho, a postconquest addition (p. 22). Akyantho "is the god of foreigners and commerce. . . . he looks like a light-skinned foreigner wearing a hat and carrying a pistol. . . . He is also responsible for the existence of foreign objects such as medicine, hard liquor, cattle, horses, and disease" (p. 65). Jesus Christ (Hesuklistos) is recognized as a minor, though foreign, deity (p. 70), but not one to be worshiped by the Lacandon (p. 126).

Most Maya, however, have converted to one form of Christianity or another. Consequently, many of their rituals, while materially the same as those of prehispanic ones, serve as the expressive core of a different ideology and religion. For example, in the Yucatán village of Chan Kom, Robert Redfield and Alfonso Villa Rojas (1934:83) note that traditional agricultural ceremonies are tied to the religious calendar of the Catholic Church, especially saints' days. Shamans (*h-menob*) lead ceremonies and use ritual equipment from the past, including crystals for divination and gourds for drinking a sacred alcoholic drink (*balche*) (pp. 74–75). They also still believe in "pagan" gods, including *balams* ("guardians of the milpa and village"), *chaacs* ("gods of rain"), and *kuilob kaaxob* ("deities of the forest") (pp. 112–113).

Shamans are also involved in the "new house" or dedication ceremony (e.g., Redfield and Villa Rojas 1934:146), a practice found throughout the Christian and non-Christian Maya world. Dedication rituals are performed to animate new houses and other objects. Part of such rituals includes the caching of objects under house floors. For example, Evon Vogt (1993:52–55) describes the two stages of the dedication ceremony during and after house construction for the Catholic Zinacantan Maya of highland Chiapas. During construction, builders bury the heads of sacrificed chickens in the floor with other offerings. Afterward, a shaman performs rites to compensate the Earth Lord for the materials he has provided as well as to "summon the ancestral gods to provide the house with an innate soul" (Vogt 1993:52). Again, more offerings are buried in the floor of the new house (Vogt 1970:78, 98; see also Wauchope 1938:143). Part of the rite includes reciting prayers to the gods, including references to the Christian God, the Virgin Mary, and Jesus Christ (Vogt 1993:53–54).

In Chichicastenango of highland Guatemala, Ruth Bunzel (1952) notes similar syncretic practices. The Quiché Maya, while mostly Catholic, also still conduct "housebuilding" ceremonies (p. 37) led by a shaman (p. 77). They classify power into at least nine realms, which involve both Christian and non-Christian elements (pp. 266–267): "The World"; phenomena of nature; saints; "idols" (ancient); "forces of destiny. . . . The 'twelve-thirteen moons and stars' (i.e., time and destiny); the 260 days of the sacred . . . and the life-token animals of individuals"; death bringers—"The Lord of Sickness and Pain"; masters of useful activities, including the patron deities of agriculture, weaving, business, industry, writing, midwifery, medicine, divination, and sorcery; Lords of Justice (e.g., deceased *alcaldes* or leaders); and souls of the dead—the "first people," the common souls, and one's own ancestors.

The ancestors are the most important supernatural component in the life of the Quiché Maya, however, as well as among other Maya groups. "The powers whose influence on human affairs is continuous and unremitting are the ancestors, who represent the great moral force" (Bunzel 1952:269). Bunzel details the importance of ancestors in everyday life (p. 18) and their role in the continuance of fertile land, rain, plentiful crops, and good health (p. 56). Among the Zinacantecos, ancestral gods are even more important than the Earth Lord (Vogt 1970:6). Ancestor veneration rites are thus performed to honor and thank ancestors. Part of such rituals involves keeping an ancestor's remains close to home and making offerings. Although ancestors live in sacred places such as caves or mountains, at least through colonial times their physical remains and offerings were kept close to home, buried in the floors of houses, as Bishop de Landa describes for colonial Yucatán (Tozzer 1941:130). In the ethnographic present, most people are buried in cemeteries or in plots near the home; but as R. Jon McGee (1990:117, 1998) describes among the Lacandon, the dead are still buried with grave goods; "A variety of grave goods including both food and the deceased's personal possessions are left at the gravesite" (1990:117).

Termination rites are part of the renewal ceremony—for the new year, for example, or after the death of a family member when life must begin anew. For example, in the Lacandon village of Najá, if a dead person's spirit does not leave people in peace, the family moves to a new house (McGee 1990:115). Termination rituals also are performed to deactivate or deanimate houses or objects, thus releasing their soul before being renewed. Part of such rituals includes breaking objects, partially destroying houses, and burning incense. For the new year in colonial Mexico, Bishop de Landa notes, "To celebrate it with more solemnity, they renewed on this day all the objects which they made use of, such as plates, vessels, stools, mats and old clothes and the stuffs with which they wrapped up their idols. They swept out their houses . . ." (Tozzer 1941:151) and deposited old items as contaminated sacred trash outside of town (p. 152). Similarly, among the Lacandon, a feature of the renewal ceremony is the manufacture of new incense-burners, the building of new fires, and the use of new utilitarian goods (Tozzer 1907:106). Old incensarios, jars, and other items are "terminated," taken out of habitation areas to a nearby cliff, and deposited in a specific place below a ledge, thus signifying the end of the termination/renewal ceremonies (Tozzer 1907:146–147).

"Smashing objects [also] constitutes one way of deactivating, or de-animating, them and releasing the soul" (Stross 1998:37). For example, throughout Mesoamerica, ritually abandoning a house involves pulling down parts of the house (e.g., corner posts, roof), burning incense, reciting prayers, and making offerings (Stross 1998). Among the Lacandon of Najá, when god pots—incense burners—are replaced with new ensouled/animated/dedicated ones, the old ones are ritually killed and discarded.

> During the transitional period before new god pots are completed, the old incense burners, which are about to die, are taken down from their storage

shelf in the god house, placed on a mat of palm leaves facing east, and fed daily offerings. (McGee 1998:44)

Several days later:

The old god pots are fed offerings one last time, the stone concealed in their bowls is removed, and the pots are placed in a corner of the god house facing west and covered, an action that symbolizes their death. . . . The old incense burners, which have sat covered in the corner for the past several days, are carefully collected and taken to a dry limestone cave about an hour's walk from the community. There, amid the smoke from burning incense, the god pots are covered with palm leaves and abandoned. . . . The vessels are left in caves, which are considered sacred and dangerous places because they are passages to the Underworld. (McGee 1998:45)

Ethnographic and colonial case studies play a key role in revealing past ritual actions. The rituals just described clearly have a long history, around which varied and changing beliefs have revolved. These examples dramatically illustrate the central role that ritual plays in creating the material world, a fact also demonstrated in the archaeological record. For example, when a Maya temple was ritually destroyed, rulers and elites burned incense and left old broken items as offerings, after which a new temple was constructed over the old and dedicated with the caching of new whole objects (Freidel and Schele 1989; Garber 1986, 1989; Schele and Freidel 1990:104–108). Even though there is extreme diversity in structure configuration, size, and function among commoner houses, elite compounds, and palaces and temples, current evidence indicates that they have structurally and functionally similar depositional (ritual) histories (e.g., Becker 1992; Gillespie 2000a; Haviland 1981, 1988; McAnany 1995:97; Walker and Lucero 2000; Willey et al. 1965). This can be attributed to common dedication, ancestor veneration, and termination rituals (practices I demonstrate in Chapters 4, 5, and 6).

Identifying Ancient Maya Rituals: Expectations

Building and destroying houses relates to the life history of ancestors. The death of an important family member often represents the need for a new house, which means the old one has to be razed and terminated and a new one built and dedicated. Dedication, ancestor veneration, and termination rites thus cannot be viewed singly but must be seen as inextricably linked ritual events; they are a vital component of the construction process. It is impossible to separate ritual activities and construction events—they are practically one and the same. Consequently, the depositional histories of Maya structures reflect a continuous flow of ritual behaviors. They also reflect how critical these rites were to everyone, high and low—as well as how they were excellently suitable for political replication and expansion.

I posit that political aspirants began to expand traditional rituals during the Late Preclassic (ca. 250 BC–AD 250) and continued to do so, culminating in large-scale royal rites in the Early Classic (ca. AD 250–550) and a direct association of royal families with the supernatural or divine forces by the Late Classic (ca. AD 550–850). Incrementally, Maya rulers conducted rites in progressively larger-scale settings (e.g., houses to elite compounds to temples and palaces), incorporating ever-larger groups of people.

If Maya rulers replicated and expanded household rituals, then we should find evidence for such rituals at commoner houses, elite residences, royal palaces, and temples beginning in the Late Preclassic. Rituals should be represented in depositional histories that are *structurally* and *functionally* similar but *increase in scale*. Differences between commoner, elite, and royal ritual deposits consist of increasing quality, quantity, and diversity of deposited items and setting (structure types). For example, all members of Maya society cached exotic obsidian objects (e.g., Olson 1994): commoners cached small blades in houses, elites more and longer blades in larger houses with small public courtyards, and royals more and longer blades as well as skillfully carved objects in palaces and temples (Krejci and Culbert 1995). Obsidian was used for multiple purposes—as cutting implements, for bloodletting, and perhaps as small versions of "eccentrics." Whatever their function, the point is that everyone, rich and poor, relinquished forever—sacrificed—items acquired through long-distance exchange networks. Before the advent of monarchs, all people in society cached more or less the same quantities of similarly shaped obsidian in their houses. During the rise of rulers, one begins to see increasing diversity in form and quantity in commoner, elite, and royal caches. The caching of obsidian never left the home but was taken to new levels in conjunction with the rise of rulers in larger public forums (e.g., Hendon 1999; Ringle 1999).

Termination deposits and dedication caches are typically found in the centers of rooms (e.g., Garber 1986, 1989). Burials are typically found in the southeast corner of small residences (e.g., Willey et al. 1965) and the eastern structures of elite plazuelas or compounds (e.g., Belize Valley, southeastern Petén) (Garber et al. 1998). Caches, other ritual deposits, and burials in palaces and temples are often located at the primary axis on top of or under floors and stairs (Ashmore 1991; Loten and Pendergast 1984:5; Pendergast 1998).

Dedication caches are found *under* floors and usually consist of burned or unburned whole objects such as jade, obsidian, groundstone fragments, lithic eccentrics, and ceramic vessels (some lip-to-lip) (Becker 1992; Coe 1959:77−78, 1965a; e.g., Chase and Chase 1998; Garber 1989:98; Mock 1998). Major differences among commoner, elite, and royal caches include the quality, quantity, and diversity of offerings and location. For example, I would expect to find shell beads in houses, jade beads in elite structures, and more diverse forms and quantities of jade objects in public monumental temples and palaces (e.g., Garber 1989:67).

Evidence for ancestor veneration rites consists of burials and offerings under structure floors (e.g., Gillespie 2000a; McAnany 1995:535). Again, major differences among nonelite, elite, and royal burials include location and the quality, quantity, and diversity of grave goods. Commoner Maya buried their dead in the floors of their houses. In elite residences, the Maya built shrines to their ancestors, usually the eastern structure of their residential compound. Royals took this practice to new heights and buried their dead in a special place, the royal acropolis. The Maya buried the most powerful royal personages in funerary temples (e.g., Temple of the Inscriptions, Palenque).

Termination deposits are found *on top of* floors and are typically broken and burned, such as smashed ceramic vessels and burned items (Coe 1965a; Garber 1986, 1989; e.g., Rice 1999). Major differences among commoner, elite, and royal deposits include the quality, quantity, and diversity of offerings and location. I expect to find a few smashed vessels in commoner houses, greater numbers and fancier polychrome vessels in elite residences, and more diverse forms and quantities of vessels with incised or painted hieroglyphs from monumental architecture. In addition, termination rituals in monumental public architecture are evidenced by the destruction of stone and stuccoed sculpture, the effacing of painted and carved portraits of rulers and deities, and the whitewashing of painted walls (Becker 1992; Garber 1989:9).

Concluding Remarks

During the Postclassic period (ca. AD 950−conquest), after rulers disappeared from the southern Maya lowlands, the Maya continued to conduct rituals where they originated, in the home. Instead of participating in household, community, and royal rites as they did beginning in the Late Preclassic through the Late/Terminal Classic periods, Maya farmers now only participated in household and community rites (the latter still funded and organized by wealthy landowners or elites). This pattern is evidenced throughout the postcollapse Maya world (e.g., Lucero and Brown 2002; Lucero, McGahee, and Corral 2002; Masson 1997; Willey et al. 1965).

In this chapter I have attempted to illustrate the key role of ritual in daily life, past and present. The critical importance of ritual lends itself to manipulation by ambitious political agents. Rituals served to show that political change was beneficial to all, as were its proponents—emerging rulers.

The increase in scale and the public setting of dedication, ancestor veneration, and termination rituals associated with the rise of Maya rulers can be assessed in the archaeological record in domestic and monumental structures at minor, secondary, and regional centers. This pattern is particularly noticeable at sites with long occupation histories spanning the periods before, during, and after the advent of rulership, which I illustrate in the following chapters. I also incorporate ritual data from other southern lowland centers to examine structurally and functionally similar ritual histories.

CHAPTER 4

Community and the Maya:
The Ritual History of Saturday Creek

In this chapter I detail the distinguishing features of community organizations (see Table 1.1) and Maya minor centers, which have several factors in common (see Table 2.1). I also present the history of ritual activities at Saturday Creek, a minor river center without rulers or any other royal trappings. My intent is to show that all Maya conducted the same rites, whether or not they were taxpayers, and whether or not they were royal.

Community Organization

In community organizations, farmers live in villages and practice swidden or small-scale intensive agriculture as well as hunt and fish. Relatively low population densities result in fewer demands on the land. Farmers depend on seasonal rainfall and do not rely on water or agricultural systems. Wealth differences exist and are expressed in differential access to resources, exotics, labor, and other goods. Political power typically does not develop, because resources are relatively extensive, stable, and plentiful (e.g., Kirch 1994). Consequently, there is no need for capital to maintain water/agricultural systems, though elites can provide food to people in need from their own stores. Elites typically attain greater wealth as a result of their being the first settlers and monopolizing the best resources (e.g., Carmean and Sabloff 1996; Marcus 1983). As a result, their power lies in the respect they are shown as founding families, for example, in making decisions involving the entire community (e.g., lineage chiefs, village headmen). Land is corporately owned, though chiefs/elites may own other means of production, such as fishing canoes. Relations are typically heterarchical, since wealth differences do not translate into a monopoly on political power. "Heterarchy may be defined as the relation of elements of one another when they are unranked or when they possess the potential for being ranked in a number of different ways" (Crumley 1995b:3). For example, Marajo Island at the mouth of the Amazon was occupied for approximately a millennium, until ca. AD 1100 (Roosevelt 1999:23):

> The general picture from the Marajoara cultural remains . . . is of populous, wealthy, but apparently uncentralized, societies. Their populations lived in sometimes sizable, long-term communities atop large-scale earth construc- tions, taking sustenance from fish, horticultural crops, and orchards. They cre- ated highly elaborate and often monumental art, and craft objects that were available to all residential groups, although in somewhat different quality and quantity.

A major factor that prevented the development of centralized power is that in- habitants of Marajo Island had the option to flee into uninhabited jungle areas.

Elites, as landowners or owners of other critical resources, compensate people for goods and services rendered, including manufacturing prestige goods, work- ing elites' land, and building their homes, shrines, and community structures (e.g., ritual architecture). Compensation comes in the form of food and access to resources and/or prestige goods, which the elites obtain as participants in a regional elite interaction sphere (long-distance exchange). Commoners, how- ever, also are involved in the exchange of utilitarian and prestige items with their cohorts, typically without elite interference. An element of choice is in- volved since people can choose for whom and when to perform tasks for others who can afford to pay. Patron-client relations can fall in this category, even though over time clients may have little choice but to work for a patron due to debts owed. Patrons, however, also have obligations to their clients to take care of them in times of trouble or need.

A key issue is that there is *more than one* wealthy individual or family rather than a sole political leader (Fried 1967:26–32; Marcus 1983). To promote soli- darity in the face of wealth differences, however, elites sponsor community feasts, performances, and religious rites and organize the building of small- scale public works (e.g., religious structures, terraces, and canals). These activ- ities also serve to increase their prestige as pillars of the community. Household rites typically involve ancestors and fertility, since they are critical to everyone's survival (Fried 1967:138). Ancestors are typically represented in a stylized man- ner in various media, such as body decoration, sacred items, shields, and ban- ners (e.g., clan totems or emblems) (Durkheim 1995 [1912]:111–117). People have no need of writing or recording systems, because each lineage is respon- sible for maintaining and passing on family oral histories.

Communities may or may not interact with a centralized or integrative po- litical system. For example, rulers of the Kedah state in Malaysia (AD 700–

1500) had peer relations with foreign trade partners (e.g., from China, Vietnam, Thailand, and India) and equal, heterarchical relations with inhabitants of the forest far upstream, with whom they exchanged foreign goods for forest products (e.g., timber) necessary for trade (Allen 1999). Whether or not they interact with larger polities, small-scale raiding for food and land (and some political reasons) is endemic but regulated (Fried 1967:178). Feuding is kept in check by lineage elders, village headmen, and any other person of respect (e.g., Leach 1970 [1954]:184–185). There are various reasons why elites do not have much political power in addition to the material factors mentioned above. David Small (1995) discusses how external trade can prohibit the development of hierarchical organization, because opportunities to participate are open to all. For example, the kula ring (interisland trade) of the Trobriand Islands is accessible to all men for trading and creating alliances (Johnson and Earle 2000: 272). Other social organizations that keep relations nonhierarchical are kinship systems, age-sets, and specialists (magicians, sorcerers, rain-makers), as found among several precolonial African societies, including Tellensi farmers and Nuer and Logoli Bantu cattle herders and farmers (Evans-Pritchard 1940; Fortes 1940; Wagner 1940).

Communities are stable and have lengthy histories, as long as there are enough resources to sustain people and as long as people can adapt to changing conditions (e.g., long-term climate change). And "because of their broader, grassroots base, heterarchical formations appear to achieve more political stability and cultural longevity than hierarchical systems imposed from above by small ruling groups" (Roosevelt 1999:14). For example, in the Maya lowlands, many communities continued long after the collapse of the political hierarchy, with little change. At Laguna de On in northern Belize, Marilyn Masson (1997) posits that communities rather than the earlier civic-ceremonial centers became the focal point for political, social, and economic organization.

I illustrate a community organization through a brief description of the Trobriand Islanders (Johnson and Earle 2000:267–280). The Trobriand Islands are located north of New Guinea, with unvaried resources. Islanders practice intensive agriculture (e.g., taro gardens) and fish. However, they do not build water/agricultural systems. Important staples are yams, which are stored, and taro. They are dependent on seasonal rainfall, and periods of drought can result in famine. When this happens, chiefs' stores of yams become critical. Trobriand Islanders live in village clusters, and chiefs reside in larger villages. Each lineage (*dala*) has a chief, and the lineages are ranked. Chiefly lineages are wealthier than other lineages, indicated by their larger houses and storage facilities. They acquire part of their wealth through dowry, a particularly lucrative strategy, as chiefs have several wives—not to mention more alliances and exchange partners. Chiefs also own canoes necessary for fishing but do not own land. Land is corporately owned by each *dala*. Consequently, there are no chiefly territories per se, only alliances and ties with nearby villages. Some men have the means and connections (alliances) to participate in the kula ring for subsistence and prestige goods (see Malinowski 1984 [1922]), which they exchange with people who do not participate in the kula ring. Chiefs, while they do not necessarily acquire tribute, do demand payment for use of their canoes and for food provided during famine. Raiding can occur during times of famine as well as for "political purposes" (Johnson and Earle 2000:271).

Household and village rites revolve around ancestors and clan totems (Malinowski 1984 [1922]:63, 72–73). Garden magicians and other ritual specialists act for the entire community, and each village has one (p. 59). Public rites take place in open, ceremonial areas, located in chiefly villages. Ceremonies involve the ancestral spirits critical to Trobriand life (pp. 421–424). Symbols represent clan totems, spirits, and witches (e.g., Anderson 1989 [1979]:Figure 5.3).

The Trobriand Islanders traditionally live in a relatively stable society because they do not over-use resources and have social mechanisms to offset food shortages and other seasonal problems (e.g., sharing stored foods).

Such societies have several factors in common with the Maya who lived in minor centers during the Late Classic (ca. AD 550–850), particularly the lack of political leaders and material conditions that were not conducive for the emergence of rulers.

The Maya: Minor Centers

Minor centers such as Barton Ramie and Saturday Creek are located on the Belize River on a relatively broad alluvium (1–2+ km wide) on the eastern periphery of the southern Maya lowlands (see Figure 2.1). They appear to be some of the earliest and longest-occupied settlements (e.g., 900 BC–AD 1500), which is not surprising given their prime location in an area with plentiful water and land. These centers are located in lower elevations (20–40+ m asl) and have higher annual rainfall than the majority of regional centers (Figure 4.1)—216 cm at Saturday Creek, similar to that of Barton Ramie, 25 km away. The naturally moist alluvial soils on the terraces above the river are excellently suited for cash crops such as cacao and cotton (Gómez-Pompa et al. 1990), not to mention maize, beans, and squash. The relatively dispersed settlement suggests that ancient Maya farmers planted fields interspersed among their houses (Drennan 1988; Killion 1990) or that landlords or estate owners living in the center or absentee limited settlement and set or determined planting schedules. Farmers did not need to use water/agricultural systems, because water was plentiful;

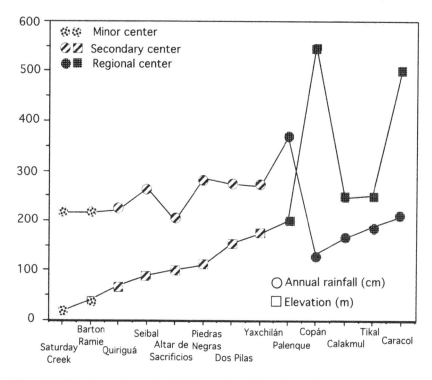

Figure 4.1. Elevation and annual rainfall at southern Maya lowland centers

farmers relied on the annual rising and subsiding of rivers for agriculture (recession agriculture). Annual inundation of the poorly drained soils of the lower terraces deterred the Maya from building or planting too close to the river. For example, at Saturday Creek occupants lived dispersed on the upper terraces along the Belize River and avoided the lower, poor-draining terraces that are seasonally inundated (Lucero n.d.b).

The Belize valley, due to its location and elevation, also benefited from annual runoff from Guatemala, Mexico, and western Belize, which supplied enough water for everyone throughout the year. The downside of runoff is that it often results in flooding and the deposition of clayey soils, which can remain saturated for most of the year. For example, in 1998 at Saturday Creek the lower river terrace was inundated during May and June, the end of the dry season. In May and June of 1999, however, the lower terrace was completely dry. The lower terrace was also devoid of prehispanic settlement, suggesting that the terrace was frequently inundated in the past. The Maya probably planted several crops a year as farmers do at present, indicating a lesser need for storage, which would explain why we do not find evidence for storage facilities (Lucero n.d.a).

These communities were composed of relatively low densities of dispersed farmsteads (e.g., 100–151 structures/km²; Lucero et al. 2004; Rice and Culbert 1990: Table 1.1; Willey et al. 1965:573). A major factor preventing elites from acquiring political power was their inability to restrict plentiful water and extensive alluvium and integrate dispersed farmers. Further, even if elites owned all the land, farmers clearly had the option to leave if elite demands became too onerous. Not relying on water/agricultural systems meant that there was no need for farmers to rely on the benevolence of political leaders to supply capital to repair damage. Communities, however, may have been subsumed under a regional polity, depending on factors such as distance from major centers and accessibility (e.g., Scarborough et al. 2003). For example, Olivier de Montmollin (1989:203) suggests that some valley areas around Tenam Rosario in the Usumacinta lowlands might have been elite or royal cotton and cacao estates. This might have been the case in other valley areas. Current evidence does not indicate involvement in warfare; if inhabitants did participate in aggressive acts against others, their involvement likely related to whether or not they were involved in regional politics.

Wealth differences account for various-sized residences and other signs of wealth rather than political power (e.g., Carmean and Sabloff 1996); elites compensated the workers who built their larger homes and worked their fields rather than exacted tribute (e.g., with prestige goods and access to land) (e.g., Potter and King 1995). Elites attained their wealth as a result of being the first settlers and owning the best and/or the largest plots of land; they acquired status as founding families, which was expressed by how members reacted to their community-wide decisions (e.g., Carmean and Sabloff 1996; McAnany 1995: 96–97; Tedlock 1985:204–205; Tozzer 1941:25–26). Consequently, greater wealth was not concentrated in the hands of one person or family but dispersed among several elite families. Elites participated to some degree in the elite interaction sphere through personal ornamentation, ceremonies, and long-distance exchange (e.g., exotic goods such as small jade and obsidian items) (Chase and Chase 1992).

Farmers and elites also traded their produce with Maya living in different areas. For example, in the upper Belize River area, there is evidence that valley farmers, who may or may not have been beholden to rulers at the nearest centers of El Pilar or Yalbac, acquired ceramic vessels and chert tools from Maya living in the foothills. The foothills have less productive agricultural soils, but plentiful raw materials for ceramic and lithic production (chert outcrops, clays, and tempers) (Ford 1990, 1991a; Lucero 2001:65–67). This type of exchange took place without elite interference (e.g., Scarborough et al. 2003). Consequently, even if Maya at minor centers were not integrated within a larger political system, they still interacted with their peers in other areas; after all, they were still members of a broader society and so identified themselves by acquiring value-laden items recognizable throughout the Maya world.

Elites sponsored local small-scale public rituals and feasts at small temples, usually not exceeding 10 m in height and relatively small plazas, and organized the construction of public works to promote solidarity in the face of wealth differences (Arie 2001; Lucero et al. 2004). Maya farmers also conducted rites in their homes, agricultural fields, and sacred places (e.g., caves and water bodies). There is no obvious public iconographic evidence for water imagery or rulers at such centers, which, by contrast, is pervasive on monumental architecture, sculpture, and mobile goods at some secondary and all regional centers. Elites did not keep a written record; nor did they have the means, or right, to make use of emblem glyphs.

Terminal Classic (ca. AD 850 – 950) events were pretty much the same as during the Late Classic. Minor centers were stable and lasted as long as there were enough resources to sustain people (Lucero 2002a). For example, the Maya occupied Saturday Creek and Barton Ramie long after they deserted secondary and regional centers, though population size gradually decreased throughout the Postclassic (ca. AD 950 – 1500) (Conlon and Ehret 2002; Willey et al. 1965). The long occupation histories (ca. 900 BC – AD 1500) raise the question as to why rulers did not emerge, an issue I address in Chapter 7.

Ritual History of Saturday Creek

Saturday Creek is located along the Belize River on an extensive floodplain (20 m asl) in central Belize on the eastern periphery of the southern Maya lowlands (see Figure 2.1).[1] Settlement was dispersed (100 – 151 structures/km^2; Lucero et al. 2004) and consisted of solitary mounds (67%, n = 53), mound groups or plazuelas, a ball court, and small temples (up to ca. 10 m tall) (Figure 4.2). The Valley of Peace Archaeology (VOPA) project, which I directed, mapped 79 structures within a 0.81 km^2 area bounded by roads on the north side of the river. Most of the site is located in a plowed field that is currently intensively cultivated by Mennonite farmers; they plow it at least twice a year and plant maize, beans, watermelon, or black-eyed peas. Consequently, mounds in the plowed field have been reduced in height and spread in areal extent. A large portion of the site (ca. 350 × 300 m), including the center core, has not been plowed. The core area has not been mapped in its entirety due to dense secondary growth (noted in Figure 4.2). Saturday Creek's former inhabitants included farmers, part-time specialists (e.g., potters had ample supplies of clay and water), and elite landowners. Elites procured exotics, such as obsidian and jade items, albeit small and simple ones. Commoners also acquired these objects

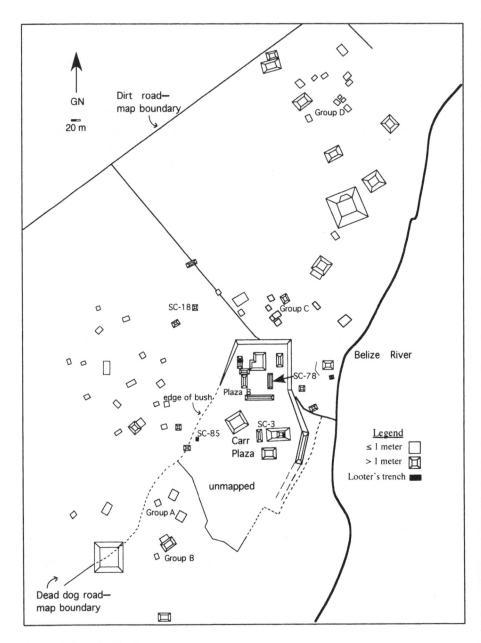

Figure 4.2. Saturday Creek

but in even smaller sizes and quantities—either as gifts or compensation from elites or through exchange with peers in other areas. Elites also organized the building of the ball court and temples.

There were no rulers, no tribute payments, no water or agricultural systems, no royal palaces, and no inscriptions; neither did Saturday Creek's residents create public iconography or use emblem glyphs. Saturday Creek was a stable and long-lasting community that was occupied from at least 900 BC through AD 1500 (Conlon and Ehret 2002). The nearest center is Yalbac, a secondary center 18 km to the northwest, and inhabitants of Saturday Creek may have had some kind of interaction with them. Even if the Maya at Saturday Creek were not politically incorporated into a larger polity, they were without question members of a larger society and interacted through social and economic exchanges (e.g., lithic tools from foothill or upland areas). Surface collections and excavated materials from Saturday Creek residences and from houses up-river indicate their relative wealth, not to mention long-distance contacts (e.g., Pachuca obsidian from central Mexico, polished hematite items, jade, and marine shell) (Lucero 1997, 2002b).

To maximize the range of ritual activities, in 2001 we excavated several structure types: two solitary mounds or commoner residences, SC-18 and SC-85; an eastern structure of an elite compound, SC-78; and a temple ball court, SC-3 (Lucero 2002b) (see Figure 4.2). In general, at each structure we began by bisecting the mound with a 2-meter-wide trench. At the two solitary mounds, we then horizontally exposed several living floors, excavating about 60% of SC-18 and 75% of SC-85. The large size of SC-78 only permitted us to bisect its width with a 2-meter-wide trench and excavate several 2 × 2 m test pits placed within structure rooms (determined using post-hole testing). This method resulted in our exposing about 20% of the mound. We excavated a 1-meter-wide trench at SC-3, bisecting the temple, platform, and ball-court side wall and alley.

We excavated following natural stratigraphy and used the Harris Matrix method of recording strata to highlight depositional sequences (see Harris 1989). Ceramic analysis was conducted concurrent with excavations resulting in chronologies for each mound in 100- to 200-year increments (Conlon and Ehret 2002). Analysis particularly focused on ceramic assemblages and their contexts because the Maya used them as ritual paraphernalia for dedicatory caches, grave goods, and termination deposits (Lucero 2003).

SC-18 (10 × 8 m, 1.24 m high) (Figure 4.3) is a commoner residence located ca. 150 m northwest of the site core on prime alluvium. It has at least six construction phases dating from ca. AD 400 through 1150 (Lucero and Brown 2002). The Maya constructed several thin plaster floors (most with cobble ballasts 2–5 cm thick), one on top of the other. Single or double-course boulder walls provided the foundation for thatch or wattle-and-daub structures. Some

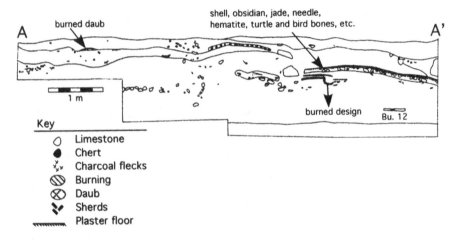

Figure 4.3. Commoner residence SC-18 with foundation walls and floors (in the sidewalls) visible; the locations of burials mentioned in text are noted. The east wall profile highlights some of the ritual deposits mentioned.

of the boulders were faced on the side facing inside. It has been plowed several times, and we do not know how much of the mound has been sheared off.

The occupants of SC-18 apparently were relatively well off farmers who acquired exotics, including small obsidian objects, jade inlays or mosaic pieces, and worked and unworked marine shell, hematite, and slate items. We also recovered a celt, bark beater, spindle whorls, bone needles, and a candelario.

SC-85 (6 × 4 m, 1.34 m in height) (Figure 4.4) is a commoner house located ca. 100 m southwest of the site core on more clayey soils. It also has six construction phases, consisting of a series of thin plaster floors with less substan-

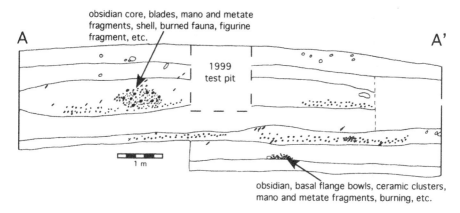

Figure 4.4. Commoner residence SC-85 with a cobble surface visible as well as a termination deposit. The north wall profile highlights some of the ritual items mentioned.

tial ballasts, one cobble surface, earthen surfaces (the earliest), and unshaped foundation boulder walls (one to three courses) for wattle-and-daub structures (Lucero, McGahee, and Corral 2002). We recognized five of the six surfaces by their termination deposits rather than plaster floors; the surrounding clays erode plaster. The Maya occupied SC-85 from at least ca. AD 400 through 1150. It is located in an area of secondary growth just east of the plowed Mennonite fields and does not appear to have been plowed.

Residents of SC-85 were less wealthy than their counterparts at SC-18, a result of their having lived surrounded by clayey, less productive soils. The Maya

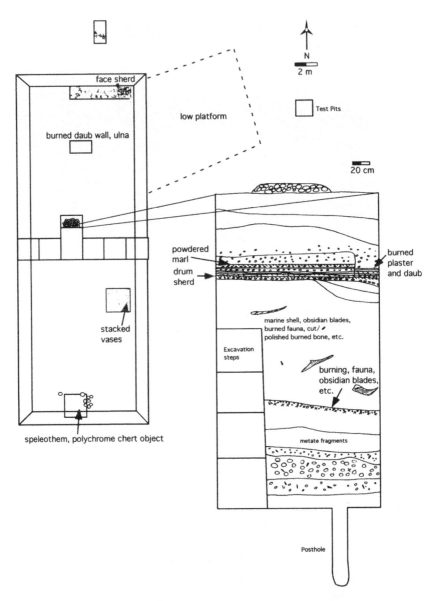

Figure 4.5. Plan of SC-78 and the north wall profile from the center excavation unit.

that lived here, however, acquired exotics and other specialized items, albeit small and simple, including Colha chert tools, worked and unworked marine-shell objects, obsidian blades, jade inlays or mosaic pieces, and hematite items.

SC-78 (Figure 4.5), the eastern structure of an elite plaza group in the site core up on one of the terraces, consists of a stepped platform (29.4 × 9.5 m,

3.85 m in height) with several relatively substantial domestic and specialized structures, especially on its north side. Some structures have thick plaster floors, ballasts, and standing walls with cut stone blocks. The Maya also used wattle-and-daub buildings (Lucero, Graebner, and Pugh 2002). It has not been plowed, as far as we know, but was being used as a milpa in 2001. The Maya lived at Saturday Creek at least by 600 BC through AD 1500, though ceramics dating to ca. 1000 BC were found in lower fill contexts. While domestic artifacts were recovered from several contexts, their frequency and density are noticeably lower than at SC-18 and SC-85. Their relative scarcity might indicate that fewer people lived here and/or that some structures had specific functions (e.g., a kitchen, storeroom, work area, shrine, or sweat bath).

SC-3 (Figure 4.6) is a temple (5 × 5 m, 2.44 m in height) oriented 10° west of north on top of a stepped platform (48 × 24 m, 3 m in height). It lies in the site core surrounded by two plazas and has not been plowed. The last major construction phase of the temple consists of a stone façade with a clay fill; some blocks are shaped, and some surfaces are plastered. We exposed an additional ten strata. A large looter's trench runs from the far northern edge of the temple down to the southern edge of its substructure or platform, extending about 10 m roughly north-south, 1.5 m to 3.5 m wide and from 1 to 2.5 m deep. The western side of the platform contained the eastern half of a ball court (Jeakle 2002; Jeakle et al. 2002).

The 1-m-wide excavation trench revealed several major construction phases, including steep, tiered walls and a platform with several construction phases and plastered steps (Figure 4.7). Due to time constraints, we were not able to reach sterile at SC-3. Excavated material, however, dates from at least ca. 300 BC to AD 1500, though ceramics dating as early as 600 BC were found in fill deposits. We also excavated a 1 × 1-m test unit on the top center of SC-2 (26 × 17 m, ca. 3 m high), the western half of the ball court, which likely dates to the Late Classic period.

Due to the relatively limited extensive excavations undertaken at Saturday Creek, I use ritual data from other comparable sites (Barton Ramie and Cuello) to illustrate that dedication, ancestor veneration, and termination rites have a long history extending from before rulers to after they had long disappeared. I have no doubt that further excavations at Saturday Creek would have yielded ritual evidence similar to what I present from other sites.

The Preclassic (1200 BC–AD 250)

The only clear evidence for dedication rites at Saturday Creek occurs at the elite structures (Table 4.1), which in all probability began as commoner structures, or at the very least houses not distinguishable from other early residences. Con-

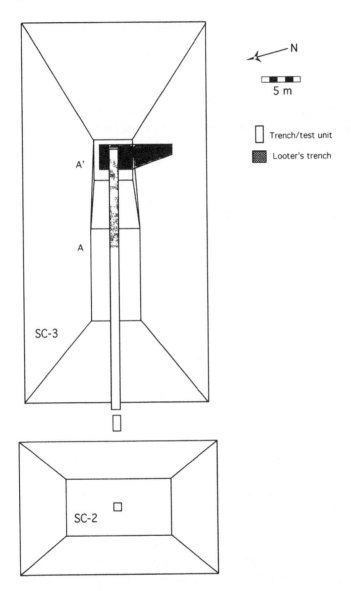

Figure 4.6. Plan of SC-3.

struction fill of commoner houses from the small, early secondary center of Cuello in northern Belize between the New and Hondo Rivers, however, yielded several caches—from a single bowl and a spindle-shaped limestone hammerstone, chalcedony flakes, and a biface tool to two pairs of lip-to-lip vessels, one containing a child's skull and the other a jade bead (Hammond and

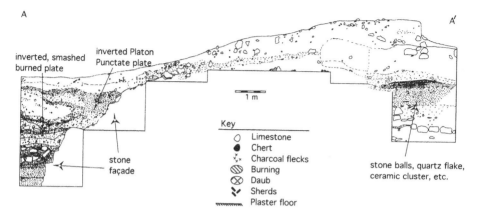

Figure 4.7. North wall profile of temple and platform SC-3 (A-A').

Gerhardt 1991) (see Figure 2.1; this area is little more than 10 m asl, and water is abundant; one can just dig a little and hit water almost anywhere). At SC-78, the elite residence, the thick clay construction fill, dating from 300 to 100 BC, yielded a dedication cache that included marine shells, a cut and polished burned bone, notched and unnotched obsidian blades (Figure 4.8), biface thinning flakes, a chert core, tool, and blade, and burned faunal remains (Lucero, Graebner, and Pugh 2002) (see Figure 4.5). In the ball-court alley fill at SC-3 we recovered a chert core, a notched obsidian blade, burned bone, and a mosaic jade piece.

No Preclassic burials were recovered at Saturday Creek, but burial data from the small secondary center of Cuello provide some of the best evidence available for Preclassic burial patterns. During the Early Middle Preclassic (1200–700 BC), most burials are located in house floors along with shell, ceramics, and some jade items (Hammond 1995, 1999). A common grave good consisted of an inverted bowl placed over the head. In the Late Middle Preclassic (700–400 BC) jade is found only in burials of males. In addition, burials start to appear in ancillary structures and community plazas. Finally, in the Late Preclassic (400 BC–AD 250), a large platform became the major locus for ceremonial activities and elite burials, the majority of which are males buried with exotic goods (Hammond et al. 1991; Robin and Hammond 1991). Domestic burials, in contrast, remained similar to those of earlier periods, usually including inverted vessels over the head as well as more diverse and exotic goods.

Barton Ramie, a minor center along the Belize River similar to Saturday Creek and heavily plowed by Mennonite farmers, also yielded Preclassic elite burials. For example, the elite residence BR-123 (33 × 23 m, 2.75 m high) had

Table 4.1. Preclassic ritual deposits

Site	Structure, Type	Ritual Type*	Context and Materials	Date**	Reference
Cuello	Str. 307, commoner residence	D	In floor; set of lip-to-lip vessels containing a child's skull	250 BC– BC/AD	Hammond and Gerhardt 1991
Cuello	Str. 306, commoner residence	D	In floor; bowl	250 BC– BC/AD	Hammond and Gerhardt 1991
Cuello	Str. 305, commoner residence	D	In floor; child's skull under inverted bowl, set of lip-to-lip vessels containing a jade bead	BC/AD– AD 250	Hammond and Gerhardt 1991
Cuello	Str. 304, commoner residence	D	In floor; 2 bowls	BC/AD– AD 250	Hammond and Gerhardt 1991
Cuello	Str. 303, commoner residence	D	In floor; spindle-shaped limestone hammerstone, chalcedony flake, Colha-type biface tool	BC/AD– AD 250	Hammond and Gerhardt 1991
Saturday Creek	SC-3, ball court alley	D	Fill; core, notched obsidian blade, burned bone, mosaic jade piece	AD 1–250	Jeakle et al. 2002
Saturday Creek	SC-78, elite residence	D	Fill; marine shell, notched obsidian blades, chert biface thinning flakes, core, tool, and blade, burned fauna, cut-polished-burned bone	300–100 BC	Lucero et al. 2002a
Cuello	Str. 352, commoner residence	AV	Burial 27; decapitated adolescent in floor; 2 vessels Burial 110; adult, in floor; 4 vessels Burial 112; adult, in floor; 2 vessels Burial 113; adult, in floor; vessel	250 BC– BC/AD	Robin and Hammond 1991
Cuello	Str. 304, commoner residence	AV	Burial 83; adult, in floor; vessel Burial 81; adult, in floor; vessel Burial 85; adult, in floor; vessel	BC/AD– AD 250	Hammond et al. 1991

Table 4.1. (*continued*)

Site	Structure, Type	Ritual Type*	Context and Materials	Date**	Reference
Barton Ramie	BR-123, elite residence	AV	Burial 30; adult, in floor; 3 vessels, jade bead, 2 shell discs, 40 *Spondylus* shell beads	100 BC– AD 250	Willey et al. 1965:551
Barton Ramie	BR-123, elite residence	AV	Burial 31; adult, in floor; 3 vessels, shell effigy jade pendant	100 BC– AD 250	Willey et al. 1965:551
Cuello	Str. 317, commoner residence	T	On floor; perishable structure burned, jade beads scattered	250 BC– BC/AD	Hammond et al. 1991
Cuello	Str. 307, commoner residence	T	Front terrace burned; pit with charcoal and sherds	250 BC– BC/AD	Hammond et al. 1991
Saturday Creek	SC-3, temple	T	Foot of temple; surface burning, sherds	100 BC– AD 200/250	Jeakle et al. 2002
Saturday Creek	SC-78, elite residence	T	Surface; burned sherds and areas, obsidian blade fragments, tool, ground-stone fragments	AD 1–250	Lucero et al. 2002a
Saturday Creek	SC-78, elite residence	T	Fill; burned areas, obsidian blade, tool, metate fragment	AD 1–250	Lucero et al. 2002a

*D = Dedication; AV = Ancestor Veneration; T = Termination.
**Saturday Creek dates were determined using ceramic chronology (type-variety) (see Conlon and Ehret 2002).

some of the earliest "lavish" burials in the Belize Valley, dating to ca. 100 BC–AD 250, including some of the earliest Maya polychrome pottery and jade beads and pendants (Willey et al. 1965:531). Burial 30, an adult male, was buried with three vessels, a jade bead, two shell discs, and forty *Spondylus* shell beads (p. 551).

The only Preclassic termination rituals at Saturday Creek consisted of smashed and burned sherds at the foot of the temple (SC-3) dating to 100 BC–AD 250 and at SC-78 on floor surfaces (burned sherds and areas, obsidian blade and chert tool fragments, and mano and metate fragments). However, there is solid evidence for domestic termination rituals at Cuello. Throughout the several construction phases of residences (and temples), the Maya burned floors and destroyed architectural features by at least 900 BC (Hammond et al. 1991).

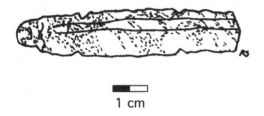

1 cm

Figure 4.8. Example of a notched obsidian blade.
Drawing by Rachel Saurman.

Later the Maya would scatter jade beads on some burned residential surfaces
(e.g., Str. 317).

The Early Classic (ca. AD 250–550)

At the commoner residence SC-85, dedicatory fill deposits dating to ca. AD 400 –
600 yielded chert cores, marine shell, notched and unnotched obsidian blades,
drilled marine shell, faunal remains, mano and metate fragments, perforated
sherds, and ceramic sherd clusters (Lucero, McGahee, and Corral 2002)
(Table 4.2). In addition to the same items listed above, elite caches at SC-3 and
SC-78 included speleothems (stalagmite or stalactite fragments from caves,
considered sacred to the Maya as portals to the underworld or Xibalba), chalcedony and obsidian cores, quartz pebbles, stone balls, and a concave sherd
containing human phalanges, some of which were twisted and deformed (Jeakle
et al. 2002; Lucero, Graebner, and Pugh 2002). A partially reconstructible
Early Classic (ca. AD 290 –550) polychrome plate was found in the fill of the
temple superstructure (SC-3).

Both of the Early Classic burials at Saturday Creek have grave goods. Burial 5 (Figure 4.9) consists of an extended and supine adult, sex unknown, with
filed incisors (Piehl 2002) buried underneath a floor with a metate fragment
over the right knee, a mano next to the metate, and a deer antler underneath
the pelvis area (Sanchez and Chamberlain 2002). Parts of the skeleton have
eroded and are indicated by dark stains (e.g., the thorax, pelvic girdle, and ver-
tebral column). Burial 6 (Figure 4.10) is an extended and prone adult, likely a
male, buried with an undecorated poorly fired (friable) plate with little temper
inverted over the chest. No burials were found at SC-3 or SC-78, which is not
too surprising given our limited excavations. At an elite Barton Ramie structure (BR-123), however, a male adult (Burial 13) was buried under a floor with
three vessels and a jade effigy pendant (Willey et al. 1965:90, 550).

Burned surfaces were recorded for every construction phase at Saturday
Creek, including that over burials (e.g., Burial 5, SC-18), indicating a consistent

Table 4.2. Early Classic ritual deposits

Site	Structure, Type	Ritual Type	Context and Materials	Date (AD)	Reference
Saturday Creek	SC-85, commoner residence	D	Fill; burned materials (daub, charcoal, cobbles), perforated sherd, chert core, mano, marine shell, drilled marine shell, notched obsidian blades, fauna; Burials 8, 10	400–600	Lucero et al. 2002b
Saturday Creek	SC-85, commoner residence	D	Fill; obsidian, mano, metate fragments	400–600	Lucero et al. 2002b
Saturday Creek	SC-85, commoner residence	D	Ballast; circular pit containing ceramic cluster	400–600	Lucero et al. 2002b
Saturday Creek	SC-78, elite residence	D	Fill; ground-stone fragments, speleothem	400–600	Lucero et al. 2002a
Saturday Creek	SC-78, elite residence	D	Fill; chalcedony core, obsidian core, marine shell	400–600	Lucero et al. 2002a
Saturday Creek	SC-78, elite residence	D	Fill; chert core, quartz pebbles, marine shell, fauna	400–600	Lucero et al. 2002a
Saturday Creek	SC-3, temple	D	Fill; core, notched obsidian blades, stone balls, ceramic cluster, quartz flake	400–600	Jeakle et al. 2002
Saturday Creek	SC-3, temple	D	Fill; basal flange bowl sherds	290–550	Jeakle et al. 2002
Saturday Creek	SC-3, platform	D	Fill; human feet and hand bones (phalanges, some twisted and deformed, inside a concave sherd), metate fragment	400–600	Jeakle et al. 2002
Saturday Creek	SC-18, commoner residence	AV	Burial 5; adult with filed incisors, in floor; metate fragment over right knee, mano, deer antler underneath pelvic area	400–600	Piehl 2002; Sanchez and Chamberlain 2002; Sanchez and Piehl 2002
Saturday Creek	SC-85, commoner residence	AV	Burial 6; adult, perhaps male, in floor; poorly fired inverted plate over chest	400–600	Sanchez and Chamberlain 2002; Sanchez and Piehl 2002
Barton Ramie	BR-123, elite residence	AV	Burial 13; adult, in floor; 3 vessels, jade effigy pendant	300–400	Willey et al. 1965:550
Saturday Creek	SC-18, commoner residence	T	Fill; circular burned area over left arm of Burial 5	400–600	Lucero and Brown 2002

(continued)

Table 4.2. (*continued*)

Site	Structure, Type	Ritual Type	Context and Materials	Date (AD)	Reference
Saturday Creek	SC-78, elite residence	T	Surface; burning throughout, notched obsidian blade fragments, fauna (some burned)	400–600	Lucero et al. 2002a
Saturday Creek	SC-3, temple base	T	Surface; burned layer of corozo nuts	400–600	Jeakle et al. 2002
Saturday Creek	SC-3, temple platform	T	Top of destroyed temple platform; layer of burned daub, fire-cracked chert	400–600	Jeakle et al. 2002

ritual behavior. We also found notched and unnotched obsidian blade fragments and metate pieces on burned surfaces. At SC-3, there were at least two major burning events at the upper temple and its platform. The first consists of a layer of burned corozo palm nuts at the base of the temple, and the second of burned daub, fire-cracked chert and charcoal-flecked soil on top of the partially collapsed (destroyed) platform substructure (Figure 4.11).

The Late Classic (ca. AD 550–850)

At Saturday Creek, dedication caches were recovered from all four structures (Table 4.3). Those found at the two commoner residences (SC-18, SC-85) are similar to those of earlier periods, but with slightly more diverse items—notched and unnotched obsidian blade fragments, mano and metate fragments, polished stone, bone needles, a miniature jar, polished and shaped bone, drilled marine shell and bone, chert cores, spindle whorls, a polished celt, a bark beater, marine shell, burned and unburned faunal remains, figurine fragments, ceramic discs, ceramic sherd clusters, and a few small jade and hematite inlay or mosaic pieces (Lucero and Brown 2002; Lucero, McGahee, and Corral 2002). A ceramic cluster at SC-85, consisting only of body sherds, may include pieces of heirloom vessels, since their dates range from 300 BC to AD 600. At SC-18 we also found a possible burned wooden post fragment, as well as some kind of design burned onto a surface, which was then buried (Figure 4.12).[2] In addition to items found at commoner houses, elite structures (SC-78, SC-3) also yielded quartz pebbles and flakes, complete notched and unnotched obsidian blades and cores, ceramic beads, a deer antler, mica, complete chert and obsidian blades, coral, speleothems, and spider monkey hand bones (Jeakle et al. 2002; Lucero, Graebner, and Pugh 2002). At SC-78 we also recovered stacked vases

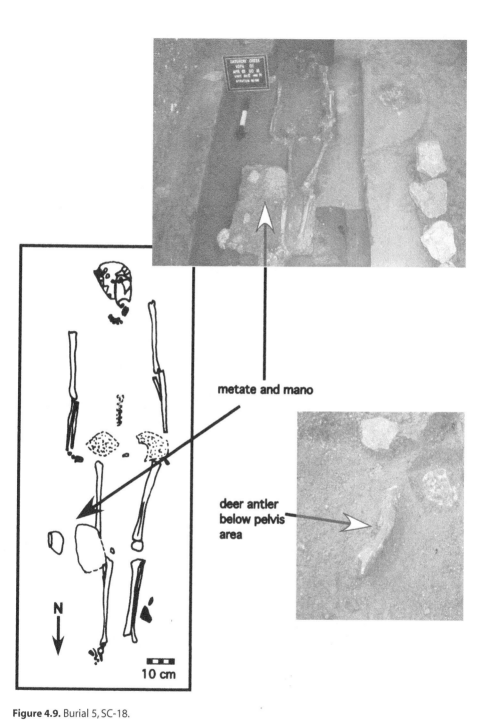

metate and mano

deer antler
below pelvis
area

Figure 4.9. Burial 5, SC-18.

Burial 6
being
exposed

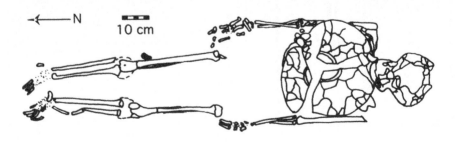

Figure 4.10. Burial 6, SC-85.

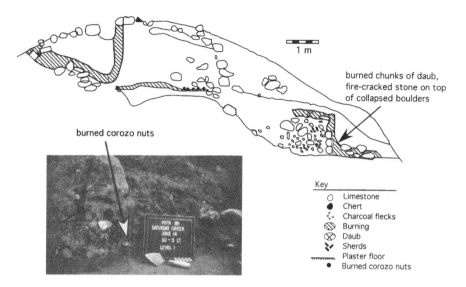

burned chunks of daub, fire-cracked stone on top of collapsed boulders

burned corozo nuts

Key
○	Limestone
●	Chert
⁙	Charcoal flecks
⧈	Burning
⊗	Daub
⋙	Sherds
⌇	Plaster floor
●	Burned corozo nuts

Figure 4.11. East wall profile of SC-3 looter's trench with burned corozo nuts and burned and destroyed platform.

with bases, but without rims; in the two examples shown in Figure 4.13, three vases are stacked, one inside the other. Of the two ceramic sherd clusters noted at SC-78, 7% ($n = 13$) are rim sherds from nine different vessels; 93% ($n = 164$) are body and base sherds. And while we did not recover a ball-court marker from the center of the alley at SC-3, the Maya had dug a pit in which they burned a large quantity of unknown organic material.

Eight Late Classic burials were recovered from the two smaller residences, four with grave goods (Sanchez and Chamberlain 2002). The three burials at SC-18 all have grave goods, including an adult, likely female (Burial 7), interred with a bowl over the knees, an olla, and freshwater shell disc beads (Figure 4.14). We are not completely sure of the sex because the burial was disturbed during the interment of Burial 11; the Maya removed everything above the pelvis and reinterred only the arm bones near Burial 11. The skull and the rest of the upper body are missing. Two of the three burials are seated, which might indicate high status (McAnany 1998; Sanchez and Piehl 2002). One seated adult, perhaps male (Burial 11), was interred with an inverted dish over the skull (see Figure 4.14), and the other (Burial 2), a young adult (14–20 years, sex unknown), with a large inverted dish over the skull, an olla near the right knee, a hammerstone next to the olla, an inverted plate over the left knee, and marine shell disc beads near the right ankle (Figure 4.15). The sole burial (Burial 8) with grave goods at SC-85, likely of an adult male, includes a dish near the skull, an olla near the chest, a mano fragment, marine shell, two heavily eroded (poorly

Table 4.3. Late Classic ritual deposits

Site	Structure, Type	Ritual Type	Context and Materials	Date (AD)	Reference
Saturday Creek	SC-85, commoner residence	D	Fill; obsidian core, notched blades, mano and metate fragments, polished stone, figurine fragment, marine shell, fauna (burned, deer, bird); Burials 1, 3	700–900	Lucero et al. 2002b
Saturday Creek	SC-18, commoner residence	D	Fill; bone needle, chert core, notched obsidian blade, spindle whorl, figurine fragment, shell	700–900	Lucero and Brown 2002
Saturday Creek	SC-85, commoner residence	D	Fill; chert core, marine shell, notched obsidian blade, fauna; Burials 4, 6	800–900	Lucero et al. 2002b
Saturday Creek	SC-85, commoner residence	D	Fill/possible living surface; ceramic disc, notched obsidian blades, fauna, ceramic cluster (20 body sherds, some dating to 300–100 BC, and AD 400–600—basal flange)	600–800	Lucero et al. 2002b
Saturday Creek	SC-18, commoner residence	D	Fill; obsidian blade, polished celt	800–900	Lucero and Brown 2002
Saturday Creek	SC-18, commoner residence	D	Fill; burned-in design, marine shell, notched obsidian blades, ceramic disc, drilled marine shell, polished-shaped bone, drilled burned bone, turtle carapace with cross-hatch cut marks, fauna	600–700	Lucero and Brown 2002
Saturday Creek	SC-18	D	Fill; notched obsidian blades, marine shell, daub	600–700, 700–900	Lucero and Brown 2002
Saturday Creek	SC-18	D	Ballast; core, possible burned wooden post; Burial 2	700–900	Lucero and Brown 2002
Saturday Creek	SC-18, commoner residence	D	Fill; marine shell, notched obsidian blades, bone needle, jade tooth inlay, hematite disc fragment, pieces of turtle carapace, bird bone	800–900	Lucero and Brown 2002
Saturday Creek	SC-18, commoner residence	D	Fill; ground-stone fragment, bark beater, fauna	650–750	Lucero and Brown 2002
Saturday Creek	SC-18	D	Ballast; core	700–900	Lucero and Brown 2002

Table 4.3. (*continued*)

Site	Structure, Type	Ritual Type	Context and Materials	Date (AD)	Reference
Saturday Creek	SC-78	D	Fill; mano, core, tool	600–900	Lucero et al. 2002a
Saturday Creek	SC-78, elite residence	D	Fill; burned plaster, charcoal, fauna (turtle), chert core, blade, notched obsidian blades, mano and metate fragments, quartz flake, ceramic bead, figurine fragment, 2 ceramic clusters, one of which has 13 (7%) rims from 9 different vessels (and 159 body and 5 base sherds); the other cluster has 2 jar rims and 7 body sherds	800–900	Lucero et al. 2002a
Saturday Creek	SC-78, elite residence	D	Floor; burned area, mano, bone cluster (monkey feet/hand bones), speleothem	700–800	Lucero et al. 2002a
Saturday Creek	SC-78, elite residence	D	Fill; vase cluster with complete base and without rims, marine shell, chert core, notched obsidian blade	800–900	Lucero et al. 2002a
Saturday Creek	SC-78, elite residence	D	Fill; 3 stacked vases with complete bases and without rims, notched obsidian blades, 2 obsidian blades, obsidian flakes, marine shell, metate	700–900	Lucero et al. 2002a
Saturday Creek	SC-78, elite residence	D	Fill; burned plaster, obsidian blades, ground-stone fragments, chert core and blade	700–900	Lucero et al. 2002a
Saturday Creek	SC-3, platform, foot of temple	D	Fill; metate fragment	700–900	Jeakle et al. 2002
Saturday Creek	SC-3, platform, foot of temple	D	Fill; burned bone flake, bone	800–900	Jeakle et al. 2002
Saturday Creek	SC-3, platform	D	Fill; chert blades, marine shell, ground-stone fragments, notched obsidian blade, antler, bone	800–900	Jeakle et al. 2002
Saturday Creek	SC-3, ball court	D	Fill; obsidian core	600–700	Jeakle et al. 2002

(*continued*)

Table 4.3. (*continued*)

Site	Structure, Type	Ritual Type	Context and Materials	Date (AD)	Reference
Saturday Creek	SC-3, ball court	D	Alley fill; burned pit with organic matter	650–750	Jeakle et al. 2002
Saturday Creek	SC-3, ball court	D	Fill; chert core and blade, white mica	800–900	Jeakle et al. 2002
Saturday Creek	SC-18, commoner residence	AV	Burial 2; seated adult (14–20 years) in floor; large dish inverted over skull, inverted olla near right knee, inverted plate over left knee, hammerstone, shell disc bead anklet	800–900	Sanchez and Chamberlain 2002; Sanchez and Piehl 2002
Saturday Creek	SC-18, commoner residence	AV	Burial 7; adult female in floor; bowl over the knees, olla, freshwater shell disc beads	700–800	Sanchez and Chamberlain 2002; Sanchez and Piehl 2002
Saturday Creek	SC-18, commoner residence	AV	Burial 11; seated adult, perhaps male, in floor; dish inverted over skull	600–700	Sanchez and Chamberlain 2002; Sanchez and Piehl 2002
Saturday Creek	SC-85, commoner residence	AV	Burial 1; adult female in floor with filed incisors	700–900	Piehl 2002; Sanchez and Chamberlain 2002; Sanchez and Piehl 2002
Saturday Creek	SC-85, commoner residence	AV	Burial 3; adolescent (10–12 years) in floor	600–700	Sanchez and Chamberlain 2002; Sanchez and Piehl 2002
Saturday Creek	SC-85, commoner residence	AV	Burial 4; child (1–4 years) in floor	800–900	Sanchez and Chamberlain 2002; Sanchez and Piehl 2002
Saturday Creek	SC-85, commoner residence	AV	Burial 8; adult, perhaps male, in floor; dish near the skull, olla near chest, polished bone near mandible, mano, marine shell, and two poorly fired temperless vessels over upper legs	700–900	Sanchez and Chamberlain 2002; Sanchez and Piehl 2002
Saturday Creek	SC-85, commoner residence	AV	Burial 9; adult female in floor	700–900	Sanchez and Chamberlain 2002; Sanchez and Piehl 2002

Table 4.3. (*continued*)

Site	Structure, Type	Ritual Type	Context and Materials	Date (AD)	Reference
Barton Ramie	BR-260, elite residence	AV	Burial 3; adult in floor; 3 vessels, 3 obsidian blades, 3 carved bones, jaguar-shaped jade pendant, polished celt	600–800	Willey et al. 1965:557
Barton Ramie	BR-123, elite residence	AV	Burial 18; adult in floor; 4 vessels effigy tooth pendant, bone needle fragment	700–900	Willey et al. 1995:550
Saturday Creek	SC-18, commoner residence	T	On surface; 3 layers of smashed and burned vessels interspersed with a possible burned mat/textile; some date to 400–600; majority are body sherds (96%, n = 209)	650–750	Lucero and Brown 2002
Saturday Creek	SC-85, commoner residence	T	Fill surface; plain miniature jar	600–700	Lucero et al. 2002b
Saturday Creek	SC-85	T	Fill/living surface; 2 ceramic clusters, 1 with 2 large mammal long bone fragments inside (1 rim/67 body; 24 body sherds), burned daub	600–700, 700–900	Lucero et al. 2002b
Saturday Creek	SC-85	T	Top of fill/living surface: 6 ceramic clusters (rim and body sherds, but no complete vessels); Majority are body sherds (84%, n = 138)	700–900, 800–900	Lucero et al. 2002b
Saturday Creek	SC-85, commoner residence	T	Burned surface; Colha-chert tool, ceramic bird or fish figurine fragment, obsidian blade, marine shell, shaped serpentine, metate fragment, 10 ceramic clusters (some not well-fired; most with only a few or no rim sherds; some dating to 250–400); majority are body sherds (88%, n = 350)	700–900	Lucero et al. 2002b
Saturday Creek	SC-85, commoner residence	T	Surface; obsidian blades, mano and metate fragments, burning, complete broken basal flange bowl (250–400), 4 ceramic clusters, the majority body sherds (58%, n = 148)	600–900	Lucero et al. 2002b

(*continued*)

Table 4.3. (*continued*)

Site	Structure, Type	Ritual Type	Context and Materials	Date (AD)	Reference
Saturday Creek	SC-18, commoner residence	T	Burned pit; charcoal, marine shell, polished-shaped-burned bone, 3 clusters of smashed, burned ceramics (possible association with Burial 5), 2 of which are all body sherds (66, 37), and the other with 17 rim and 106 body sherds	650–750	Lucero and Brown 2002
Saturday Creek	SC-18	T	Fill surface; circular burned area, burned daub	700–900	Lucero and Brown 2002
Saturday Creek	SC-18, commoner residence	T	Pit in floor; burned soil, obsidian core	700–900	Lucero and Brown 2002
Saturday Creek	SC-18, commoner residence	T	Surface; 3 layers of smashed burned sherds, majority body sherds (97%, n = 266); 1 complete vessel, marine shell, 2 large burned mammal bones	700–900	Lucero and Brown 2002
Saturday Creek	SC-18, commoner residence	T	Surface; polychrome sherds, burning	700–900	Lucero and Brown 2002
Saturday Creek	SC-78	T	Floor; burned area; surface—face jar neck sherd against step; notched obsidian blade	600–700	Lucero et al. 2002a
Saturday Creek	SC-78, elite residence	T	Floor; burned plaster (and daub)	700–900	Lucero et al. 2002a
Saturday Creek	SC-78, elite residence	T	Floor; powdered marl on surface	700–900	Lucero et al. 2002a
Saturday Creek	SC-78, elite residence	T	Surface; burned daub wall on top of ceramic cluster (41 body sherds); human ulna on plate, drilled-carved marine shell pendant, slipped miniature jar	800–900	Lucero et al. 2002a
Saturday Creek	SC-78, elite residence	T	On floor; ceramic drum sherd	650–750	Lucero et al. 2002a
Saturday Creek	SC-3, platform	T	Surface; smashed ceramics	700–900	Jeakle et al. 2002
Saturday Creek	SC-3, platform, foot of temple	T	Fill surface; 3 ceramic clusters on burned area, 2 of which consist of body sherds, 1 with 5 rims and 21 body sherds (some with charcoal inside) (96% total body sherds, n = 114)	650–750, 700–900	Jeakle et al. 2002

Table 4.3. (continued)

Site	Structure, Type	Ritual Type	Context and Materials	Date (AD)	Reference
Saturday Creek	SC-3, platform, foot of temple	T	Top of fill; burned area and daub, fire-cracked rocks	700–900	Jeakle et al. 2002
Saturday Creek	SC-3, platform	T	Surface (foot of temple); inverted Platon Punctate (no rims) plate, burning	800–900	Jeakle et al. 2002:56–57

fired) untempered vessels over the upper legs, and a polished bone near the mandible (Figure 4.16). Burial 3 at SC-85 is a bundle burial of an adolescent (ca. 10 –12 years of age) without grave goods (Figure 4.17). The extended and prone adult female at SC-85 (Burial 1) has filed incisors but was not buried with any grave goods (Piehl 2002) (Figure 4.18).

Due to the limited excavations at Saturday Creek elite structures, we did not find any burials. At Barton Ramie, however, elite burials yielded, in addition to jade beads, at least three jade effigy pendants as well as typically more goods per burial (Willey et al. 1965:90, 549–552). For example, grave goods interred with an adult (Burial 3) at BR-260 (ca. 40 × 30 m with four mounds up to 2 m high) included three vessels, three obsidian blades, three carved bones, a jaguar-shaped jade pendant, and a polished celt (pp. 267–270, 557).

We found termination deposits at all four structures, which are similar to earlier periods. They consist of smashed and burned vessels on surfaces. For example, at SC-18 we recovered three layers of burned and smashed ceramics, mostly body sherds (96%), some of which date to AD 400–600. They had been deposited on top of a textile or mat of some sort, which also had been burned (Figure 4.19). In a later termination event at SC-18, the Maya again burned and smashed three layers of largely rimless ceramic sherds (8 rims or 3%; and 266 body sherds or 97%); we also found a complete but broken bowl in the same deposit, as well as burned bone and marine shells. Similarly, at SC-85, the Maya broke and burned several items, including daub and ceramics; some sherds contain the long bones of a large mammal, likely a deer. They also placed an undecorated miniature jar on a burned surface at ca. AD 600–700. In what appears to be a major termination event, the Maya at SC-85 burned and smashed ceramics (10 different clusters, some not well-fired, with only a few rims) and offered a Colha-chert tool, a ceramic bird or fish figurine fragment, an unnotched obsidian blade, marine shell, shaped serpentine, and a metate fragment (Figures 4.20 and 4.21). Some of the ceramics were possible heirloom vessels, since they dated to as early as ca. AD 250.

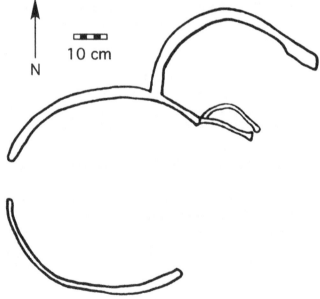

Figure 4.12. Burned symbol on a surface at SC-18.

Figure 4.13. Two examples of stacked vases without rims at SC-78.

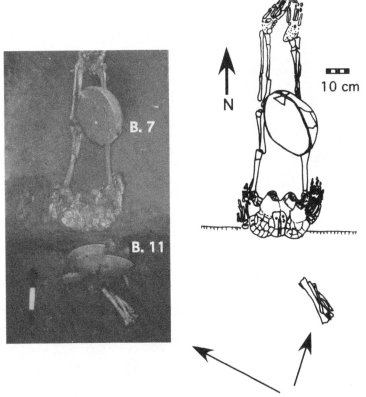

Redeposited B. 7 arm bones found 33 cm below original burial

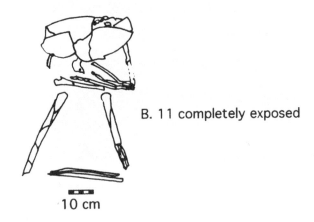

B. 11 completely exposed

Figure 4.14. Burial 7 (and Burial 11), SC-18.

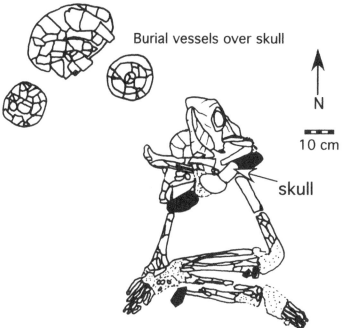

Burial vessels over skull

N

10 cm

skull

Figure 4.15. Burial 2, SC-18. The plate over the left knee has been removed and is not shown in the photograph.

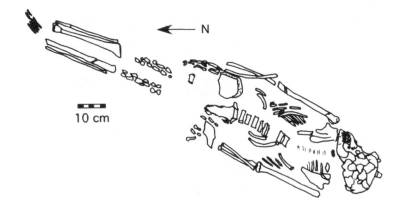

Figure 4.16. Burial 8, SC-85. The upper photograph shows the grave goods found on top of the remains (mano, olla, and two poorly fired vessels).

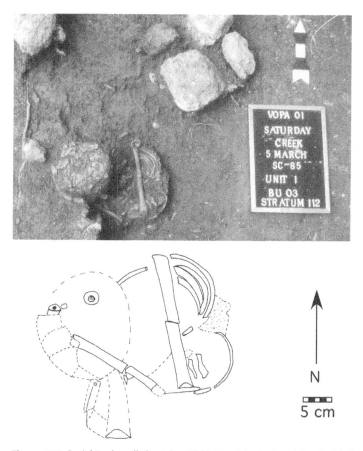

Figure 4.17. Burial 3, a bundle burial at SC-85. Vandals displaced the skull before we could draw it.

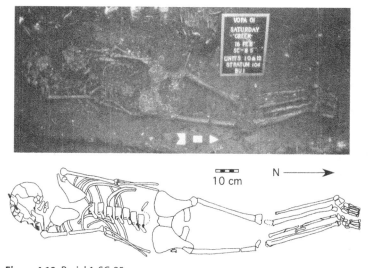

Figure 4.18. Burial 1, SC-85.

Figure 4.19. Termination deposit at SC-18, consisting of three layers of smashed and burned ceramics. The outline of a burned textile or mat is visible.

Figure 4.20. Termination deposit at SC-85, consisting of burned and smashed ceramics and other items. The lower deposit is located east of the upper one and one floor below.

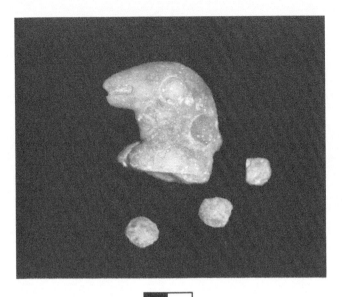

1 cm

Figure 4.21. A bird or fish figurine fragment at SC-85 that was part of the termination deposit in Figure 4.20.

The major difference between commoner and elite termination deposits is the types of vessels smashed. At SC-18 and SC-85, the Maya smashed vessels usually consisting of plain or monochrome slipped bowls, jars and plates, and only a few polychrome sherds, as well as the other items just described. In many cases, however, the smashed ceramic clusters in both elite and commoner contexts largely consist of body sherds with few or no rims. The elite structure and temple yielded, in addition to the above, drum vases, polychrome vessels, molded ceramic pieces, drilled and carved marine shell, powdered marl, burned plaster fragments, and human bone. For example, sometime during the ninth century AD, the Maya at SC-78 burned an entire structure of wattle-and-daub (Figure 4.22). One wall collapsed on a deposit of several burned and smashed decorated vessels (all body sherds), a human ulna placed on top of a large rimless plate, an incised drilled marine shell pendant, and a drilled shell (Figure 4.23). On the north edge of the platform at about AD 600–700, the Maya placed a molded-face jar neck sherd and a notched obsidian blade against the lower platform step near a burned patch of plaster floor (Figure 4.24). In another case, at the foot of the temple at SC-3, an inverted Platon Punctate rimless plate was burned (Figure 4.25; see Figure 4.7 for location) (Jeakle 2002:56–57). This ceramic type was not found anywhere else at Saturday Creek (Conlon and Ehret 2002), and James Gifford et al. (1976:257) note that it was only found in burial contexts at Barton Ramie.

upper
ceramic
cluster

detail of human
ulna on a rimless
plate

Figure 4.22. Termination deposit at SC-78, consisting of a collapsed burned daub wall (removed) over smashed and burned ceramics and other items, including a human ulna on a rimless plate.

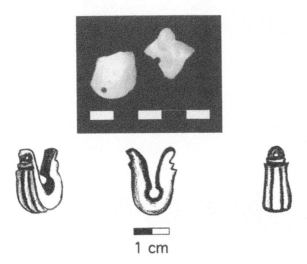

1 cm

Figure 4.23. Drilled and carved marine shells from a termination deposit at SC-78. 1 cm scale. Drawing of pendant by Gaea McGahee.

The Postclassic (ca. AD 950–1500): The Story Continues

The Maya continued to conduct the same traditional rites in the home long after royals and upper elites ceased conducting theirs. At Saturday Creek, for example, the occupants of one of the small houses (SC-18) expanded the structure south; within fill dating to ca. AD 900–1150, we found a notched obsidian blade (Table 4.4). In another expansion episode in the same area and period, the Maya added more fill and another floor, within which they had placed a polished celt and an unnotched obsidian blade (Lucero and Brown 2002). The other commoner house (SC-85) yielded a Postclassic burial (Burial 10) of a seated individual facing south (Figure 4.26). Time constraints prevented us from completely excavating the burial, but we were able to remove the offering, a complete large red dish (Daylight orange) that the Maya had inverted over the head. We do not know if there were more offerings, since we only exposed the head and shoulders.

Evidence for even later rites comes from the elite compound at Saturday Creek (SC-78). From a fill deposit dating to ca. AD 1150–1500 on the far south of the mound, we recovered a chert blade tool and a shaped and polished multicolored chert flake (Figure 4.27) (Lucero, Graebner, and Pugh 2002). An earlier fill deposit (AD 900–1150) on the north side of the platform mound yielded a piece of jade. In a final example from Saturday Creek, we recovered cores, marine shell, and notched obsidian from a fill deposit of the platform of the temple ball court (SC-3) that dates to ca. AD 900–1150 (Jeakle et al. 2002). Ritual

original position
of face sherd

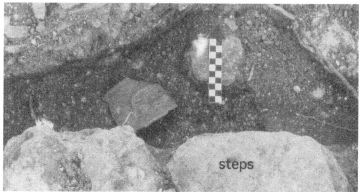

steps

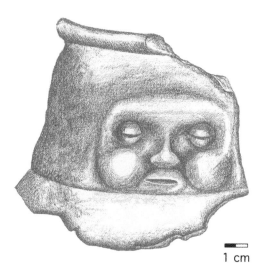

1 cm

Figure 4.24. A face jar neck sherd recovered against a step on the north side of SC-78. Drawing by Gaea McGahee.

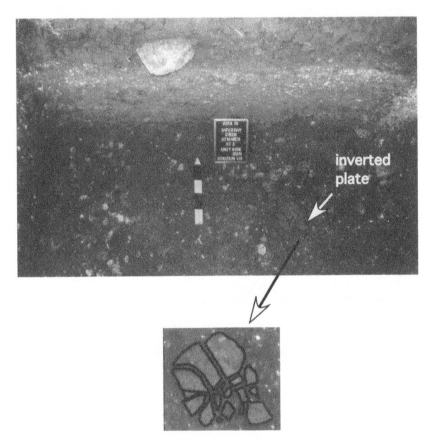

Figure 4.25. An inverted Platon Punctate rimless plate at the foot of temple SC-3.

deposits at SC-78 and SC-3 began by at least 300 BC (and very likely earlier) and continued through the Postclassic period, from AD 1150 to 1500.

Similar patterns were noted at Barton Ramie, especially for burials. BR-1, a mound 2 m in height and 28 m in diameter with 12 occupation phases dating from ca. 100 BC to AD 1200 (Willey et al. 1965:36), yielded an unbroken sequence of ritual events. For example, in the last period of occupation at this house, an infant or child was interred with small beads (Burial 5, p. 545).

At an elite residence, BR-123, Gordon Willey and his crew found thirty-five burials in the thirteen occupation levels (pp. 90, 112), two of which date to the Postclassic (Burials 27 and 33). Neither was buried with grave goods, though one of the burials might be that of a male (pp. 551–552), a pattern that contrasts sharply with earlier burial practices at this mound (see Tables 4.1, 4.2, 4.3).

This pattern differs from BR-144 (1.5 m high, 35 × 35 m). The Maya lived here from ca. AD 0–1200 but only appeared to have two major construction epi-

Table 4.4. Postclassic ritual deposits

Site	Structure, Type	Ritual Type	Context and Materials	Date (AD)	Reference
Saturday Creek	SC-18	D	Fill; notched obsidian blade	900–1150	Lucero and Brown 2002
Saturday Creek	SC-18	D	Fill; polished celt, obsidian blade	900–1150	Lucero and Brown 2002
Saturday Creek	SC-3, platform	D	Fill; cores, marine shell, notched obsidian blade	900–1150	Jeakle et al. 2002
Saturday Creek	SC-78	D	Fill; jade piece	900–1150	Lucero et al. 2002a
Saturday Creek	SC-78	D	Fill; obsidian blade, polychrome-polished-shaped chert flake, blade tool	1150–1500	Lucero et al. 2002a
Saturday Creek	SC-85	AV	Burial 10; not excavated; seated, facing south, large dish inverted over head	900–1150	Sanchez and Chamberlain 2002
Barton Ramie	BR-1, commoner	AV	Burial 5; infant or child; small beads	900–1200	Willey et al. 1965:545
Barton Ramie	BR-144, commoner	AV	Burials 1, 5; 2 female (one with limestone crescent, one with a vessel)	900–1200	Willey et al. 1965:553–554
Barton Ramie	BR-123, elite residence	AV	Burials 33, 27; 2 adults (one a possible male)	900–1200	Willey et al. 1965:551–552

sodes (or perhaps it was quite late in construction and the ceramics from fill contexts came from elsewhere). There are seven burials, all of which date to either ca. AD 800–900 or 900–1200 (pp. 553–554). Only two burials, both of female adults (Burials 1 and 5), have grave goods; the former was buried with a "crescent-shaped object of limestone" (p. 553), and the latter with one vessel. While we did not recover obvious Postclassic termination deposits at Saturday Creek, the Maya likely still performed rites at the end of an object's life. This pattern continues into the Colonial period and into the present, as illustrated in Chapter 3. Also, both Barton Ramie and Saturday Creek have been heavily plowed during the last few decades, which has likely destroyed much evidence for Postclassic termination and other ritual activities. Postclassic rituals are scarce or nonexistent, however, at major centers such as Tikal and Altar de Sacrificios. Their purpose as a place for royal rites decreased in significance when rulers lost power and centers were largely abandoned in the AD 900s.

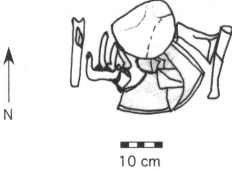

N

10 cm

Figure 4.26. Burial 10, SC-85.

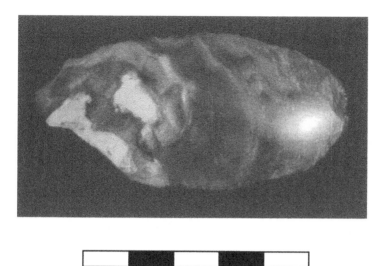

Figure 4.27. A polychrome polished chert flake tool from the south side of
SC-78. 1 cm scale.

Summary and Discussion

At Saturday Creek, ritual deposits at commoner residences SC-18 and SC-85
remained basically the same throughout their entire occupation (ca. AD 400–
1150). The earliest ritual deposits at the elite structure SC-78 (fill dating to ca.
300–100 BC) are similar (that is, simpler and smaller in scale) to those found at
the two solitary commoner mounds (SC-18 and SC-85) throughout both commoner houses' entire occupation (e.g., marine shell, obsidian blade fragments,
and undecorated vessels). This pattern signifies that earlier, commoner ritual
deposits at SC-78 are the same as at the two commoner residences and that
later, elite buildings have increasingly more diverse goods. As to the significance of notched obsidian blades, they may have served as smaller or commoner
versions of eccentrics. The ceramic clusters with only a relatively few rim sherds
need explaining; perhaps depositing ceramics without rims was a way to kill
vessels in both dedication and termination rituals. In addition, the inclusion of
older vessels as termination offerings might indicate the sacrifice of heirloom
objects (e.g., R. Joyce 2000).

Evidence for ancestor veneration rites does not noticeably change at commoner residences in over 500 years at Saturday Creek and longer elsewhere. It
appears that only select people were buried in houses, particularly adults of both
sexes, but mostly males (Sanchez and Piehl 2002; e.g., Haviland 1997). These
practices are similar to those seen at small residences at Cuello, Barton Ramie,

Altar de Sacrificios, and Tikal (see Chapters 5 and 6). While the burial patterns presented in this chapter are simple, they actually involve complex ritual behaviors. For example, when the residents of SC-18 buried the adult of Burial 5, they first dug a pit, which they filled with flakes and burned and broken pottery (Lucero and Brown 2002). They placed the antler in the center of the pit, after which they put in fill and the deceased individual. They added more fill and then burned and smashed more ceramics. Afterward, they added the mano and metate fragments and more ceramics and placed more fill (dirt). Finally, they burned more items and placed vessels just south of the skull and burned the entire deposit again.

The Maya conducted small-scale rituals inside the home for family members. Some rituals were conducted privately in the elite compound, and some probably involved community members. Its location on a terrace facing a plaza overlooking the majority of Saturday Creek's inhabitants provided both privacy (it is not visible from below) and an arena for public participation. The more diverse and exotic offerings also distinguished elites at SC-78. Communal or voluntary labor likely built the temple ball court. There is evidence (faunal remains, decorated serving vessels) of feasting near or in the ball-court alley, which elites sponsored for Saturday Creek's inhabitants. In her analysis of Spanish Lookout (AD 700–900) ceramic forms and faunal remains from the platform and ball-court alley, Julie Jeakle (2002) found noticeable differences between SC-3 assemblages and those from houses, especially the commoner ones. While SC-3 had the lowest ceramic density of the four excavated sites, it yielded a high proportion of large serving vessels. Further, several kinds of bowls were only found at SC-3 and were probably used during feasts. Finally, Jeakle noted that excavated materials from the ball-court alley yielded the highest percentage of large mammal remains (e.g., deer) and turtle carapaces. No faunal remains were recovered from the temple on top, where Maya elites conducted private dedication and termination (and probably ancestor veneration) rituals not visible from the ball-court alley below, at least in the Classic period, when the platform was built up. A similar scenario likely occurred at Barton Ramie.

With plentiful water and land throughout the year, the Maya at Saturday Creek lived a comfortable existence without the worry and bother of outside interference. The lack of obvious water systems and public imagery does not indicate a lesser reliance on gods and ancestors for rain, but rather a lesser need for assistance from other mortals. As members of a larger society, however, they participated in creating and defining Maya social and cultural worldviews. Despite the fact that kings did not emerge at Saturday Creek, elites still conducted traditional rituals at the community level to offset potential conflict in the face of wealth differences and to promote solidarity.

In conclusion, we can better understand how the Maya lived at minor centers through knowledge of their community organization. The only noticeable difference between the general definition of community organization and minor centers is that we do not know about land ownership per se, though it was probably both corporate and private. We must assume that, even if the Maya did not fight as warriors, there was probably some type of conflict (e.g., feuding). And while there is no political iconography or obvious decorative element on monumental architecture, decorations on portable items (e.g., vessels and incised bone) were significant to the Maya and still reflected the critical importance of ancestors and the gods.

CHAPTER 5

Local Rulers and the Maya:
The Ritual History of Altar de Sacrificios

In this chapter I detail the distinguishing features of local polities (see Table 1.1) and secondary Maya centers, which have several factors in common (see Table 2.1). I also present a history of ritual activities at Altar de Sacrificios, a secondary Maya center.

Local Polity

Depending on individual circumstances, a local polity can be viewed as several politically integrated communities—versus economically integrated ones, which they typically are. Farmers, who live in dispersed but densely settled villages, rely more on intensive agriculture, including small-scale water/agricultural systems. They still must deal with the vagaries of annual rainfall, including periodic drought, flooding, or rain damage. These polities have both concentrated (e.g., trade ports) and unrestricted (e.g., dispersed fertile land) resources. Hereditary leaders, whose positions are institutionalized, can acquire some tribute because of their ability to monopolize critical resources, especially when seasonal food shortages or weather damages occur (Gilman 1981). Their main economic role, however, is not so much in ownership of the means of production but in their abilities to provide food from their own stores or via trade and capital for the common good. Leaders live in central places such as large villages or towns. Elites and political leaders (e.g., a paramount chief) participate in the elite interaction sphere and regional politics. If local polities are in the same area as a regional polity, they may be politically subsumed by the larger entity, though material conditions typically prevent their leaders from becoming monarchs of a centralized or integrative polity themselves. Territorial extent includes the immediate area, including farmsteads and communities; and chiefs sponsor and coordinate warfare for political purposes—to incorporate more people and labor (Johnson and Earle 2000:249).

Political leaders participate in external exchange, particularly since nonlocal goods, information, and ties play a major role in maintaining political power (Helms 1979). Consequently, such societies typically have trade ports and differential distribution of exotic goods, most of which are found in trade centers and less so at lower-order settlements. For example, Small (1995) describes how the Yapese incorporated West Caroline Islands through controlling exchange via patron-client relationships. Consequently, access to exotics and external ties distinguish leaders (Helms 1993). Commoners, however, still participate in the exchange of utilitarian and prestige goods with members of other communities and local polities, free from elite interference.

Everyone participates in traditional household and community ancestor rites. In addition, chiefs perform rituals in public arenas large enough to hold people from several villages or communities that usually revolve around chiefly ancestors as descendants of gods (Johnson and Earle 2000:266), as well as fertility, rain, and war gods, which are depicted in the iconography. Individual people, however, are not portrayed, and writing or recording systems are not used.

Internal relations check chiefs' power and include subjects' loyalty to their own descent groups, social mobility, chiefly councils, competing chiefly or noble lineages, magicians, age-sets, warrior and secret societies, and ritual specialists. External relations also often act to curb centralized power; for example, in several precolonial African societies, subordinate chiefs are physically beyond the reach of paramount chiefs and can break away if tribute demands are too onerous or if the paramount chief is unjust (e.g., Zulu, Ngwato, Bemba, Banayankole, Kede) (Fortes and Evans-Pritchard 1940). Chiefs lead warfare parties of a few military specialists and part-time soldiers drawn from the ranks of villages during agricultural downtime to incorporate more tribute-payers, versus killing people and taking their land. Leaders have various kinds of relations with other groups, both equal and unequal. For example, as mentioned in Chapter 4, rulers of the Kedah state in Malaysia (AD 700–1500) had peer relations with foreign trade partners and equal, heterarchical relations with inhabitants of the forest far upstream, with whom they exchanged foreign goods for forest products (e.g., timber) necessary for trade (Allen 1999). In addition, Kedah rulers also had hierarchical relations with inland dry-land farming communities and secondary centers mid-river who owed tribute to Kedah leaders (prestige goods and rice), who in turn provided them with foreign goods and access to the foreign market for their rice.

In local polities, disruptions in political relations, elite interaction (e.g., diminishing prestige-goods exchange), climate regimes, and resource availability reverberate throughout the political system (Flannery 1972), but not necessarily the economic system (subsistence practices and wealth differences). For example, in precontact Hawaii (Johnson and Earle 2000:282–294), political instability occurred after the death of a paramount chief because succession rules did not exist. Consequently, different chiefly lines competed to lay claim to wearing the feather cloak of the paramount chief. The subsistence base, however, remained stable. In the Kedah case in Malaysia, though, over-use of non-irrigated farmlands beginning about AD 900 resulted in decreasing supplies of staple foods necessary to support tribute demands; in addition, silt build-up cut off coastal ports by ca. AD 1200 (Allen 1999).

I illustrate a local polity through a brief description of Hawaiian chiefdoms. The Hawaiian Islands consist of seven islands in the Pacific. At the time of contact in 1778, there were four competing chiefdoms. The largest of the islands is Hawaii, on which I focus. It is environmentally diverse, with three different zones extending from the coast inland: the "shallow offshore bays," uplands and alluvium, and forests (Johnson and Earle 2000:287). While overall population density was relatively low, it increased in areas with fertile soils, which are unevenly distributed across the island. Islanders practiced intensive agriculture, especially taro production, as well as some shifting agriculture and fishing. There is an uneven distribution of rainfall across the island as well as "periodic flooding and tidal wave damage" (p. 289). Subsistence technology was relatively small-scale, and much of it was handled at the village level. Hawaiians used small-scale terraces, irrigation, drainage systems, and taro pond fields (Earle 1978:193). Households were basically self-sufficient, with some intracommunity exchange across the different zones, as well as small, nonextensive markets for extracommunity exchange. Villages were dispersed and varied in size and density. Economic stratification existed, where chiefly lineages were wealthier than others.

The paramount chief (PC), a sacred person, supported military and religious specialists, to whom he allotted lands for services rendered, and lorded over district chiefs, community chiefs, and village land managers. The PC also provided capital to rebuild irrigation systems destroyed by heavy rainfall (Earle 1978:74). Since mature taro can be stored in the field for up to eighteen months, its continuous supply "largely eliminated the need for storage facilities and minimized the periodicity of labor in agriculture" (p. 118). The PC owned all the land and seafaring canoes used to obtain maritime resources and for trade and organized the construction of agricultural systems. He also allotted land to communities (p. 157). In exchange for use of the PC's land, fishponds, and canoes, people contributed food, labor, and specialized goods. Paramount chiefs organized war parties to conquer people, to increase the amount of tribute at their disposal.

Religious institutions and rituals played a large role in consolidating the PC's control over the region, especially since competition for power was intense. The PCs, "gods on earth" (Earle 1997:169), conducted rites to key gods, including Ku, the god of war, and Lono, the god of "land and fertility" (Johnson and Earle 2000:291), throughout the land on a ceremonial circuit at shrines (stone enclosures), where representations of gods made of wicker were used (e.g., the Makahiki ceremony) (Earle 1978:188; 1997:172). Many deities were once chiefly ancestors (Kirch 1984:66). Communities built smaller shrines at which to worship, and people also had their own house gods (Earle 1997:175). "[R]ituals directed to ancestors made up a large part of religious practice" (Kirch and Green 2001:245). Farmers also conducted rituals at every stage of the agricultural process (Kirch 1984:38).

The only politically unstable periods were during the transition to a new PC, when the various district chiefs vied for the powerful position, as mentioned above. The end of the Hawaiian way of chiefly life was due to external causes— their exposure to Western culture and eventual takeover by the United States.

Such societies have many factors in common with the Maya who lived in secondary centers during the Late Classic (ca. AD 550–850), especially the extent of power at a ruler's disposal—that is, the number of subjects.

The Maya: Secondary Centers

Histories of secondary centers show great variability, which is to be expected given their secondary status. They differ from minor centers in several ways. For example, Lamanai, Altar de Sacrificios, Yalbac, Seibal, Yaxchilán, El Pilar, Quiriguá, Bonampak, Cuello, Dos Pilas, Piedras Negras, Xunantunich, Toniná, and other centers are typically found along or near rivers in hilly areas with limited or dispersed pockets of agricultural land and may have been subsumed in a regional polity or at least interacted with it (see Table 2.1). A common factor among them is access to rivers or river trade routes. Secondary centers are typically found in lower elevations than regional centers (70–175 m asl). Annual rainfall ranges from over 200 cm to over 280 cm (see Figure 4.1). At most secondary centers, residents lived above rivers on ridges and hills, which meant that saturated hillsides during the rainy season posed problems and influenced building plans and agricultural schedules (Turner 1974). Many rivers were fast flowing and dangerous during the height of the rainy season and low and difficult to travel during the dry season (Gill 2000:254). For example, Wendy Ashmore (1981:89) suggests that the Maya at Quiriguá may have built artificial levees and/or canals to control flooding and to offset poor drainage.

Because of the dispersed agricultural soils, Maya farmers used scattered small-scale water/agricultural systems, including *aguadas*, dams, canals, and drainage ditches (e.g., Dunning et al. 1997; Fedick 1994). Their scale and scattered distribution suggest that they did not have a major role in politics. Moreover, even if rulers owned land throughout the area, they could have only kept an eye on things in the immediate vicinity. For land beyond their reach, they compensated farmers for their labor with prestige items and a portion of the crop rather than demanded corvée labor as they did near the center (Lucero n.d.a). Since warfare was small-scale for the most part, there really was not much need for rulers to provide protection from attack, although they sometimes did; other options existed, such as fleeing into the jungle or to other areas.

Water may have played a crucial role in access to harbors and the potential to monopolize the trade of exotics such as obsidian and jade. For example, occupants of Quiriguá, located along the lower Río Motagua, were involved in trading jade and obsidian from highland to lowland areas. Even though Yaxchilán lacks a riverfront (Andrews 1975:145), former inhabitants still controlled trade between the highlands of Guatemala and Chiapas and the lowlands. Altar de Sacrificios is located at the confluence of the Pasión and Chixoy Rivers (Usumacinta River), an ideal spot for trade since canoe travel was possible; however, its agricultural fields were subject to flooding (Willey and Smith 1969:3, 46–47). Rulers of Yalbac and El Pilar, located along perennial streams that drain into the Belize River, had access to trade items, not to mention good pockets of agricultural land nearby (Ford 1990; Lucero 2004; Lucero et al. 2004).

Many areas of the Usumacinta Basin, however, have poor passage. At Piedras Negras, the current is swift and dangerous, but it is surrounded by ca. 32 ha of alluvium as well as dispersed pockets of fertile land (Houston 1998; Houston et al. 1998, 2003) that provided the means for rulers to expand the political economy. As of yet, no obvious agricultural systems have been found in the immediate vicinity of Piedras Negras (Charles Golden, personal communication, 2004).

Dos Pilas is located in a politically circumscribed area, Petexbatún. Although it is not situated on a river, it has a perennial spring close to the main plaza. Inhabitants also had access to underground water at caves near El Duende, the major temple (Brady et al. 1997; Demarest 1997), both of which were controlled by the political elite. The site itself is located in an area with poor agricultural soils, however, although better soils are found within 10 km (O'Mansky and Dunning 2004). Matt O'Mansky and Nicholas Dunning (2004) posit that rulers monopolized trade along the Pasión River. Whatever the material basis for power, specific historic events played a major role in the emergence of rulership when a branch from the Tikal royal family moved to Dos Pilas and later allied with Calakmul, a major rival of Tikal. Consequently, the kings of

Dos Pilas were more noticeably involved in long-distance interactions with re-gional rulers than many other secondary kings.

At Quiriguá, occupants may have planted cash crops like cacao on the lower river terraces, which are devoid of settlement (Ashmore 1981:77–85). A similar scenario likely existed at Seibal, located on a bluff overlooking the Rio Pasión with rich but small pockets of alluvial soils available on the other shore of the river (Mathews and Willey 1991). At Lamanai, David Pendergast (1981:40) sug-gests that inhabitants may have planted crops in the seasonally inundated har-bor area, based on core data "that show corn-pollen frequencies many times nor-mal." Secondary centers had access to agricultural produce in various amounts, as long as they could find the labor to work their fields; they implemented cor-vée labor demands on commoners in the immediate vicinity of centers and compensated laborers for their work on plots of land farther away and out of their reach.

Further, since water/agricultural systems were small-scale there was less need for a ruler's assistance in repairing damage caused by heavy rainfall since it was handled at the household or community level. Further, *chultuns* (storage facilities dug into the limestone bedrock) are small-scale and cluster at elite and noble residences (Ford 1991b). Their distribution and size indicate food stores for household members or perhaps for feasts (Lucero n.d.a). Rulers supplied water to people from *aguadas* rather than the larger artificial reservoirs near or within centers at the height of the dry season. The common farmers had some leverage since they could have lived/survived away from centers or opted to gift their surplus goods and labor elsewhere.

Settlement is typically dense near centers (e.g., up to 275 structures/km^2; Loten 1985; Tourtellot 1990) and less so in hinterland areas due to the scattered nature of agricultural soils (e.g., 145 structures/km^2; Ashmore 1990; Rice and Culbert 1990:Table 1.1). Rulers conducted public ceremonies to acquire what tribute they could from the surrounding populace. For example, the vibrantly painted murals of Bonampak depict tribute payments (e.g., "five 8,000 bean counts of cacao"; Miller 2001:210), as well as ritual dancing that took place "on the adjacent plaza or possibly a courtyard" (p. 215). The murals also depict other royal activities, including a major battle, the sacrifice of captured victims, and an heir designation.

When regional rulers temporarily or permanently lost political power, sec-ondary rulers benefited and, for a time, became primary rulers (see Webster 1998, 2000). For example, the events at Dos Pilas mentioned above occurred during a long "hiatus" at Tikal (ca. AD 593–672), when monumental architec-ture and inscriptions ceased (Mathews and Willey 1991). In another example, Buts' Tiliw of Quiriguá captured Copán's ruler Waxaklajuun Ub'aah K'awil in

AD 738, perhaps with a little help from Calakmul's king (Looper 1999). The ruler of Toniná witnessed a similar victory when he defeated Palenque's ruler in the 700s (Martin and Grube 2000:172–174, 182). However, these periods of primary rulership were relatively brief due to external factors (including competition and changing seasonal weather) and internal ones (including inadequate numbers of tribute-payers to support a primary royal lifestyle).

These centers arose as "secondary" polities when local rulers participated in the royal interaction sphere established by regional rulers through alliances, writing, intercenter marriages, warfare, prestige-goods exchange, and royal dynastic rites (cf. Blanton et al. 1996; Iannone 2002; Marcus 2003). This pattern is borne out in the inscriptions, where regional dynastic histories begin earlier (AD 292–435) than secondary ones (AD 450 and later) (see Martin and Grube 2000). Kings at some secondary centers also adopted emblem glyphs, signifying their claim of political supremacy within a specific, more limited, realm. Rulers built ball courts, palaces, temples, and a few funerary temples, sometimes emulating the layout of regional centers (e.g., Quiriguá mirroring Copán and Xunantunich mirroring Naranjo) (Ashmore and Sabloff 2002). Public iconography is ornate, sometimes even more so than at regional centers, perhaps because rulers were in a more precarious political position that required continuous display and public negotiation.

Kings also realized that farmers could opt to leave or contribute to other rulers or even leave the political realm altogether. For example, Anabel Ford (1991a; Fedick and Ford 1990) cites a noticeable increase in Late Classic occupation in the foothills of the Belize River area in west-central Belize, an area with marginal agricultural soils. The foothills also have a relatively low settlement density compared to the valley and upland areas, where secondary centers are located, as well as a predominance of solitary structures. Occupants were generally less wealthy and pursued more diversified economic activities in addition to farming, including ceramic and stone tool production (Lucero 2001: 65–66). The Maya perhaps chose to live in a more marginal area rather than contribute to political coffers at El Pilar, though they could still have supplied utilitarian goods to their wealthier neighbors. Admittedly, the Maya may have moved to the foothills in response to growing population and the need to expand into areas previously unoccupied.

Whatever the political relations, commoners exchanged goods with peers in other communities independent of elite control. Crumley (2003:141; emphasis in original) states it best: "While the Maya *political* system was organized vertically, the *economy* would appear to have been shaped by environmental constraints and characterized by fluidly networked interregional exchanges" (e.g., Kunen and Hughbanks 2003; Lewis 2003).

As is the case elsewhere, farmers also performed traditional rites in the home, agricultural fields, and sacred places, including caves and water bodies. At some centers rulers and water symbolism (e.g., water lilies) are found on monumental architecture and stelae as well as portable goods (e.g., ceramic vases) (e.g., Hellmuth 1987; Rands 1953), indicating the important link between water and royal power. When inscriptions are present, they typically highlight ties to regional rulers, such as marriages, battles, and royal visits (Schele and Mathews 1991).

Terminal Classic events varied at secondary centers and were related to the level of involvement of secondary rulers with those at larger, regional centers, since nonlocal royal ties played a major role in maintaining political power. Any change in external relations—such as regional centers' loss of power, trade disruption, or diminishing prestige-goods exchange—reverberated throughout the royal interaction sphere. Local subsistence practices and wealth differences were not necessarily affected as long as resources held out. Consequently, there were varied responses to the collapse of power at regional centers. Many secondary centers where rulers had close ties with regional rulers were largely abandoned by the ninth or tenth century, but not necessarily their hinterland areas (e.g., Quiriguá, Yaxchilán, El Pilar, Yalbac, and other centers). Altar de Sacrificios was abandoned for good in the AD 900s, though its last fifty years of occupation (ca. AD 900–950) may have been by non-Petén Maya (Adams 1971, 1973; Mathews and Willey 1991; Willey and Shimkin 1973). Recently, however, Gair Tourtellot and Jeremy Sabloff (2004) have suggested that outsiders came from Ucanal (southeastern Petén) and occupied Seibal and surrounding areas ca. AD 830, perhaps in an effort to revitalize trade.

As a result of weakening power at regional centers at the end of the Late Classic, several secondary rulers claimed independence. For example, Quiriguá became independent from Copán, and Yaxchilán broke from Palenque and Tikal (Ashmore 1984; Mathews and Willey 1991). In such cases, rulers did not immediately lose power, so neither their centers nor surrounding hinterlands were abandoned. Clearly, several means underwrote political systems, such as the monopolization of nearby agricultural land, trade in nonexotics, and the use of alternative trade routes and partners. Kings at some secondary centers even prospered. For example, rulers at Seibal and Xunantunich witnessed a brief florescence—ca. AD 830–890 for Seibal and ca. AD 780–890 for Xunantunich (LeCount et al. 2002; Mathews and Willey 1991; Tourtellot and González 2004). Farmers who did not emigrate continued to live near, or even at, centers but without any royal demands to worry about. Petexbatún centers, such as Dos Pilas and Aguateca, were abandoned in the latter part of the eighth century and early part of the ninth century as a result of political conflict in the densely

packed region. But why did the political vacuum remain in the southern Maya lowlands? I address this question in Chapter 7.

Ritual History of Altar de Sacrificios

Altar de Sacrificios is located on high ground in a semi-swampland at the confluence of the Pasión and Chixoy Rivers (Usumacinta River) in Guatemala at about an elevation of 100 m asl (Willey and Smith 1969:3) (see Figure 2.1). While the site was an ideal trade port due to its location and the relative ease of canoe travel, it was subject to flooding, especially in its agricultural fields as well as at the site core (Smith 1972:5; Willey and Smith 1969:3, 46–47). Tourtellot and Sabloff (2004) suggest that inhabitants may have traded in locally manufactured pottery and perishables such as quetzal feathers and salt. Because of its location at the confluence of two rivers, the site is restricted in extent (ca. 1.1 × .8 km) and has a density of ca. 90 structures per sq. km (Figure 5.1). The core area, consisting of about thirty structures, includes temples (the tallest being 13 m high), a ball court, and palace complexes (Strs. B-IV and A-I).

Seasonal flooding and poor drainage resulted in a problem with leached soils (Willey and Smith 1969:39). Annual rainfall is about 176 cm but can range dramatically from year to year. For example, from 1924 to 1934, average annual rainfall ranged from 99 to 237 cm (p. 40). Nor is there a noticeable dry season, though it does rain less at times. "There are also suggestions of rainfall 'cycles,' with three or four wet years being followed by the same number of dry ones" (p. 40). There is no obvious evidence for terraces or raised fields in the Pasión region (Dunning 1996). When writing about the Pasión region in general, Stephen Houston (1993) notes that soils in the immediate vicinity of the river are "suitable for non-intensive agriculture without the addition of substantial quantities of fertilizer" (p. 11) and that soil farther upland is even less fertile; centers are typically fund on the boundary of these two soil zones (p. 72).

Altar de Sacrificios had kings until at least AD 662 (Culbert 1991), an emblem glyph, and carved and inscribed monuments (stelae, altars, censer altars, and architectural panels) (Graham 1972:86–88). It "has the longest monument sequence of any site in the Pasion region . . ." (Mathews and Willey 1991:42) and the earliest (Graham 1972:119)—from AD 455 to AD 849. The Maya lived at Altar de Sacrificios from ca. 900 BC through AD 950. While it is near Dos Pilas (see Figure 2.1) and has inscriptions that include emblem glyphs from Yaxchilán and Dos Pilas or Tikal probably representing royal visits (Marcus 1976:93; Schele and Mathews 1991), it appears to have been an independent polity never completely subsumed by a regional center. Thus, inhabitants were less involved in warfare. Rulers and elites acquired exotics such as jade, obsidian, and marine shell items, as did everyone else to a lesser extent. Commoners acquired prestige goods as compensation for work or gifts from elites and obtained utilitarian and some prestige items through exchange with Maya in other areas. Kings are depicted in the iconography, and gods are included in the inscriptions (e.g., sun god, Stela 4), as well as Cauac symbols (e.g., Stelae 1 and 5) (Graham 1972: 13, 18, 20).

Altar de Sacrificios began to use "foreign" ceramic designs between ca. AD 850–909, after which the Maya apparently abandoned the site (Mathews and Willey 1991) for a short time. It was briefly reoccupied, perhaps by a different Maya group, based on the presence of different ceramics at ca. AD 909–948, who built small structures on monumental platforms with thatch and reused redstone and limestone blocks (Smith 1972:6).

Group B is the earliest monumental complex built, dating to ca. 600 BC; the Maya continued to enlarge and rebuild it until AD 524 (the last dated monument) but likely used it long afterward (Smith 1972:72–73). Its façade consists of redstone quarried from ca. 9 km away (p. 6). Str. B-I is the tallest temple and structure at Altar de Sacrificios (13 m). Monumental construction shifted to Group A in the Early Classic and continued through the Late Classic but was used long after the last stone was placed (Willey and Smith 1969:26). It consists of two large plazas (north and south) surrounded by range structures, temples, and an acropolis, much of which has eroded into the Pasión River. The plazas are separated by the only ball court at Altar de Sacrificios. Extensive excavations by the Harvard crew revealed much about monumental construction histories and ritual activities.

A. Ledyard Smith and his team also tested nearby and surrounding settlements, consisting of solitary mounds and plazuela groups (numbered 1–40) or commoner and elite residences. Excavation units typically were placed on the top center of mounds. This strategy revealed much evidence about ritual activities. Here I focus discussion on ritual activities in Groups A and B and the elite compounds and commoner mounds located in the immediate vicinity.

The Preclassic (ca. 900 BC–AD 250)

Much Preclassic ritual evidence was recovered at Altar de Sacrificios, especially at structures near and in the core (Table 5.1). For example, a solitary commoner mound (no. 22) 2.8 m in height and 20 × 20 m in extent yielded a dedication deposit dating from ca. 300 to BC/AD containing a human pottery face, a sandstone ball, a redstone figurine, and a possible bark beater (Smith 1972:168). Elite caches from the same period consist of a red-slipped bowl (mound 2 directly west of Group B, 2 m high, 30 × 25 m) (pp. 131, 242) and a red-slipped bowl inverted over a human arm bone at mound 7 (2 m high, 35 × 20 m), the

Table 5.1. Altar de Sacrificios Preclassic ritual deposits

Structure, Type	Ritual Type*	Context and Materials	Date	Reference
Mound 22, commoner residence	D	Human pottery face, sandstone ball, redstone figurine, bark-beater-like stone	300 BC–BC/AD	Smith 1972:168
Mound 2, elite residence	D	Cache 57; red-slipped bowl	300 BC– BC/AD	Smith 1972:131, 242
Mound 7, elite residence	D	Cache 58; red-slipped bowl inverted over human arm bone	300 BC–BC/AD	Smith 1972:178, 242
Group B plaza near corner of main stairway	D	Cache 60; vessel containing 4 obsidian blades	300 BC–AD 150	Smith 1972:242
Str. B-I, temple	D	Cache 37; fill under altar caches; 1 jade bead, 6 red slipped bowls, 1 cylinder vase	300 BC–AD 150	Smith 1972:73, 238
Str. B-I, temple	D	Cache 44; fill; 1 jade bead in a plain vessel over which 4 red-slipped vessels were inverted	BC/AD–AD–150	Smith 1972:73, 239–240
Str. B-I, platform	D	Cache 45; fill; incised red-slipped plate	BC/AD–AD–150	Smith 1972:73, 240
Str. B-I, temple	D	Cache 39; fill; 3 slipped and unslipped bowls, 2 of which are lip-to-lip and contain ocelot bones, 2 canines, and other faunal remains	BC/AD–AD–150	Smith 1972:73, 239
Str. B-I, temple	D	Cache 33; under floor of stairway base; 2 red-slipped bowls lip-to-lip	BC/AD–AD–150	Smith 1972:73, 238
Str. B-I Const. B or C near Cache 33	D	Cache 41; under floor near Cache 33; black bowl	BC/AD–AD–150	Smith 1972:73, 239
Str. B-I, temple	D	Cache 42; under floor; inverted flaring-sided bowl	BC/AD–AD–150	Smith 1972:73, 239

(continued)

Table 5.1. (*continued*)

Structure, Type	Ritual Type*	Context and Materials	Date	Reference
Mound 38, elite residence	D	"Alligator" bone, turtle carapaces, chert flakes	BC/AD–AD–300	Smith 1972: 164–165
Mound 7, elite residence	AV	Burial 131; adult male; cranial deformation; jade effigy pendant in mouth, miniature bowl inverted over skull	600–450 BC	Smith 1972:268
Str. B-II, temple	AV	Burial 129; adult male; cranial deformation, some teeth greenish; large red bowl inverted over skull, deer antler fragment, celt, and purple substance under a sherd	600–300 BC	Smith 1972:268
Str. B-II, temple	AV	Burial 124; under *tierra quemada***; adult female; jar partially inverted over skull; bones stained with red pigment	600–300 BC	Smith 1972: 265–266
Str. B-I, temple	AV	Burial 127; below floor; 3 infants/children; teeth stained green, red bowl inverted over one skull, small red bowl over another skull, and sherds over the other under which a chert core placed; black bowl	450–300 BC	Smith 1972:73, 266
Str. B-II, temple	AV	Burial 125; 0–4 yrs; jar fragments placed over remains, armadillo armor plates, fish teeth	450–300 BC	Smith 1972:265
Mound 8, elite residence	AV	Burial 136; 0–4 yrs; cream bowl inverted over skull, red bowl, miniature bichrome bowl	300 BC–BC/AD	Smith 1972:176, 269
Mound 2, elite residence	AV	Burial 31; adult female; chert biface	300 BC–BC/AD	Smith 1972:248
Mound 2, elite residence	AV	Burial 8; adult male with 4 upper incisors notched; red-slipped bowl	300 BC–BC/AD	Smith 1972:244

Table 5.1. (*continued*)

Structure, Type	Ritual Type*	Context and Materials	Date	Reference
Mound 18, elite residence	AV	Burial 104; adult; fluted bowl inverted over skull—worked sherds, quartzite river stone, chert fragment all on top of bowl; jar, red bowl, cream bowl	300 BC–BC/AD	Smith 1972:158, 260–261
Mound 17, elite residence	AV	Burial 107; adult female; red bowl inverted over skull, tubular jade bead in mouth	300 BC–BC/AD	Smith 1972:155, 262
Mound 40, elite residence	AV	Burial 41; adult male; large red bowl inverted over skull, red bowl, miniature jar, jade bead fragment	300 BC–AD 150	Smith 1972:181, 250
Str. B-II, temple; cist with redstone blocks	AV	Burial 119; adult male; large red vase containing skull, red bowl inverted over chest, another over pelvis, jade tubular bead near mouth	300 BC–AD 150	Smith 1972: 264–265
Str. B-II, temple	AV	Burial 108; below floor; adult; most of skull missing; traces of red pigment on bones	300 BC–AD 150	Smith 1972:262
Str. B-III, temple, redstone crypt, corbel arch	AV	Burial 105; adult male; copal fragment in mouth, jade tubular bead at throat, teeth stained green, bones covered in red pigment; 2 red bowls	300 BC–AD 150	Smith 1972:93, 261
Str. B-I, temple	AV	Burial 53; in pit; adult female	300 BC–AD 150	Smith 1972:73, 251
Mound 10, commoner residence	AV	Burial 130; adolescent	BC/AD–AD 150	Smith 1972:176, 268
Mound 26, commoner residence	AV	Burial 97; adult male and child; red bowl, bone tube	BC/AD–AD 150	Smith 1972:147, 259
Str. B-II, temple	AV	Burial 110; under wall 1; adult	BC/AD–AD 150	Smith 1972:262
Mound 25, commoner residence	T	Pit with charcoal	900–600 BC	Smith 1972:142

(*continued*)

Table 5.1. (*continued*)

Structure, Type	Ritual Type*	Context and Materials	Date	Reference
Str. B-III, temple	T	Ash layer	600–300 BC	Smith 1972:93
Str. B-III, temple	T	Extensive surface burning; also a "refuse" deposit with stones, snail shells, dumbbell-shaped redstone, all on layer of ash	600–300 BC	Smith 1972:93, 97
Str. B-III, temple	T	Layer of ash, carbon, chert pieces, burned bone, charred beans at bottom of shaft	600–300 BC	Smith 1972:97
Mound 7, elite residence	T	Burned earth, Xe (900–600 BC) figurine fragment	600–450 BC	Smith 1972:179
Mound 40, elite residence	T	"This occupation may have been terminated by fairly extensive burning"; burned seeds	300 BC–BC/AD	Smith 1972:184
Mound 20, elite residence	T	Extensive carbon layer	300 BC–BC/AD	Smith 1972:159
Mound 2, elite residence	T	"Refuse" over Burial 8; mussel shells, turtle carapaces, faunal remains, deer antler	300 BC– BC/AD	Smith 1972:131
Str. B-III, temple	T	Burning episode associated with Burial 105; ash, carbon, burned earth layer over burial	300 BC– BC/AD	Smith 1972: 98–99
Str. B-III, temple	T	Burned lens 10 cm thick	300 BC– BC/AD	Smith 1972:97
Mound 26, commoner residence	T	2 pits; one with limestone blocks in a line, other with pots, flakes, bone fragments, "calcified deposit," and "three beds of charcoal and fired soil cross the pit at intervals"	300 BC–AD 150	Smith 1972:147
Str. B-III, temple	T	Layer of ash with bone, sherds, and carbon above crypt Burial 105	300 BC–AD 150	Smith 1972:261

*D = Dedication; AV = Ancestor Veneration; T = Termination.
**Tierra quemada* is a hard, fired clay (Smith 1972:124).

eastern structure of a plazuela group (pp. 172, 242). Caches from monumental architecture have more diverse and better-made items. A vessel containing four obsidian blades was found under a plaza B floor that dates to somewhere between 300 BC and AD 150 (p. 242). Some of the earliest construction events at Altar de Sacrificios occur at Str. B-I, a temple eventually reaching 13 m in height and 40 × 38 m in size; the Maya cached six red-slipped bowls, a cylinder vase, and a jade bead (pp. 73, 238). Other Str. B-I caches more firmly dated to ca. BC/AD–AD 150 yielded an incised red-slipped plate (p. 240), a jade bead within a plain vessel over which four red-slipped vessels had been inverted (pp. 239–240), and three bowls, two of which were lip-to-lip and contained ocelot bones, two canines, and other faunal remains (p. 239). Other caches in Group B are similar.

There is even earlier evidence for ancestor veneration, especially in elite contexts. At mound 7, for example, an adult male with cranial deformation was interred (Burial 131) ca. 600–450 BC with a jade effigy pendant in his mouth and a miniature bowl inverted over his skull (p. 268). Str. B-II, a small temple (6 m high, 22 × 20 m) on the west side of Group B, yielded three Middle Preclassic burials that deserve mention. Burial 129, an adult male with cranial deformation and some teeth stained greenish, was buried sometime between 600 and 300 BC with a large red-slipped bowl inverted over the skull as well as a deer antler fragment, a celt, and a purple substance underneath a sherd (p. 268). From the same period, an adult female (Burial 124), whose bones the Maya stained red, was interred with a jar partially inverted over the skull (pp. 265–266). Adults were not the only ones privileged with such burials. Burial 125 (450–300 BC) consisted of an infant/child buried with armadillo armor plates, fish teeth, and jar fragments placed over the remains (p. 265). Burial 127 at Str. B-I included three infants/children with their teeth stained green (p. 266). Red-slipped bowls were inverted over two of the skulls and a sherd over the other, under which a chert core had been placed. The final grave object was a black bowl.

The earliest obvious commoner burials at Altar de Sacrificios date to ca. BC/AD–AD 150. Excavations at mound 10 (4.7 m high, 24 × 18) revealed an adolescent (Burial 130) without any grave goods (pp. 176, 268). Burial 97 from mound 26 (2 m high, 30 × 24 m) consists of an adult male and child buried with a red-slipped bowl and a bone tube (pp. 147, 259).

There are several elite burials. For example, mound 2 yielded two burials from the same period (ca. 300 BC–BC/AD), one (Burial 31) consisting of an adult female buried with a chert biface (p. 248) and the other (Burial 8) of an adult with notched upper incisors buried with a red-slipped bowl (p. 244). Other elite burials from the same period were more ornate and included more vessels (e.g.,

Burials 135, 104, and 41) (pp. 250, 260–261, 269), jade (e.g., Burials 107 and 41) (pp. 250, 262), and other items such as quartzite (e.g., Burial 104). The scale increases further in monumental contexts. For example, Burial 119, a redstone cist tomb in Str. B-II (ca. 300 BC–AD 150), enshrined an adult male buried with a large red vase containing his skull, a red bowl inverted over the chest, another over the pelvis, and a jade tubular bead in the mouth (pp. 264–265). In a redstone corbel arch crypt in Str. B-III (a temple 5 m high, 23 × 23 m in size) dating to the same period, another male adult (Burial 105) with green-stained teeth and bones covered in a red pigment was buried, this time with a piece of copal in his mouth, a jade tubular bead at his throat, and two red bowls (pp. 93, 261). Interestingly, there are also simple burials with few or no grave goods in monumental contexts, usually under floors (e.g., Burial 108, Str. B-II, and Burial 65, Str. B-I, both dating to ca. 300 BC–BC/AD) (pp. 253, 262) or walls (e.g., Burial 53, Str. B-I, dating to ca. BC/AD–AD 150) (p. 251). They may have been sacrificial victims (e.g., Burial 108 was missing most of its skull).

There is also evidence for Middle Preclassic termination rites at Altar de Sacrificios. In a pit dating to ca. 900–600 BC, the Maya burned something and built over it at mound 25 (2.3 m high, 22 × 20 m) (p. 142). Other early deposits are found in elite and monumental contexts. For example, mound 7 has a lens of burned earth dating to 600–450 BC with a Xe (900–600 BC) figurine fragment (p. 179). There is also extensive burning at Str. B-III dating between 600 and 300 BC, consisting of layers of ash and "refuse" or broken items (pp. 93, 97). For example, at the bottom of a shaft in Str. B-III excavators found a layer of ash, carbon, chert pieces, burned bone, and charred beans (p. 97). This pattern continues into the Late Preclassic; at a commoner house, mound 26 (2 m high, 30 × 4 m), there were two pits dating between 300 BC and AD 150, one with limestone blocks in a line, and the other with pots, flakes, bone fragments, and a "calcified deposit"; finally, "[t]hree beds of charcoal and fired soil cross the pit at intervals" (p. 147). And sometime between 300 BC and BC/AD, at the elite platform structure 40 (1.7 m high, 32 × 20 m located in the core), "occupation may have been terminated by fairly extensive burning," including charred seeds (p. 184). There are also termination events directly related to ancestor veneration. For example, there is a layer of ash, carbon, and burned earth over Burial 105, the crypt burial mentioned above (pp. 98–99, 261).

The Early Classic (ca. AD 250–550)

Early Classic dedication caches at Altar de Sacrificios are similar to Preclassic ones but increase in scale, especially in monumental contexts (Table 5.2). Commoner deposits more or less remain similar to those of earlier periods. For example, at mound 21 (3.5 m high, 30 × 28 m), a single bowl was found upright

Table 5.2. Altar de Sacrificios Early Classic ritual deposits

Structure, Type	Ritual Type	Context and Materials	Date (AD)	Reference
Mound 38, elite residence	D	Cache 55; possible "heirloom" dish inverted over ground stone disc	150–450	Smith 1972:164, 241–242
Mound 5, elite residence	D	Figurines and worked "alligator" mandible	150–450	Smith 1972:179
Mound 21, commoner residence	D	Upright bowl in southwest corner	150–450	Smith 1972:171
Str. B-I, temple	D	Cache 40; fill; sherds; Late Plancha (0–AD 150) Usulután sherds and 28 discs, some burned and with carbon	150–450	Smith 1972:73, 239
Str. B-II, temple	D	Cache 54; below wall; red-slipped bowl containing fish bones, turtle carapaces, carbon, and a small stone sphere	150–450	Smith 1972:84, 241
Str. B-I, temple	D	Caches 8–30; stairway fill; 46 red-slipped or plain bowls, most lip-to-lip	300–450	Smith 1972:73, 237
Mound 31, elite residence	D	Inverted white bowl, complete but broken orange bowl, modeled black effigy vessel and resist painted effigy vessel; the latter two in 2 hearth lenses	450–534	Smith 1972:151
Mound 8, elite residence	AV	Burial 134; child; orange bowl inverted over skull, 6 perforated shell tinklers near skull	150–450	Smith 1972:269
Mound 38, elite residence	AV	Burial 113; adult; orange bowl with kill hole inverted over skull; possibly remains of burned vegetable matter (e.g., possibly maize cobs)	150–450	Smith 1972:164, 263

(continued)

Table 5.2. (*continued*)

Structure, Type	Ritual Type	Context and Materials	Date (AD)	Reference
Str. B-III, temple	AV	Burial 99; center shaft; adult male; cranial deformation; possibly wood over trunk and upper legs, drilled *Spondylus* shell covered neck and mouth, stingray spine, shell adorno, "disc or rosette" with iron pyrite, 1 jade tubular flaring bead, 1 raw jade piece, 1 bone bead	150–450	Smith 1972: 259–260
Mound 36, commoner residence	AV	Burial 118; adult male; orange bowl inverted over skull	350–500	Smith 1972:264
Mound 2, elite residence	AV	Burial 12; child; tetrapod bowl inverted over skull, olla fragments underneath skull	450–500	Smith 1972:245
Mound 2, elite residence	AV	Burial 7; adult with 4 upper incisors notched; polychrome bowl inverted over skull; black bowl, greenstone bead, and blackstone bead	500–554	Smith 1972:244
Mound 18, elite residence	AV	Burial 103; adult; plain bowl	500–554	Smith 1972:260
Mound 20, elite residence	AV	Burial 106; adult; red bowl inverted over skull	500–554	Smith 1972:159, 262
Mound 36, commoner residence	AV	Burial 116; adult female; orange polychrome bowl, stingray spine, 4 jade tubular beads, 3 shell beads, pink stone fragment	500–554	Smith 1972:264
Mound 36, commoner residence	AV	Burial 115; adult male; polychrome bowl with kill hole inverted over skull; tripod cylinder vase with slab feet and lid, orange bowl containing miniature redstone censer altar, obsidian blades, 2 mussel shells with traces of red paint, shell adorno with jade, shell adorno with jade and shell mosaic of a human face	500–554	Smith 1972: 263–264

Table 5.2. *(continued)*

Structure, Type	Ritual Type	Context and Materials	Date (AD)	Reference
Mound 37, commoner residence	AV	Burial 117; adult male	500–573	Smith 1972:170, 264
Mound 20, elite residence	AV	Burial 122; adult; basal-ridge polychrome bowl inverted over skull	500–573	Smith 1972:265
Str. B-III, temple	T	Redstone altar fragments on terrace walls and platform; 2 large concentrations of incensario sherds in front of terrace wall and platform	150–450	Smith 1972: 99–100
Mound 36, commoner residence	T	Carbon-ash layer probably associated with Burial 118	350–500	Smith 1972:169
Str. B-I, temple	T	Butts of stelae 10 (AD 455) and 11 (AD 475) in fill; also chert pieces in groups of 9 and 13	500s	Smith 1972: 73, 82
Str. B-I, temple	T	Butt of stela 13 (inscribed AD 495) on west edge of Stairway 1	500s	Smith 1972: 73, 81
Mound 37, commoner residence	T	Layer of carbon over Burial 117	500–573	Smith 1972:264

in the southwest corner that dates to ca. AD 150–450 (Smith 1972:171). Elite structures typically have more ornate caches. For example, mound 31 (2.6 m high, 22 × 20 m), associated with a large platform structure (no. 33), yielded an inverted white bowl, a complete but broken orange bowl, a modeled black effigy vessel, and a resist-painted effigy vessel, all dating to ca. AD 450–534 (p. 151). Str. B-I yielded a cache dating to ca. AD 150–450 that included heirloom Usulután sherds (ca. BC/AD–AD 150) and 28 sherd discs, some burned and with surface carbon (p. 239). In a later deposit (ca. AD 300–450) at Str. B-I stairway 1, 46 red-slipped or plain bowls were recovered, most lip-to-lip (p. 237). Excavations below a wall at Str. B-II revealed a cache consisting of a red-slipped bowl containing fish bones, turtle carapaces, carbon, and a small stone ball (p. 241). Ancestor veneration rites also continue and expand in scale, though less so in commoner contexts. For example, Burial 117 (ca. AD 500–573), an adult male buried at mound 37 (3.3 m high, 22 × 20 m), did not have any grave goods (pp. 170, 264). Many commoner burials, however, have grave goods. For example, Burial 118 (ca. AD 350–500) from mound 36 (<1 m high, 16 × 20 m), an adult male, was buried with an orange bowl inverted over his skull (pp. 169, 264). At the same mound but dating slightly later (ca. AD 500–554), the Maya buried an adult male (Burial 115) with a polychrome bowl with a kill hole inverted over the skull, a tripod cylinder vase with slab feet and a lid, an orange bowl containing a miniature redstone censer altar, obsidian blades, two mussel shells with traces of red paint, a shell adorno (ornament) with jade inlays, and a shell adorno with a jade and shell mosaic of a human face (pp. 263–264). In a later burial (Burial 114) at the same mound (no. 36, ca. AD 554–573), a large polychrome plate had been inverted over the skull of an adult (p. 264). Other grave goods included an incised bowl, an orange bowl, and two jade beads. These commoner burials are similar to elite ones. For example, Burial 106 at mound 20 (4 m high, 36 × 32 m), associated with mound 19, included an adult with a red bowl inverted over the skull (pp. 159, 262). Burial 103 at mound 18 (2.4 m high, 25 × 17 m), the western structure of an elite compound, consisted of an adult buried with a plain bowl. Other elite burials, however, differ from commoner ones. For example, mound 2 yielded an Early Classic (ca. AD 500–554) burial (Burial 7) of an adult with notched upper incisors, a polychrome bowl inverted over the skull, a black bowl, a jade bead, and a blackstone bead (p. 244).

Early Classic burials in monumental architecture are also diverse. For example, from a shaft burial (Burial 99) in Str. B-III dating to ca. AD 150–450, an adult male with cranial deformation was placed with what looks like wood over the torso and upper legs, a drilled *Spondylus* shell covering the neck and mouth, a stingray spine, a shell adorno with iron pyrite, a jade tubular flaring bead, a piece of raw jade, and a bone bead (pp. 259–260). Also noticeable are the child burials; they represent either human sacrifices or special posthumous treatment for royal family members. For example, from below a floor dating to ca. AD 554–573 of Str. A-I, an acropolis 8 m in height and more than 80 (eroded by the river) × 36 m in size, Burial 100 was found, consisting of an infant/child with a polychrome bowl inverted over the remains, as well as a possible heirloom bowl (pp. 12, 260).

Termination rites at Altar de Sacrificios also continue through the Early Classic, mostly consisting of carbon and ash lenses and broken items. They are also associated with burial rites (e.g., commoner Burials 118 and 117) (pp. 169, 264). Monumental architecture yielded the most ornate evidence. Construction ceased at Group B in the Early Classic (ca. AD 500) (Smith 1972:6) and was terminated with parts of destroyed stelae. For example, butts of stelae 10 (dated AD 455) and 11 (dated AD 475) were found in the construction fill of Str. B-I, as well as chert pieces in groups of nine and 13 (p. 82, Table 2). The butt of stela 13 (dated to AD 495; Table 2) was placed at the edge of stairway 1 of temple Str. B-I (p. 81). On top of the terrace wall and platform of Str. B-III, the Maya placed fragments of a redstone altar, as well as incensario sherd clusters in front of the wall and platform (pp. 99–100). These deposits likely represent the termination of the stelae and altars and the dedication of the last construction event.

The Late Classic (ca. AD 550–850)

Late Classic dedication deposits at Altar de Sacrificios are similar to those of earlier periods, though monumental architecture has more diverse and ornate ritual deposits (Table 5.3). Commoner structures continue to house the simplest caches. For example, mound 19 (2 m high, 22 × 18 m), associated with a much larger structure (no. 20), yielded a small carved sandstone incensario and a mano fragment dating to ca. AD 554–613 (Smith 1972:163). Mound 36, another commoner house, had a cache dating to ca. AD 573–613, with two polychrome bowls (p. 241). From a deposit dating to the same period at mound 38, an elite structure, archaeologists recovered "alligator" bones (actually crocodile or caiman) and mano fragments (pp. 164–165). Dedication caches become more ornate in monumental contexts. For example, in the central axis of stairway 1 fill of Str. A-I at ca. AD 613–671 the Maya cached nine chert eccentrics (one with traces of red pigment), two *Spondylus* shells with traces of red pigment, two stingray spine fragments, and six pieces of jade (p. 238). A cache in the fill over Burial 128 (see below) in Str. A-III (a temple platform 10 m high and 100 × 30 m in size), dating to ca. AD 700–771, consists of a jade bead, five stingray spines, seven shells, twenty-seven small pieces of jade, fish vertebrae, bones of two different bird species, and one crab claw (pp. 56, 242). Smith starts to distinguish "nicked" and notched obsidian pieces in caches (e.g., Caches 50 and 47, Str. A-III, ca. AD 771–948) (pp. 240–241).

Ancestor veneration increases in scale, especially in Group A structures. Elite and/or royal rites shifted to Group A in the Early Classic from Group B, where construction ceased. As Table 5.3 illustrates, Late Classic commoner and elite burials are similar in scale to earlier ones. There are also indications of human sacrifice in Group A, based on the presence of skulls (or remains without skulls). For example, under a floor at Str. A-I in a deposit dating to ca. AD 573–613, the skull of an adult male (Burial 6) with notched upper incisors was recovered (p. 247). Two other skulls (adult males) with notched upper incisors (Burials 35 and 49) were recovered under floors or walls in Str. A-II dating to ca. AD 700–771 (pp. 251, 256–257). The Burial 49 skull had been placed in a small cist. Simple burials of adults and infants/children with few or no grave

Table 5.3. Altar de Sacrificios Late Classic ritual deposits

Structure, Type	Ritual Type	Context and Materials	Date (AD)	Reference
Mound 19; kitchen?	D	Small carved sandstone incensario, mano fragment	554–613	Smith 1972:163
Mound 36, commoner residence	D	Cache 52; 2 polychrome bowls	573–613	Smith 1972:169, 241
Mound 38, elite residence	D	"Alligator" bones, carbon, mano fragments	573–613	Smith 1972:164–165
Str. A-I, acropolis	D	Cache 34; fill of stairway 1 axis; 9 chert eccentrics, 1 with traces of red pigment, 2 *Spondylus* shells with traces of red pigment, 2 stingray spine fragments, 6 pieces of jade	613–771	Smith 1972:12, 238
Mound 24, commoner residence	D	"Quantities" of figurines	700–771	Smith 1972:172
Mound 6, elite residence	D	Figurines	700–771	Smith 1972:178
Str. C-I, platform temple	D	Cache 59; unslipped bowl	700–771	Smith 1972:107, 242
Str. A-III, platform temple	D	Cache 56; fill above Burial 128; 1 jade bead, 5 stingray spines, 7 shells, 27 small pieces of jade, fish verte-brae, 2 species of bird bones, 1 crab claw	700–771	Smith 1972:56, 242
Str. A-III, platform temple	D	Cache 46; fill; probably deposited same time as Burial 88; 16 plain, slipped, polychrome vessels (7 plates, 2 cylinder vases, 7 bowls)	771–850	Smith 1972:240
Mound 15, elite residence	D	Cache 51; 2 large jars	771–909	Smith 1972:155, 241

Table 5.3. (*continued*)

Structure, Type	Ritual Type	Context and Materials	Date (AD)	Reference
Str. A-X, east temple	D	Cache 1; southeast corner of structure; bowl containing 670 chert flakes	771–909	Smith 1972:235
Mound 19; kitchen?	D	Chert and obsidian fragments, scraper, axe, 3 human figurine whistles, animal whistle	771–909	Smith 1972:163
Str. A-III, platform temple	D	Cache 50; fill; 58 obsidian blades and blade fragments (45 "nicked" or notched)	771–909	Smith 1972:241
Str. A-III, platform temple	D	Cache 47; hole in wall; 30 obsidian blades (19 "nicked" or notched)	771–948	Smith 1972:240
Mound 36, commoner residence	AV	Burial 114; adult; large polychrome plate inverted over skull; incised bowl, orange bowl, 2 jade beads	554–573	Smith 1972:264
Mound 38, elite residence	AV	Burial 112; adult male; incisors filed and notched; basal-ridge polychrome bowl with kill hole inverted over skull; jade bead in/near mouth, incised bowl	554–573	Smith 1972:164, 263
Str. A-I, acropolis	AV	Burial 100; below floor; 0–4 years; basal-ridge tripod polychrome bowl inverted over burial; possible heirloom bowl	554–573	Smith 1972:260
Str. A-III, temple	AV	Burial 98; adult male; killed polychrome bowl with deer motif inverted over skull, jade adorno, 7 small jade mosaic pieces (near skull)	554–573	Smith 1972:259
Str. A-I, acropolis	AV	Burial 51; fill; child; bowl inverted over skull	554–573	Smith 1972:251

(*continued*)

Table 5.3. (*continued*)

Structure, Type	Ritual Type	Context and Materials	Date (AD)	Reference
Str. A-II, range structure/ palace	AV	Burial 42; below plaza floor; adult female; large red bowl inverted over skull surrounded by stones, black bowl	554–573	Smith 1972:41, 250
Str. A-I, acropolis	AV	Burial 6; below floor; adult male with 4 upper incisors notched, possibly sacrifice	573–613	Smith 1972:244
Str. A-II, range structure/ palace	AV	Burial 85; fill between walls; adult male, skull only; notched teeth; possibly sacrifice	700–771	Smith 1972:256–257
Str. A-II, range structure/ palace	AV	Burial 49; through plaza floor; adult male skull only in cist large enough for skull; incisors notched; possibly sacrifice	700–771	Smith 1972:251
Str. A-I, acropolis	AV	Burial 48; between floors; adult male	700–771	Smith 1972:250–251
Str. A-I, acropolis	AV	Burial 47; between floors; adult female; bowl inverted over skull	700–771	Smith 1972:250
Str. A-III, temple	AV	Burial 96; through terrace floor; adult female in cist lined with stones; cranial deformation; upper incisors inlaid with jade and filed and notched; upper canines notched; black plate inverted over skull; "Altar" vase-polychrome with inscribed date (AD 754), polychrome bowl, black plate, 2 jade beads, chert knife; associated with Burial 128 (possibly sacrifice)	700–771	Smith 1972:259

Table 5.3. (*continued*)

Structure, Type	Ritual Type	Context and Materials	Date (AD)	Reference
Str. A-III, temple, stone-lined crypt with beam roof	AV	Burial 128; adult female with cranial deformation, upper teeth inlaid with jade; roof beams rest on ca. 5-cm-thick layer of ca. 8,000–9,000 chert chips; small amounts of carbon found near feet, skull, and pelvic area; bichrome plate with kill hole inverted over skull with human figure on "throne" motif and glyph band; appears to have been a textile between plate and skull, conical jade bead in mouth, woven mat placed under pelvis and skull; 13 other vessels (bichrome tripod plate with green stucco rim and 12 *ahaw* in center, cylindrical bichrome vase with *ahaw* motif and green stucco interior band, bichrome bowl, black tripod plate with green stucco band on rim, bichrome bowl with green stucco band on rim and water bird motif, bichrome vase with "sunburst" motif, cylinder vase with painted stucco, bichrome bowl with stepped feet, 2 bichrome tripod plates with green stucco rim band andglyph band motif, cylinder vase with "flower" design motif, black vessel, cylinder vase with modeled-carved human figures and glyphs with stucco decoration), pottery earplugs, pottery mask, slate mirror back with red pigment on	700–771	Smith 1972: 266–268

(*continued*)

Table 5.3. (*continued*)

Structure, Type	Ritual Type	Context and Materials	Date (AD)	Reference
		one side, 4 mother-of-pearl fragments, mother-of-pearl bead, "pottery bar, perforated at each end and covered with gray-green stucco," stuccoed pottery earplugs, perforated ceramic disc with green stucco on one side and red pigment on the other, 17 stingray spines (7 with hieroglyphs incised), 8 stingray spine fragments (4 with hieroglyphs incised), 9 shell fragments, jade tubular bead, jade adorno, pottery pendant, 476 small jade disc beads, 538 *Spondylus* shell disc beads, 39 spiral shells, 10 green-stuccoed pottery beads, 11 ceramic discs, iron pyrite fragments, decayed wood, 3 obsidian flakes, obsidian core, 10 obsidian blades		
Str. A-I, acropolis	AV	Burial 39; below floor; adult female	613–771	Smith 1972:249
Str. A-III, temple	AV	Burial 88; below north platform; adult male; red pigment near skull; 35 jade beads (probable necklace; cylindrical, subspherical), jade adorno, bone pin, worked bone fragment, obsidian blade fragment, probable wooden object painted blue, 12 ceramic beads with appliqué designs, shell adorno, shell, 18 vessels (9 polychrome, 3 black with blue paint, 5 smudged, and white cylinder vase)	771–850	Smith 1972:257

Table 5.3. (*continued*)

Structure, Type	Ritual Type	Context and Materials	Date (AD)	Reference
Str. A-I, acropolis	AV	Burial 38; below floor; adult; fine orange bowl	771–909	Smith 1972:249
Str. A-III, temple	AV	Burial 74; between walls; adult male; canine notched	771–909	Smith 1972:255
Str. A-I, acropolis	AV	Burial 66; near northeast corner of platform; adult female	700–948	Smith 1972:253
Str. A-III, temple	AV	Burial 90; on floor; adult male	771–948	Smith 1972:258
Str. A-III, temple	AV	Burial 84; adolescent; skull on redstone block	771–948	Smith 1972:256
Str. A-III period 5	AV	Burial 83; adult male; canines and incisors notched or filed	771–948	Smith 1972:256
Str. A-III, temple	AV	Burial 77; near wall; 0–4 years	771–948	Smith 1972:255
Str. A-III, temple	AV	Burial 75; near wall; adult male	771–948	Smith 1972:255
Str. A-III, temple	AV	Burial 94; near wall; 0–4 years	771–948	Smith 1972:258
Str. A-III, temple	AV	Burial 86; on terrace floor; adult male	771–948	Smith 1972:257
Str. A-I, acropolis	AV	Burial 37; below floor; child	771–948	Smith 1972:249
Mound 8, elite structure	T	Burned earth, Jaina-like figures, incised bone fragment (glyphs), polychrome sherds	613–700	Smith 1972:177
Str. A-I, acropolis	T	Panel 9; reused masonry block from hieroglyphic panel, inverted, with jaguar glyph	613–771	Graham 1972: 93, 95
Mound 10, commoner residence	T	Metate fragments, shell tinkler, lance point; possibly associated with Burial 123	700–771	Smith 1972:176

goods in contexts similar to that of the skulls in Group A might also indicate sacrificial victims (Burials 86, 97, 77, 75, 37, 84, 83, 66, 90, 74, 38, 48, 47, 39, etc.) (pp. 249–258).

In contrast to these burials, others were clearly royal. For example, sometime between ca. AD 700 and 771, in Str. A-III the Maya enshrined an adult female with cranial deformation, with her upper teeth inlaid with jade in a stone-lined crypt with a beam roof (Burial 128) (pp. 266–268). The roof beams rested on a 5-cm thick layer of 8,000–9,000 chert chips. Small amounts of carbon were found near her feet, skull, and pelvic area, as well as a bichrome plate with a kill hole inverted over the skull on which a human figure on a throne motif and glyph band were painted. The Maya appear to have placed a textile between the plate and skull. Other items included a conical jade bead in the mouth, a woven mat placed under the pelvis and skull, 13 other vessels (a bichrome tripod plate with a green stucco rim and a 12 *ahaw* painted in the center, a cylinder bichrome vase with a painted *ahaw* motif and a green stucco interior band, a bichrome bowl, a black tripod plate with a green stucco band on the rim, a bichrome bowl with a green stucco band on the rim and a painted water bird motif, a bichrome vase with a painted "sunburst" motif, a cylinder vase with painted stucco, a bichrome bowl with stepped feet, two bichrome tripod plates with green stucco rim bands and glyph band motifs, a cylinder vase with a painted "flower" design, a black vessel, and a cylinder vase with modeled-carved human figures and glyphs with stucco decoration), pottery earplugs, a pottery mask, a slate mirror back with red pigment on one side, four mother-of-pearl fragments, a mother-of-pearl bead, a "pottery bar, perforated at each end and covered with gray-green stucco," stuccoed pottery earplugs, a perforated ceramic disc with green stucco on one side and red pigment on the other, 17 stingray spines (7 with incised hieroglyphs), 8 stingray spine fragments (4 with incised hieroglyphs), 9 shell fragments, a jade tubular bead, a jade adorno, a pottery pendant, 476 small jade disc beads, 538 *Spondylus* shell disc beads, 39 spiral shells, 10 green-stuccoed pottery beads, 11 ceramic discs, iron pyrite fragments, decayed wood, 3 obsidian flakes, an obsidian core, and 10 obsidian blades.

Associated with Burial 128 was another adult female (Burial 96), who might have been a sacrificial offering for the woman in Burial 128; she had cranial deformation and notched and filed teeth inlaid with jade (p. 259). The Maya placed her in a stone-lined cist and inverted a black plate over her skull. Other grave goods included a polychrome bowl, a black plate, two jade beads, a chert knife, and the famous "Altar" vase with an inscribed date of AD 754. The scene painted on the vase depicts six individuals, one of whom might be the woman in Burial 128, dancing and performing some kind of ritual (Adams 1971:68–75), perhaps a transformation ritual dance (Reents-Budet 1994:177). The hieroglyphic band includes emblem glyphs of Yaxchilán and Dos Pilas (or Tikal), which might indicate visits by their respective kings (Marcus 1976:93; Mathews and Willey 1991; Schele and Mathews 1991). In a slightly later burial (Burial 88) dating from ca. AD 771 to 850 below the north platform of Str. A-III, an adult male was buried, though not as ornately (Smith 1972:257). There was red pigment near the skull, as well as 35 subspherical and cylindrical jade beads (likely a necklace), a jade adorno, a bone pin, a worked bone fragment, an obsidian blade fragment, a possible wooden object painted blue, 12 ceramic beads with appliqué designs, a shell adorno, shell, and 18 ceramic vessels (9 polychrome, 3 black with blue paint, 5 smudged, and a white cylinder vase).

Termination rites continue much the same as in earlier periods and largely consist of burned strata and broken objects. For example, mound 8, the southern structure of an elite compound, had a burned lens dating to ca. AD 613–700 with "Jaina-like" figurines, an incised bone fragment (with glyphs), and polychrome sherds (p. 177). Metate fragments, a shell tinkler, and a lance point had been placed over Burial 123 at mound 10, a commoner house (p. 176). In a building phase dating to ca. AD 613–771 at Str. A-I, the Maya reused a masonry block from an earlier hieroglyphic panel with a jaguar glyph and inverted the block so it would not be visible (Graham 1972:93, 95).

Summary and Discussion

The majority of elite and commoner ritual deposits at Altar de Sacrificios are similar to those at Saturday Creek. Rites at monumental architecture, however, are quite different; they are more expensive and diverse. Temple rituals likely were conducted for audiences from all walks of life, whereas some ceremonies conducted in the acropolis were more restricted, for just a few people—royals and their elite underlings. But there is clear evidence that everyone practiced the same rites, which came from a long-standing tradition.

Seasonal rainfall vagaries likely meant that inhabitants of Altar de Sacrificios prayed and made offerings to gods and ancestors for rain. We begin to see the replication and expansion of traditional domestic rituals in more ornate settings, using more fancy and expensive items; at the same time we begin to see clear evidence for the appearance of the first kings in the area in the latter half of the Early Classic period. While monumental architecture appears much earlier, evidence for royal life (as at other secondary centers) occurs after the emergence of rulers at regional centers.

In addition to surplus acquired from agriculture, rulers and elites also relied on trade and participation in the elite/royal interaction sphere. Disruptions occurring elsewhere in the southern lowlands were eventually felt by kings of Altar de Sacrificios, resulting in their loss of material wealth and prestige in the eyes of surrounding farmers (not to mention the gods). Consequently, Altar de

Sacrificios was abandoned after ca. AD 950. Farmers likely survived the changing times to various degrees, but royal life did not.

In conclusion, we can better understand how the Maya lived at secondary centers through our knowledge of local polities. The only differences relate to the fact that Maya at secondary centers were members of a larger social and political society. Key factors, however, are quite similar, particularly how local material conditions impacted social, political, economic, and religious life.

CHAPTER 6

Regional Rulers and the Maya: The Ritual History of Tikal

In this chapter I describe centralized and integrative polities (see Table 1.1) and river and nonriver major Maya centers, which have several factors in common (see Table 2.1). I also present a history of ritual activities at Tikal, home to some of the most powerful Maya kings.

Centralized Polity

When Anu and Enlil [major gods] gave me the lands of Sumer and Akkad to rule, and entrusted their sceptre to me, I dug the canal Hammurabi-the-abundance-of-the-people *which bringeth water for the lands of Sumer and Akkad. The scattered people of Sumer and Akkad I gathered, with pasturage and watering I provided them; I pastured them with plenty and abundance, and settled them in peaceful dwellings.*

HAMMURABI (CA. 1792–1750 BC), TRANSLATED IN RUSSELL (1938:77)

A centralized polity is politically centralized, integrating several local polities and communities. It is largely based on a ruler's access to concentrated critical resources and concomitant nucleated, dense settlements (e.g., river valleys) (Carneiro 1970; Earle 1997; Friedman and Rowlands 1978; Gilman 1981). Examples include several ancient complex polities that arose along rivers, where leaders more easily controlled access to waterways and/or concentrated alluvium, as well as the labor of surrounding farmers who lived in farmsteads, communities, villages, or towns (e.g., China, Egypt, Mesopotamia, parts of Mesoamerica, and coastal Andean South America). Political demands are superimposed onto existing economic and social institutions. Centralized polities are what anthropologists have traditionally defined as archaic states (e.g., Marcus 1998). They have dense populations (e.g., urbanization), institutionalized rulership with power over life and death of subjects, the ability to collect tribute and raise an army, centralized storage and/or stores of capital, socioeconomic stratification, occupational specialization, specialized personnel (military, religious, and administrative personnel or bureaucrats), interdependency (e.g., protection, reliance on large-scale water/agricultural systems), and, secondarily, writing or recording and codified laws (Adams 1966; Carneiro 1970; Childe 1951 [1936]: 114–120; Engels 1978 [1884]; Fried 1967:229–240; Marx and Engels 1977 [1932]; Service 1962:180; Steward 1972 [1955]:191–196; White 1959:141–147).

Lineages, clans, or comparable groups corporately own land (Trigger 2003: 320). The largest landholders, however, are monarchs, temple estates, and aristocratic families (p. 333). While farmers typically are largely economically self-sufficient (pp. 112, 402), they—along with urban dwellers—face periodic drought, famine, and damaged crops and water/agricultural systems resulting from heavy rains. Rulers provide food from their granaries or via trade and capital to rebuild water/agricultural systems (cf. Trigger 2003:387). They also allocate water and/or resolve disputes involving water rights and protect subjects and their property from raids and invasions.

Sociopolitical relations are hierarchical and unequal, though kings have to take care not to over-exploit their subjects. Inequality results from rulers' being able to exact tribute without any obligation to compensate subjects equally. Military support is for protection from foreign threats, but, more importantly, to conquer land and incorporate more people. The presence of an army indicates that rulers could coerce compliance from farmers to pay their share in maintaining the political economy. In other words, farmers had less choice and fewer options but still resisted when they could, usually in subtle ways, with what Scott (1990) labels "hidden transcripts." For example, taxpayers express discontent and resistance through jokes, folktales, songs (p. 19), role-reversals (e.g., Carnival) (pp. 80, 173), and poaching (p. 190) and stealing from royal or elite lands.

Monarchs participate in the royal interaction sphere, including alliances, marriages, and prestige-goods exchange. Large-scale integrative events (e.g., trickle-down of exotics, ceremonies, and feasts) are necessary to legitimize rulership and promote solidarity. Corvée labor is used to build both public (e.g., stadiums) and private/restricted buildings (e.g., palaces). All members of society participate in trade independent of elite interference, either between individuals or in markets.

Regal rites revolve around royal ancestors to illustrate that they have the "mandate of heaven" (Fried 1967:238; Helms 1998). Ceremonies also acknowledge the importance of other gods, especially those in the upper echelons of the supernatural hierarchy. Rulers, because of their role in the continuance of life and society, are depicted in public iconography, often alongside powerful gods (e.g., sun and water deities), on various media from small objects (e.g., coins) to large public buildings (e.g., temples) (for example, Durkheim 1995 [1912]: 64). Everyone conducts household and community rites, which revolve around ancestors and fertility. Writing or recording systems typically emerge to record important information, including economic transactions, dynastic histories, religious rites, and myths (Postgate et al. 1995).

Centralized polities last as long as resources hold out and seasonal regimes do not change drastically for long periods. Demand for surplus production instituted by monarchs may contribute to the over-exploitation of resources, a condition that can be exacerbated by changing climate patterns. "Evidence of resource degradation is more common in periods when hierarchical, centralized polities held sway, even when overall population density in the polities was not much greater than in periods when non-centralized societies were in charge" (Roosevelt 1999:14). For example, the increased salinization of irrigated land in southern Mesopotamia likely contributed to the loss of political power, critical resources, and people in and around urban areas in the eighteenth to seventeenth centuries BC (Jacobsen and Adams 1958; Postgate 1992:181; Yoffee 1988). However, as mentioned, it is a rare occurrence when regions are largely abandoned.

I illustrate a centralized polity through a brief description of one of the "largest desert areas in the world" (Kemp 1991:8), Egypt during the New Kingdom (1540–1070 BC). Egyptians lived along the Nile River, a rich, fertile area replenished each year during annual flooding. Intensive agriculture, as well as the herding of cattle (and sheep and goats) and the capture of riverine life (fish and fowl), supported densely settled villages, towns, and cities (including temple towns) (Baines and Yoffee 1998). Since farmers depended on the annual rising and subsiding of the Nile for their livelihood, famine was always a concern, caused either by drought or by flood damage (Hassan 1994). Canals and earthen embankments (dikes) diverted water to fields, which were built under both local and government supervision. By the New Kingdom, the *shaduf* was introduced, a water-lifting device that expanded available farmland. Potential food shortages were mitigated by the use of granaries, which pharaohs, temple estates, and wealthy individuals built and stocked (Kemp 1991:296). In addition, many residential compounds had wells.

Stratification was undeniable, in terms of both wealth (palace, temple, and noble estates) and political power, with the pharaoh ruling from the top and with various high officials and temples priests vying for wealth and power. The pharaoh owned large amounts of land, as did temple priests, officials, and wealthy families. Elites also owned the ships vital for trade. However, everyone owed tribute to the pharaoh. In addition, the royal household controlled the vast wealth from conquered lands, including, for example, gold from Nubia. Pharaohs supported a standing army as well as foreign mercenaries to conquer rich areas and to protect their people and territory from invasion (Kemp 1991: 228). Egyptians had access to trade and other goods in the markets as well as through local exchange independent of royal supervision (p. 259).

Monumental architecture was closely tied to religious and political venues, including temples that housed divine images and royal tombs that served as royal ancestral cults (Kemp 1991: 21, 53), both of which collected tribute (p. 235). In addition, each deity had its own temple and priests, all of whom vied for material support. At the household and community level, rites revolved around ancestors at family tombs and various deities from the vast pantheon of Egyptian gods. Villages also commemorated "the gods they favoured" (p. 304) (e.g., Amun, Amun-Ra). If able, elites built small shrines in their garden in honor of the royal family (p. 301). Royal and religious rites were grand public affairs to celebrate and honor gods as well as the divine ruler. The importance of gods and the pharaoh is also reflected in public iconography, which is dominated by the inscribed life stories of gods and rulers, conquests, and festivals, not to mention the annual height of the Nile flood (Kemp 1991: 23). The relationship between king and deities and the cosmos was also detailed in the written record.

Political power has changed hands numerous times throughout Egypt's long history, but it has always been densely settled and is still going strong today.

Integrative Polity

To be a god does not necessarily mean to have more license, but rather to have more duties: divinité oblige.
HOCART (1970 [1936]: 151–152)

A major difference between centralized and integrative polities is that the former exhibit greater centralized and hierarchical power structures, whether they are city-states (e.g., Mesopotamia), territorial states (e.g., Egypt), or empires (e.g., Inka). One system gives the appearance of a unified front through high culture (i.e., civilization) (Baines and Yoffee 1998), and the other actually is more politically unified. The confusion has arisen when scholars conflate civilization and the state (Yoffee 1988). A civilization shares a "great tradition" or an elite and royal culture. Centralized polities have one primary ruler, whereas integrative ones have several relatively autonomous ones. In integrative polities, periods of centralization, if any, are brief; but they have a common political ideology expressed via monumental iconography, writing, and royal public rites. Marcus (1998) mentions some of these factors in her dynamic model. While she argues that most archaic states go through cycles of centralization and decentralization, I argue that in many instances periods of decentralization are a normal state of affairs for integrative polities (cf. Demarest 1992; Feinman 1998). In some cases "success" (centralization) is achieved, but usually only briefly or not at all (e.g., Angkor and the Classic Maya).

Another major difference between centralized and integrative polities has to do with the material basis for political power (see Table 1.1). Unlike in a centralized polity, it is more challenging for kings of integrative polities to access completely the dispersed critical resources, resulting in a decentralized subsistence economy (e.g., Fox 1977:54; de Montmollin 1989:17–19; Kunen n.d.). As a result, farmers live in farmsteads or villages scattered throughout the landscape, making it difficult for leaders to bring people together to organize work parties, feasts, and ceremonial events (e.g., Java; Miksic 1999). Integrative polities also lack large-scale and centralized storage facilities—for food, at least; water storage and allocation is another matter. Without centralized storage, rulers cannot assist their subjects in times of need, unless they have the means to import food. Hereditary rulers, however, still involve themselves in supporting large-scale water/agricultural systems, which are critical in the face of seasonal concerns such as drought, floods, and water allocation. Other economic systems, such as trade, also can be garnered to support rulership. But monarchs bring people together, for example, in regal-ritual centers (Fox 1977) by sponsoring elaborate ceremonies and feasts at monumental temples, temple-palace complexes, stadiums, and arenas. The goal is to create obligatory relationships and impose taxation on those who congregate at royal centers.

> The population of the city consists of those bound to the court by kinship, official duties, or craft specializations. . . . The life-style is defined by the calendrical round of state rituals, kingly ceremonies, coronations, funerals, preparations for war, royal feasts, and divine sacrifices, rather than by individualism and secularism. (Fox 1977:53)

Consequently, competition exists among rulers to *attract* and keep followers. Of course, everyone still performs household and community rites. Rulers, however, are better able to communicate with the supernatural world and highlight their contention that the continuance of their rule benefits everyone.

Kings are depicted in the iconography to emphasize their ties to gods, especially sun and rain or water deities. This relationship is often recorded via carved inscriptions for all to see but not usually to read and comprehend. Writing systems do not record economic transactions as much as they do royal and supernatural events (cf. Postgate et al. 1995). Rulers still need funding, however, to support the political system. When possible, they amass an army to incorporate more labor and for protection, though coercion is politically unstable (Earle 1997:7–8; Scott 1990:109; Trigger 2003:222). Warfare typically thus is small-scale and ceremonial in nature, often related to status rivalry (Webster 1998; e.g., Geertz 1980:252). Nor do they have much of a bureaucracy, if at all (e.g., Geertz 1980:132). Rulers are heavily involved in a far-flung royal interaction sphere to bolster their rights of power over others (e.g., Helms 1993). In addition, while they cannot force compliance, people often listen to their advice because of what leaders provide in return. For example, when corporate kin groups no longer can resolve disputes involving nonkin members, rulers can adjudicate intergroup problems (e.g., water and land disputes) (Hocart 1970 [1936]:133). The king thus is a lineage elder writ large.

"Galactic polities" of Southeast Asia (Tambiah 1977) exemplify such a system, the traits of which are summarized by Arthur Demarest (1992:150):

The most salient characteristic . . . is the great importance of ritual performances in their ceremonial centers and the awe (and authority) that these displays generated. . . . Other important features include (1) the organization of hegemonies into capital centers loosely controlling a cluster or galaxy of subordinate centers; (2) a redundancy of structure and functions between the capital center and dependencies; (3) an emphasis on control over labor and allegiance rather than territory; (4) little direct control by the rulers over local economic infrastructure; (5) an extreme dependency on the personal performance of the ruler in warfare, marriage alliances, and above all, ritual; and (6) the tendency of these states to expand and contract in territory, reflecting the dynamics resulting from all of these features, as dependencies struggle against authority or shift allegiances or as expanding capitals impose short-lived attempts at centralization.

Another noticeable feature of integrative polities is the degree of leverage that farmers have over ruling elites, which is more than in centralized polities. Michael Adas (1981:218), based on his research on precolonial and colonial Southeast Asia polities, argues that political power actually

. . . is in reality severely restricted by rival power centers . . . by weaknesses in administrative organization and institutional commitment on the part of state officials, by poor communications, and by a low population-to-land ratio that places a premium on manpower retention and regulation.

In precolonial times, rivalries existed among elites for labor control as well as the rivalry between rulers and regional lords. Marriage alliances served to cement ties between elite/royal families and benefited both sides. Further, since administrators "at all levels" kept a portion of taxes collected rather than being paid a salary per se, institutionalized corruption was rampant. Monarchs also found it difficult to control much beyond the capital city and hinterlands, especially at the village level. They found it challenging to compete with village headmen. Village headmen in Java and Burma, for example, generally came from local elite landholding families, who usually claimed to be descended from founding families:

> Their control over local affairs rested on the extent of their holdings, the number of laborers and artisans dependent on the use of their land and their patronage, the wisdom they demonstrated in village councils, and their ability to defend the interests of their communities in dealings with supravillage officials and their agents. (p. 222)

In Java:

> Most of the remaining families in the village were attached as clients, with varying degrees of dependence, to one of the [elite] households. The clients . . . worked the [elites'] fields for a customary share of the harvest yield, performed domestic and artisanal services, and in some cases actually lived in dwellings provided by their patron. (p. 226)

Kings could not do much about this situation because of the lack of a military force powerful enough to guarantee compliance. Elite officers commanded troops of poorly trained and equipped conscripted peasants. It was also difficult to control regional lords and collect taxes, not to mention organize large-scale labor-intensive projects.

> Thus, precolonial rulers were compelled to rely mainly upon adherence to state cults centering on the ruler's powers to protect and to grant fertility, on chains of patron-client clusters extending from the court to local notables, and on the cooperation of village leaders, rather than on military clout, to ensure that taxes were collected and order maintained. (p. 223)

These conditions in precolonial Southeast Asia, in turn, provided the means for farmers to avoid excessive demands through several strategies, which rarely included outright revolt and violence. It was not usually necessary in the face of other options farmers had. They migrated, chose other patrons, or fled to temple estates/monastic orders or to rival kingdoms. Farmers could always return if rulers or patrons lessened their tribute demands. Since the success of patrons (royal or not) was based on their prosperity—brought to them through the labor of others—attracting and keeping laborers was critical. Patrons thus had to demand enough taxes and labor to demonstrate their success without making the demands too onerous. Clearly, farmers had leverage, since the loss of labor was detrimental to royal and noble power and prestige. Consequently, competition for their loyalty and labor was intense. "The flight of the peasantry came to be seen in most African and Asian cultures as a sign of dynastic weakness and socioeconomic decline" (Adas 1981:234). Monarchs traveled throughout their domain to interact ritually with their subjects.

An integrative polity is thus less politically integrated than centralized polities because material wealth is inadequate in and of itself to support the political system, as are integrative events. Consequently, rulers must continually maintain their power through feasts, ceremonies, and elaborate displays. This system consequently is more susceptible to any type of fluctuation—climatic, economic, political, or social. As long as resources and climate regimes are stable, however, the economic system is relatively stable or unaffected by cyclical or changing political histories.

I illustrate an integrative polity through a brief description of nineteenth-century Balinese kingdoms. Wet rice intensive agriculture supported the entire population but not political power per se, since individual "irrigation societies" (*subak*s, consisting of up to 100 farmers) were economically independent and self-sufficient and crosscut dispersed hamlets or residential units (Geertz 1980: 50; Lansing 1991:4). The island of Bali is covered with rivers, streams, springs, and rich agricultural land but has no urban centers. Water is scarcer in the north part of the island (Hauser-Schäublin 2003). Water allotment was crucial, since farmers relied on the "seasonal flow of rivers and springs" (Lansing 1991:38) during the five-month rainy season. Priests at water temples found throughout Bali allocated water, which was staggered and couched in ceremonial proceedings (Geertz 1980:82; Lansing 1991:117–118). This system was critical, since up to 100 *subak*s relied on the same river (Lansing 1991:4). Husked rice was stored in storehouses built by *subak* members (Hauser-Schäublin 2003). Various forms of clientship existed: between higher and lower ruling lineages, between ruling and priestly lineages, and between ruling lineages and communities (Geertz 1980:34, 37–38). The irrigation systems, consisting of dams, canals, dikes, dividers, tunnels, aqueducts, reservoirs, and terraces, were owned by *subak*s (Geertz 1980:69), though the land was owned by the gods (p. 128); and "the king was represented as the prime 'guardian,' 'custodian,' or 'protector,' *ngurah*, of the land and its life . . ." (p. 129). While there was no bureaucracy per se, there was an official (*perbekel*) who served to link hamlets to kings (Geertz 1980:54).

Several kingdoms competed for tribute. For example, in the nineteenth century the Dutch recognized eight kingdoms (Lansing 1991:17). The Balinese participated in foreign trade with other Southeast Asian countries to acquire exotics. People also acquired goods at local, regional, and large rotating markets (Hauser-Schäublin 2003). Kingdoms were funded by clients, rent, trade, and taxation, in exchange for which farmers could use agricultural land (Lansing 1991:31, 103). Labor obligations also were owed to the king (p. 27). In addition, each temple implemented tribute demands in exchange for their services in keeping the water flowing (p. 107). Politics particularly came into play when temples competed for tribute, especially during the dry season and/or during drought, when temples were not "working" and rival temples claimed that they could provide the needed water (pp. 107–108). Competition also existed between temple priests and "princes" (p. 90). Sometimes competition escalated to war, which, according to Clifford Geertz (1980:256), consisted of a "series of brief lance and dagger skirmishes" with few casualties. Warfare clearly had a ritual aspect to it.

Bali had six great (regional) water temples (Geertz 1980:40; Lansing 1991: 44); in addition, each *subak* maintained a water temple (Lansing 1991:81). And of course each palace had a temple (p. 109). Each temple had a god, and these gods controlled water and irrigation (Lansing 1991:53). Water and fertility rites took place at all temples, with increasing grandeur and scale (Geertz 1980:40). "[A]ll traditional Balinese social units, from households to kingdoms, possess their own altars or temples, where regular offerings are made to the gods concerned with their affairs . . ." (Lansing 1991:50). "Ancestor shrines for commoners may have from one to three *meru* roofs, high-caste aristocrats, five or more, with the highest rank of eleven roofs reserved for consecrated kings" (Lansing 1991:71). Royal ancestors were important in the lives of all Balinese and were acknowledged in various rites (Hauser-Schäublin 2003). The importance of gods was reflected in the iconography, where major Indic (Hindu-Buddhist) gods (e.g., the supreme god, Siva, or the sun god, Surya), as well as traditional gods, were represented (Geertz 1980:105; Lansing 1991:63). Kings were also represented in the iconography, and they left inscribed edicts throughout the land detailing settlement and temple borders, royal regulations, and required offerings for particular shrines and temples (Hauser-Schäublin 2003).

The king himself was a "ritual object" (Geertz 1980:131). "The extravagance of state rituals was not just the measure of the king's divinity . . . it was also the measure of the realm's well-being. More important, it was a demonstration that they were the same thing" (Geertz 1980:129). This fact, however, could not prevent their conquest by the Dutch in the mid-nineteenth century when the traditional Balinese royal system collapsed (Lansing 1991:19). Ironically, the disastrous consequences of the 1970s Green Revolution (use of modern technology and fertilizers and planting crops at the same time) demonstrated the critical importance of water temples, priests, and rituals (and formerly kings) in the allocation of water to prevent the spread of disease and pests (Lansing 1991:111–126).

In sum, centralized and integrative political systems differ from one another in the way in which the distribution of resources affects how people settle and subsist, which in turn relates to political organization. Resources that are more easily accessed and where people are tied to the land facilitate the development of more centralized hierarchical political systems, whereas dispersed and diverse resources typically do not. Another crucial element is seasonal rainfall—too much or too little. All systems, however, are similar in that rulers often provide capital and sustenance (food and/or water) during times of need as well as allocate water and provide protection when necessary. Finally, political demands are superimposed on existing social and economic institutions that consequently are less affected by cyclical political histories. A greater reliance on large-scale water/agricultural systems in the face of seasonal vagaries and an ill-adaptive government can also be a formula for disaster.

Late Classic (ca. AD 550–850) river and nonriver major Maya centers have several factors in common with centralized and integrative polities, as I detail below.

The Maya: Regional Centers

River Centers

Regional centers, such as Palenque and Copán, are located along or near rivers with concentrated alluvium, more in line with archaic states found in temperate zones (see Figure 2.1) (e.g., Mesopotamian city-states, China, Egypt, and coastal Andean South America). The major difference between regional and other centers is that they incorporate more people and have greater power. At present I assign only two centers to this category, though others might be added in the future (e.g., possibly Yaxchilán and Piedras Negras). The elevation of Palenque and Copán is higher than that of minor and most secondary centers and similar to that of nonriver centers, from 200 to 550 m asl. Both are located on the edges of the Maya lowlands: Palenque to the northwest and Copán to the southeast. Annual rainfall is both above and below that found at nonriver centers; 130 cm at Copán and 370 cm at Palenque (see Figure 4.1). Alluvial soils surrounding Copán are concentrated within a 24 sq km area (Webster 1999). Rulers also probably monopolized trade with highland areas for jade and obsidian (e.g., Fash 1991), especially utilitarian obsidian blades (Aoyama 2001).

Copán's kings initially had the support of Tikal's royal family to bolster their claims over others, since the founding ruler of Copán (ca. AD 426–427), K'inich Yax K'uk Mo', may have been an "elite warrior" from Tikal (Sharer 2003).

Copán's occupants also built large reservoirs, which may have been managed and controlled by the political elite, based on their distribution and analysis of water symbolism (Fash 2005). Additionally, while the presence of rural *aguadas* signifies some degree of self-reliance on the part of noncenter farmers, relatively low annual rainfall and undrinkable river water during the height of the dry season meant that local farmers relied on water management systems part of the year or even perhaps during the height of the rainy season, when heavy rains churned up sediment in the river (Davis-Salazar 2003; Fash and Davis-Salazar n.d.). As a consequence, people had fewer options and had to acquiesce to tribute demands. And since the surrounding hillsides are more difficult to plant—not to mention dealing with problems that result from heavy rainfall and erosion—farmers were more tied to the concentrated alluvium and center and hence more susceptible to political machinations. They still, however, participated in exchange with Maya in other areas independent of elite or royal supervision (e.g., Webster and Gonlin 1988). Commoners thus had some leverage, since they could either move far from the center or opt to gift their surplus to another ruler (e.g., Quiriguá).

A similar situation existed at Palenque. Palenque overlooks a fertile valley (de la Garza 1992:51–52). It sits "on a 2 × 1 sq. km plateau 100 meters above the seasonally inundated plains to the north" (Barnhart 2001:70). A sharp escarpment lies to the south, and to the east and west "the mountainside becomes more karstic and areas of habitable land appear only in isolated pockets" (p. 71). Within Palenque are over fifty streams and springs; inhabitants built aqueducts and canals to drain water away from the center—not too surprisingly, given that annual rainfall exceeds 360 cm (French 2002; French et al. n.d.). In addition, people may have constructed irrigation canals on the plains below (Barnhart 2001:101). The prevalence of water is also illustrated in the Maya name for Palenque, Lakam Ha or Big Waters (p. 100). Surrounding farmers relied on the plentiful water sources at Palenque, especially during the nonagricultural dry season.

Kings provided capital to maintain and repair water systems, especially since they were often damaged during heavy rainfall. They also handled water allocation issues or disputes. Finally, while there is little evidence for storage facilities, rulers probably supplied food from their presumed extensive fields in times of need (Lucero n.d.a).

Settlement is typically dense around centers. For example, there are 1,449 structures/km^2 within Copán's core (0.6 km^2) (Rice and Culbert 1990:Table 1.1; Webster and Freter 1990), and noticeably fewer structures in areas be-yond the alluvium (e.g., 28–99 structures/km² in rural Copán). Palenque's site core (2.2 km²) has 643 structures/km² (Barnhart 2001: Table 3.1).

Rulers collected tribute from densely settled farmers because of their ability to access concentrated resources, provide water and capital, sponsor integrative events, and incorporate lower-order centers and communities in the vicinity. As in secondary centers, *chultuns* for storage are small-scale and cluster around elite and royal residences, indicating their insignificant role in politics (Lucero n.d.a). Texts do not mention a bureaucracy or administrators, a standing army, or a formal code of laws (Fox et al. 1996). Kings, though, probably provided some degree of protection, especially to those farmers more tied to the land in the immediate vicinity; however, commoners still had the option to flee else-where in the face of conflict. Kings could at least protect large-scale water sys-tems in the site core. While rulers did not have a standing army, they still could muster enough men to capture the rulers of other centers, especially secondary ones. Victory demonstrated to subjects of the vanquished rulers that it was bet-ter to support the victor. Corvée labor built large ball courts, private palaces, temples, and funerary temples. While rulers could easily access densely settled people, they still needed to integrate them, justify their rights to demand trib-ute, and promote solidarity in the face of political and economic inequality, which they did via public ritual events. For example, up to 3,000 observers could have watched ball games at Copán and viewed other events from the Great Plaza steps (Fash 1998). Maya farmers, however, still continued to con-duct traditional rites in their homes and communities.

Kings are depicted in the iconography, as is water imagery (e.g., Fash 2005; Fash and Davis-Salazar n.d.; French 2002; French et al. n.d.; Scarborough 1998). It is interesting to note that while water lilies cannot grow in Palenque's springs and flowing streams, their obvious ubiquity in the iconography in-dicates the importance of water symbolism in political ideology and rituals throughout the Maya region (see below). However, Edwin Barnhart (personal communication, 2002) suggests that some of the artificial pools could have sup-ported water lilies. For example, he notes that an artificial pool off an aqueduct in the possible early central precinct Picota Plaza may have had water lilies, since water plants are present today, and it never dries up. Inscriptions also highlight the importance of kings and their relationship to the supernatural, watery world (Schele and Freidel 1990). Emblem glyphs of Copán and Palen-que are some of the most often mentioned outside their respective centers, probably indicating their greater power compared to other center rulers (Mar-cus 1976).

Rulers of both river centers are some of the first kings to lose political power in the Terminal Classic. Demand for surplus production instituted by rulers may have contributed to the over-exploitation of resources. For example, Copán's farmers started to plant on the less-productive hillsides at the end of the Late Classic due to either competition or resource degradation (Wingard 1996). Any decrease in surplus undermined the political system, whether it was caused by resource degradation, decreasing water supplies, or both. Kings had no choice but to abandon the trappings of what formerly defined Classic Maya political life—palaces, temples, inscribed sculpture, and dynastic rites. A disruption in the trade of exotics also would have lowered the prestige of rulers in the eyes of their subjects (e.g., Demarest 2004; Hosler et al. 1977). Consequently, Copán and Palenque, but not necessarily their hinterlands, were largely abandoned during the ninth century. While archaeologists do not agree on the occupation history of Terminal Classic and Early Postclassic Copán and its hinterlands (Fash et al. 2004; Webster et al. 2004), there is no doubt that its rulers disappeared forever. And because of their close ties, the decline of regional rulers also contributed to the disruption of royal power at secondary centers.

Nonriver Centers

Nonriver centers such as Tikal, Calakmul, and Caracol are similar to river centers except for several factors (see Table 2.1). They are located in upland areas with large pockets of dispersed fertile land without permanent water sources but with large artificial reservoirs located next to temples and palaces (see Figure 2.1). Centers are located at higher elevations than minor or secondary centers (over 245 m asl). The need for an adequate water supply is related to annual rainfall; it was typically less than at secondary and regional river centers (see Figure 4.1). For example, annual rainfall at secondary centers ranges from over 200 to over 280 cm; at Tikal it was just under 190 cm, at Calakmul just under 170, and at Caracol 210 (Neiman 1997:Table 15.1).

Regional rulers collected tribute in return for providing drinking water during the dry season, particularly from January through April or May, when for all intents and purposes rainfall was nonexistent and the jungle became a green desert (e.g., Folan et al. 1995; Ford 1996; Lucero 1999b; Scarborough 1991, 1993, 1996; Scarborough and Gallopin 1991). At Tikal, for example, there are at least six major reservoirs, all located in the site core next to palaces and temples (Scarborough and Gallopin 1991).

Peter Harrison (1993) correlates reservoir building with the accelerated construction of monumental architecture in Tikal's core, especially beginning in the Early Classic. Quarrying of reservoirs provided building materials for monumental construction projects, including limestone fill, wall facing, and plaster (Scarborough 1993). At Calakmul, which is surrounded by *bajos* (low-lying seasonal swamps), there are extensive canal systems as well as thirteen reservoirs and *aguadas* (Braswell et al. 2004; Folan et al. 1995). Caracol has at least two major reservoirs next to temples and is literally surrounded by terraced hillsides for agriculture as well as water control (Chase and Chase 1996, 2001; Healy et al. 1983). Even if some *bajos* turn out to have been perennial wetlands or lakes (e.g., Culbert 1997; Dunning et al. 1998, n.d.; Hansen et al. 2002), their location at or near major centers would have provided rulers with even more water and agricultural surplus at their disposal. This may have been more noticeable in higher elevations; Pope and Dahlin (1989) note that perennial wetlands are more common in areas below 80 m asl. Until we have better information about *bajos,* however, I take a conservative approach and treat them all the same at present (i.e., as seasonal swamps).

A challenge the Maya did face, however, was keeping standing water clean during the dry season. Standing water quickly becomes stagnant and provides prime conditions for insects and parasites to proliferate and, more significantly, can result in the build-up of noxious chemicals (e.g., nitrogen) (Burton et al. 1979; e.g., Hansen et al. 2002). The natural wetland biosphere acts to sustain clean water if a balance of hydrophytic and aquatic plants is maintained (Hammer and Kadlec 1980; Nelson et al. 1980). Maya kings organized the maintenance of reservoirs during the dry season (Ford 1996) and performed important rites to keep water clean (Fash 2005; Lucero 1999b; Scarborough 1998). In fact, Maya rulers appropriated traditional water rites and conducted them in grand settings to demonstrate their success in propitiating the gods (Scarborough 1998). Rulers conducted water rites at the sources themselves—reservoirs next to temples.

Settlement is dense around centers (e.g., 235–557 structures/km^2; Culbert et al. 1990) and in hinterland areas (e.g., up to 313 structures/km^2; Folan et al. 1995). People lived in farmsteads scattered throughout the landscape, mirroring the distribution of good land, which made it challenging for rulers to bring people together to organize work parties, feasts, and ceremonies, not to mention to extract surplus. This fact did not prevent commoners from exchanging goods with one another outside of elite or royal interference (e.g., Ford 1986). Similar to the situation at secondary centers, corvée labor probably only worked the royal plots of land in the immediate vicinity of centers. Beyond this, kings had to compensate laborers with exotics and a portion of the crop. Rulers, however, funded large-scale public rituals in plazas at the foot of temples to *attract* and integrate farmers, especially during annual drought when water shortages would have been a problem. In exchange, rulers received tribute in the form of surplus labor, goods, and food from farmers and people from lower-order centers and communities in the vicinity (Lucero 1999b). Despite participating in royal rites, Maya commoners conducted similar rites in the home on a much smaller and private scale. Again, small-scale storage facilities precluded their role in political life (Lucero n.d.a).

Rulers interacted on an equal footing with other primary rulers through alliances, marriages, and warfare and incorporated nearby secondary and minor centers. Warfare was conducted to capture fellow royals, increase their prestige in the eyes of contributors, and attract more members into their political fold. For example, after kings from Caracol defeated those of Tikal twice in the latter half of the sixth century (AD 556 and 562), possibly with a little help from their allies at Calakmul (Braswell et al. 2004; Chase and Chase 1989), many farmers appeared to have left the losing polity to join the successful one. Because of their victory, Caracol's kings were able to attract or persuade many of the Tikal's former supporters to nucleate around Caracol (and perhaps Calakmul; Marcus 2003) instead of Tikal. As a result of this population shift Caracol's kings had access to a dramatically larger labor pool, since it was obvious that Caracol's rulers had better supernatural connections than those at Tikal. Evidence for migration to Caracol includes a noticeable increase in settlement density in and near Caracol (Chase and Chase 1996), the large number of terraces that appeared relatively quickly, and an increase in inscriptions and monumental building in the site core (Chase and Chase 1989). Arlen Chase and Diane Chase (1996) estimate that population increased 325 percent over the next 130 years. Further, there are the indications that population growth slowed at Tikal (27.5% for central Tikal and 15% for its hinterlands) (Haviland 1970). Commoners moved to Caracol's realm to access the victor's better supernatural connections.

Thus, during the Classic period, "hiatus" (AD 534–593 and as late as 692 at Tikal)—defined as a lessening or a cessation of stela erection and monumental construction—probably represented labor and power shifts (e.g., Fry 1990). In other words, kings who did not have the means to attract the necessary labor could not afford to build monumental structures. Caracol's rulers, however, were not the only ones competing for labor, as recorded in the inscriptions at Late Classic centers with the increasing mention of battles, intercenter ball games, and the sacrifice of captives.

Kings distributed exotics to lower-level elites and some commoners. They also organized the construction of public works, ball courts, large administrative and private palaces, and funerary temples as well as utilized carved texts and emblem glyphs. Other than Caracol, nonriver center emblem glyphs are the most frequently mentioned at other centers (Marcus 1976; Martin 2001). In addition, E-Group and Twin-Pyramid complexes are typically found only at nonriver centers (Arie 2001:49).

Kings and water imagery were prevalent in the iconography and are visible indicators of the relationship between water and political power, especially their performance of water rituals and providing clean water (Lucero 1999b). A visible sign of clean water is water lilies. Water lilies (*Nymphaea ampla*) are sensitive hydrophytic plants that can only grow in shallow (1–3 meter), clean, still water that is not too acidic and does not have too many algae or too much calcium (Conrad 1905:116; Lundell 1937:18, 26). Thus, the presence of water lilies on the surface of *aguadas* and reservoirs is a visible indicator of clean water. A major symbol of royalty in Classic Maya society is the water lily and associated elements (e.g., water lily pads, the water lily monster, etc.), which are found depicted on stelae, monumental architecture, murals, and mobile wealth goods such as polychrome ceramic vessels (e.g., Fash 2005; Fash and Davis-Salazar n.d.; Hellmuth 1987; Puleston 1977; Rands 1953; Scarborough 1998). Ford (1996: 303) notes that Nab Winik Makna (Water Lily Lords) refers to Classic Maya kings. Water lilies often make up part of royal headdresses as well (Fash and Davis-Salazar n.d.). Often rulers have names that include "water" (e.g., Water Lily Lord of Tikal and Lord Water of Caracol). Further, kings impersonated sun, maize, and other gods through the wearing of masks and costumes; "Another deity impersonated by Maya lords . . . seems to be aquatic represented as a serpent with a water-lily bound to its head" ("water serpent"; Houston and Stuart 1996:299).

The continued supply of clean water meant that rulers were successful in supplicating gods and ancestors and that rulers had special ties to the supernatural world that benefited everyone—for a price, of course. Inscriptions and iconography amply illustrate that Classic Maya rulers had closer ties to important Maya deities, ancestors, and the supernatural world than the rest of Maya society (e.g., Houston and Stuart 1996; Marcus 1978; McAnany 1995; Schele and Freidel 1990; Schele and Miller 1986).

Farmers in hinterland areas without permanent water sources could not amass enough labor to build their own water catchment systems, since they lived dispersed throughout the hinterlands (e.g., Scarborough 2003:93). During the rainy season, it would have been easy to store water in jars or other containers, since supplies were replenished daily. They also relied on *aguadas*, but their small size would not have supported large numbers of people throughout the year. In addition, during the dry season water eventually evaporated in smaller *aguadas* (Scarborough 1996). Estella Weiss-Krejci and Thomas Sabbas (2002), however, suggest that archaeologists need to take into account small (7–722 m², 0.4–1.0 m deep) natural and artificial depressions as possible year-round household water storage systems based on their work in northwestern Belize. But only four (25%) of the sixteen depressions they excavated were "good" candidates for water storage. They suggest that the Maya may have relied on the water stored in these depressions throughout the year and perhaps prevented evaporation by using covers, for example. Weiss-Krejci and Sabbas also note that in times of particularly bad dry spells that stored water would not have lasted the entire dry season. Taken together, these factors suggest that at least during the dry season many farmers had little choice but to rely on royal reservoirs, though perhaps a few family members stayed behind. Farmers did have options as to which royal reservoir people paid to quench their thirst (e.g., the Tikal/Caracol labor shifts discussed above).

The Terminal Classic period (ca. AD 850–950) witnessed the loss of political power. As long as the water supply was adequate, rulership lasted. For example, Tikal has one of the longest political histories in the entire southern Maya lowlands (inscriptions date from AD 292 to 869). Clearly rulers were successful in expanding and maintaining their political base through providing water and sponsoring integrative events. Their source of power, however, was susceptible to fluctuations, especially in the water supply. This accounts for the abandonment of Maya royal centers by the ninth or tenth century (e.g., Braswell et al. 2004; Valdés and Fahsen 2004). For example, Arlen Chase and Diane Chase (2004) demonstrate that the Maya at Caracol continued to build monumental architecture until after ca. AD 800 and that nonroyal elites continued to live in the epicenter until ca. AD 895. They also note that when people did abandon Caracol, by ca. AD 900, they did it relatively rapidly. As long as subsistence resources were available, however, farmers did not necessarily abandon hinterland areas, since political events taking place at royal centers did not always affect them. They continued to farm in small communities, participate in local and household ceremonies, and maintain small-scale water systems (e.g., *aguadas*).

In sum, we can better understand how the Maya lived at regional centers through what we know about centralized and integrative polities. The major difference between centralized polities/river centers and integrative polities/nonriver centers is that in the former case most of the agricultural land is concentrated along rivers rather than being dispersed in areas without surface water. As a consequence, there were different settlement patterns; farmers lived near where the land is fertile. Where farmers are more dispersed, rulers continually had to maintain their ties with subjects through frequent feasts, ceremonies, and games. The nature of Maya warfare was different as well and related more to status rivalry (Webster 1998) rather than conquest for labor per se. I am sure, however, that victorious kings benefited from access to greater labor pools—not by forcibly incorporating people but by attracting them due to their success as warriors and as intermediaries with gods and ancestors. Another distinctive aspect of the Maya is the apparent lack of large-scale storage facilities. Combined factors of humidity, heat, and farming practices did not make the construction of large-scale storage facilities practical or feasible. A final difference from most other ancient societies is the lack of clear evidence for markets, though some Mayanists suggest plazas could have served as markets (e.g., Jones 1991; Scarborough et al. 2003). The nature of subsistence practices—relatively self-sufficient—and the archeological record indicate a royal and elite concern with the long-distance exchange of prestige goods rather than utilitarian ones.

Since there are many similarities between river and nonriver regional centers, especially the degree of political power that rulers had, I only detail the ritual history at one such center, Tikal.

Ritual History of Tikal

Tikal is located in the Petén district, Guatemala, on top of an escarpment (250 m asl) surrounded by swampy areas to the west and east, earthworks to the north and south (Jones et al. 1981), and large tracts of fertile land (Fedick and Ford 1990).[1] It is one of the best-known and largest Maya centers (Figure 6.1). Since it is not near lakes or rivers, its inhabitants relied on several complex reservoir systems to offset seasonal water shortages (Scarborough and Gallopin 1991), which are found next to temples and royal palaces. The central core (9 km^2) consists of a densely built landscape of public and private monumental and nonmonumental architecture (ca. 235 structures/km^2) (Culbert and Rice 1990: Table 1). Annual rainfall is less than at secondary centers and Palenque, but more than at Copán (ca. 190 cm) (see Figure 4.1).

Commoners were densely settled immediately around Tikal—for example, 181 to 307 structures/km^2 in the 7 km^2 area immediately surrounding the core and 112 to 198 structures/km^2 beyond that (Culbert and Rice 1990: Table 1). They acquired goods through exchange with other commoners elsewhere, especially for utilitarian goods, as well as prestige items (e.g., Haviland 1985). The nearest known obvious agricultural systems (terraces) are ca. 28 km away (Harrison 1993), though some of the *bajos* might have supported two or three crops per year (Scarborough 1993; e.g., Hansen et al. 2002). *Chultun*s, as is the case at other Maya centers, cluster at elite residences (see Puleston 1983 survey maps).

Tikal was ruled by a "holy" or "divine" king (*k'ul ahaw*), who implemented tribute demands. Tikal has inscriptions, its own emblem glyph, water symbolism, palaces, royal funerary temples, large ball courts, and tall temples facing large and open plazas (e.g., Temple IV is 65 m tall). Its monumental complexes are connected via *sacbeob* (causeways). The earliest inscribed stela in the southern Maya lowlands (Stela 29, AD 292) is found at Tikal, and it has one of the longest dynastic histories in the Maya area (last known inscribed date: AD 869). Rulers early on absorbed surrounding centers (e.g., Uaxactún). The earliest recorded inauguration was in AD 320 and the last in AD 768, though a founding

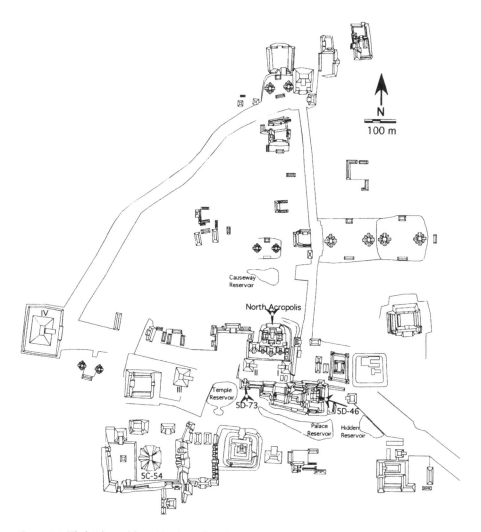

Figure 6.1. Tikal. Adapted from Martin and Grube (2000:24).

ruler is mentioned much earlier, between AD 219 and 238 (Sharer 1994:178), and kings are mentioned up to AD 869 (Martin 2003). Even if outsiders from Teotihuacan replaced or intermarried with Tikal's royal line in AD 378 (Martin 2003), they clearly adopted the use of traditional Maya rites in addition to foreign and new ones; there is no break in the ritual histories of structures. Tikal was largely abandoned in the AD 900s, as were most major centers in the southern Maya lowlands.

Tikal also has one of the longest sequences of monumental architecture in the Maya lowlands. For example, more than a thousand years of temple construction (e.g., twenty plaster floors), destruction (e.g., smashed objects and defaced monuments), and rebuilding occurred in the site's North Acropolis (Figure 6.2) (Sharer 1994:154–159). At the time of abandonment, this necropolis was approximately 100 × 80 m, with structures totaling 40 m high, though it began as a 6 × 6 m structure (Coe 1965b, 1965c, 1990) (Figure 6.3), similar in size to commoner residences at Saturday Creek. It supports at least eight funerary temples, most from the Early Classic period. On the south it faces the

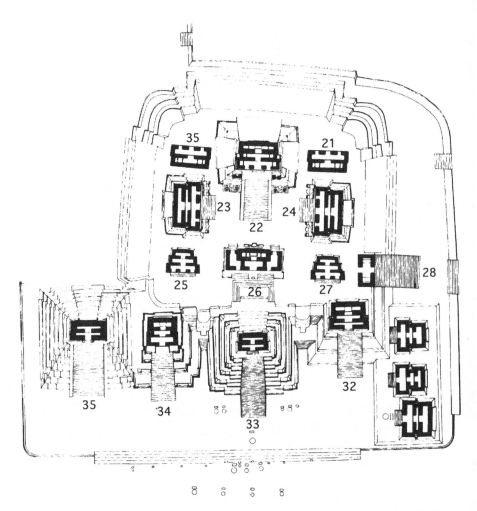

Figure 6.2. North Acropolis, Tikal. After W. R. Coe, University of Pennsylvania Museum Tikal Project, Neg. #98-5-2.

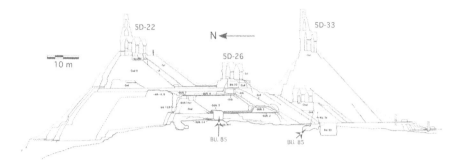

Figure 6.3. North Acropolis profile. After W. R. Coe, University of Pennsylvania Museum Tikal Project, Neg. #67-5-113.

Great Plaza (125 × 100 m), where an audience probably would have watched and participated in royal ritual performances at least until the last few centuries of occupation at Tikal, when structures were built that restricted access.

In the following section I highlight the history of royal ritual events, because they differ noticeably from Saturday Creek and Altar de Sacrificios rites and because elite and commoner ritual deposits are more similar to those at the smaller centers.

The Preclassic (800 BC–AD 250)

While ritual evidence from commoner contexts in Tikal's outskirts does not seem apparent as it does in later periods, the earliest houses and small temples actually are buried underneath later and increasingly monumental buildings. I largely focus on the ritual history of the North Acropolis because of the extensive excavations conducted there by the University of Pennsylvania team and later by Guatemalan archaeologists.

The Maya began to build the North Acropolis sometime after 600 BC by digging several pits, within which they placed a human skull and Preclassic ceramics. The earliest substantial architecture (300–200 BC) includes three successive platforms (5D-Sub.14-3rd, -2nd, -1st), each comparable in size to a large thatched house on a platform, approximately 6 × 6 m, similar in size to SC-18 and SC-85 at Saturday Creek. William Coe (1965c:12–13) describes the last of these three temples (5D-Sub.14-1st) as follows:

The roof was probably of thatch with poles at the corners. . . . This building burned, then was refloored, then charred again. . . . Beneath its floors were

three burials, an infant and two adults who were partially protected by . . .
large inverted Chuen [350 BC–AD 1] plates. Pits in bedrock in front of these
platforms yielded other insights. One contained a young adult . . . with a
necklace of shell pendants and imported jade and shell beads. . . . The other
pit contained the incomplete disarticulated remains of an adult accompa-
nied by fragments of one or more stingray spines [used for ceremonial
bloodletting].

This pattern of burning and destroying—terminating—earlier architectural
features continues throughout the building of the North Acropolis (Coe
1990:506).

The Maya also dedicated each construction event. As early as ca. AD 1–50, a
lidded jar with shell and jade beads was found on top of one of the platform
stairways associated with Str. 5D-Sub.1-1st (Table 6.1). At a contemporary
temple with four stairways (Str. 5C-54) beneath the base of the east stairway
the Maya had placed a large lidded red vessel containing a carved jade pendant depicting a bearded man (Coe 1965c). In the wall core of an early temple
dating to AD 1–150, Str. 5D-26-5th, the Maya deposited two perforated clam
shells, two obsidian blade fragments, two chert flakes, and four bone fragments
(Coe 1990:275). In the next phase (5D-26-4th), dating to AD 100–175, the Maya
dug a small pit in which they placed the sherds of a large polychrome bowl
(pp. 279–280).

The earliest clearly elite or royal burial at the North Acropolis is associated
with Platform 5D-Sub-10 (Burial 166), dating to ca. 50 BC. The Maya entombed two females in a corbel-vaulted chamber with painted designs on red-
plastered walls along with twenty vessels, some with powdered cinnabar, jade
and shell beads, stingray spines, and a carved shell pendant (Coe 1965c). Another elite burial located within Platform 5D-4-7th (No. 85, dating to AD 1–150)
consisted of a simple chamber with small slabs as a roof, within which a bun-
dled male was buried with his legs severed and without a skull. Twenty-six vessels were also interred, as well as a cylindrical jade bead, a greenstone mask with
shell eye and dental inlays, a perforated marine shell, a stingray spine, an obsidian blade, a stuccoed wood bowl, possible cinnabar dust (perhaps all that remains of a red-painted textile or mat), and other objects (Coe 1990:217–219).
Burial 85 actually might contain the remains of the first acknowledged ruler of
Tikal, Yax Ehb' Yook (?) (Martin 2003). Whether burials were public or private
events, the fact that these burials were found in monumental buildings distinguishes them from residential burials.

Commoner Maya practiced similar, though simpler, rites, as did their peers
at Saturday Creek, Altar de Sacrificios, and other Maya centers.

Table 6.1. Tikal Preclassic ritual deposits

Structure, Type	Ritual Type*	Context and Materials	Date	Reference
North Acropolis, Platform 5D-4-10th	D	Bedrock; disarticulated/ redeposited adult; stingray spines	600–350 BC	Coe 1965c, 1990:24
North Acropolis, 5D-26-5th, temple	D	Wall core; 2 perforated clam shells, obsidian blade fragments, 2 chert flakes, 4 bone fragments	AD 1–150	Coe 1990:275
5C-54, temple	D	Stairway fill; lidded vessel with carved jade pendant (of a bearded man)	AD 1–50	Coe 1965c
North Acropolis, 5D-Sub. 1-1st, temple	D	Top of platform stairway; lidded jar containing shell and jade beads	AD 1–50	Coe 1965c
North Acropolis, 5D-26-4th, small temple	D	Small pit in floor; polychrome bowl sherds	AD 100–175	Coe 1990: 279–280
North Acropolis, 5D-4-10th, temple	AV	Burial 121; adult, in bedrock; 8 shell pendants, 3 jade beads, 3 *Spondylus* beads	800–600 BC	Coe 1965c; 1990:22
North Acropolis, Platform 5D-Sub. 14-1st	AV	Burial 123; adult, platform fill; vessel	350 BC–AD 1	Coe 1965c, 1990:203
North Acropolis, Platform 5D-Sub. 14-1st	AV	Burial 122; infant, platform fill; vessel, large sherd	350 BC–AD 1	Coe 1965c, 1990:203
North Acropolis, Platform 5D-Sub. 10	AV	Burial 166; 2 adults in corbel-vaulted chamber with red-painted walls and designs; 20 vessels (some with powdered cinnabar), jade and shell beads, carved shell pendant, stingray spines	ca. 50 BC	Coe 1965c
North Acropolis, Platform 5D-4-7th	AV	Burial 85; adult (missing skull) with severed legs in chamber; might contain remains of first ruler, Yax Ehb' Yook; 26 vessels, cylindrical jade bead, greenstone mask with shell eye and teeth inlays, perforated marine shell, stingray spine, obsidian blade, stuccoed wood bowl, possible textile/mat remains	AD 1–150	Coe 1990: 217–219
North Acropolis, Platform 5D-Sub. 14-1st	T	Platform; burned floors	350 BC–AD 1	Coe 1965c, 1990:202

*D = Dedication; AV = Ancestor Veneration; T = Termination.

The Early Classic (ca. AD 250–550)

At the North Acropolis of Tikal during the Early Classic, Coe (1965c:31) notes a "plethora" of ritual deposits under floors, on the surface of floors, and in the fill, consisting of thousands of obsidian pieces, eccentric cherts, and marine objects (shell, especially carved *Spondylus*, sea-worms, stingray spines) (Table 6.2).

Lip-to-lip ceramic vessels with offerings were replaced by fancier lidded vases and other vessels, some of which are incised or painted with hieroglyphs stating who lived in the structure (e.g., stairway dedication cache, Str. 5D-46) (Harrison 1999:77–78). Within Str. 5D-26-1st, in the floor of one of the two rooms (Room 2), archaeologists found incised obsidian, obsidian blades, chert eccentrics, a mano fragment, large faunal remains, twenty-two sawfish spikes, marine shell, twenty-seven porcupine fish dermal spines, part of a tripod bowl, a censer ladle encrusted with soot, and a figurine head fragment (Coe 1990: 302). They recovered similar items in the floor of Room 1A, as well as jade mosaic pieces, a miniature clay head, three sharpened bone fragments, soft sponge, and cinnabar-coated stingray spines (Coe 1990:304–305). These caches contrast with those found in residences about 1 km to the northeast, which consist of single sets of lip-to-lip vessels (Haviland 1985:155–156).

Elite Maya distinguished their ancestors from common ones by burying their dead in eastern shrines, which first appear in the Early Classic (Becker 1999:144). For example, Burial 84 in Str. 4G-9-B, dating to ca. AD 250–550, consists of a crypt dug into bedrock sealed with stone slabs (p. 13). An adult was interred with a basal flange bowl, a fire-clouded bowl, jade beads (including a spherical one), and *Spondylus* valves (pp. 13–14). Commoner residential burials at Tikal are similar to those at Saturday Creek and Altar de Sacrificios. For example, Burial 33, just south of Str. 4F-7, includes an adult male with an incomplete vessel (Haviland 1985:134). In contrast, Burial 48, associated with temple 5D-33-1st of the North Acropolis, consisted of a chamber with a domed ceiling and walls painted with hieroglyphs (Coe 1990:118–119; Harrison 1999: 89–90) that contained three individuals (possibly including the ruler Siyah Chan K'awil and sacrificial victims), one with a severed head, placed on mats or skins, along with 30 vessels, over 400 jade beads, a metate and mano, hematite items, obsidian blades, quartzite pebbles, an alabaster vessel, about 30 different species of marine shell, and nearly 700 jade pieces (perhaps part of a mosaic) (Coe 1990:120–122). Its location at the foot of an imposing temple facing a plaza may indicate a public ceremony venerating a royal ancestor.

Termination rituals are indicated by burned floors at every residence (Haviland 1985) as well as burned and smashed items such as ceramics. Burning also occurred throughout Early Classic building events at the North Acropolis (Coe 1990). The Maya incorporated into the fill of new monumental structures

Table 6.2. Tikal Early Classic ritual deposits

Structure, Type	Ritual Type	Context and Materials	Date (AD)	Reference
Group 4F-1, Quarry 4F-1, small residential group	D D D	Fill; set of lip-to-lip vessels Fill; set of lip-to-lip vessels Fill; set of lip-to-lip vessels	250–550	Haviland 1985:155–156
Central Acropolis, 5D-46, temple	D	Stairway fill; lidded vessel inscribed with hieroglyphs	ca. 350	Harrison 1999:77–78
North Acropolis, 5D-26-1st, temple	D	Rm. 2 in floor; incised obsidian, obsidian blades, eccentric cherts, mano fragment, large fauna, 22 sawfish spikes, marine shell, 27 porcupine fish spines, figurine head fragment, censer ladle with soot, tripod bowl sherds	250–550	Coe 1990:302
North Acropolis, 5D-26-1st, temple	D	Rm. 1A in floor; similar to Rm. 2, as well as jade mosaic pieces, cinnabar-coated stingray spines, miniature clay head, 3 pointed bone fragments, soft sponge, sherds	250–550	Coe 1990: 304–305
Group 4F-2, 4F-7, small residence	AV	Burial 33; adult, outside structure; incomplete vessel	250–550	Haviland 1985:134
Group 4F-1, Quarry 4F-1 (under 4F-8, residence)	AV	Burial 34; child, east of structure in pit; incomplete vessel, chert flakes Burial 35; adult, east of structure in *chultun;* 6 vessels, animal skull, obsidian blade Burial 36; child, east of Burial 35 in pit; 2 bifaces	250–550	Haviland 1985:135
Group 4G-1, Str. 4G-9-B, elite shrine	AV	Burial 84; incomplete adult, slab-sealed crypt dug in bedrock; basal flange bowl, fire-clouded bowl, 2 jade beads (one spherical), *Spondylus* valves	250–550	Becker 1999:13–14
North Acropolis, 5D-33-1st, temple	AV	Burial 48; 3 adults (including possible remains of ruler Siyah Chan K'awil, and 1 missing the skull) placed on mat, bedrock chamber with painted hieroglyphs; 30 vessels, 400+ jade beads, metate, mano, hematite items, obsidian blades, quartzite pebbles, alabaster vessel, ca. 30 species of marine shell, 700 jade pieces	ca. 459	Coe 1990: 118–119, 120–122; Harrison 1999:89–90

(*continued*)

Table 6.2. (*continued*)

Structure, Type	Ritual Type	Context and Materials	Date (AD)	Reference
North Acropolis, 5D-34, terrace	AV	Burial 10; chamber tomb of ruler Yax Ain I; 3 turtle carapaces, headless crocodile, 2 pygmy owls, green jay, ant tanager, stingray spines, *Spondylus* shells, jade crocodile head ornament, 3 effigy vessels with Teotihuacan symbolism, ca. 25 vessels, and remains of 3 individuals	ca. 420	Harrison 1999:83–87
Group 4F-2, 4F-15-3rd, small residence	T	Burned floors, censer sherds	250–550	Haviland 1985:63
Group 4F-2, 4F-Sub. 1-1st, small residence	T	Burned floors, burned stones	250–550	Haviland 1985:69
North Acropolis, 5D-22-3rd, temple	T	On floor; layer of charcoal with burned jade fragments, mica fragments, 97 chert flakes, bone fragments, and censer sherds from 2 vessels with burned copal	250–550	Coe 1990:359
North Acropolis, 5D-22-3rd, temple	T	On floor; charcoal, red-painted plaster fragments, sherds, 2 chert fragments	250–550	Coe 1990:360
North Acropolis, 5D-26-1st, temple	T	Pit in fill; carved monument fragment (misc. stone 34), 5 chert chips	250–550	Coe 1990:314

the destroyed remains of earlier carved building fragments (e.g., Str. 5D-26-1st) (p. 314).

The Late Classic (ca. AD 550–850)

Caching behavior somewhat similar to that seen at Saturday Creek and Altar de Sacrificios is evident among smaller residences at Tikal, contrasting dramatically with what has been revealed in monumental architecture (Table 6.3). At the small residence Str. 4F-3 of Group 4F-1, three manos were placed near the house, in what Haviland (1985:156–157) calls a "votive" deposit. In a gap in a wall of Str. 4F-42, another small residence, the Maya placed a small bowl containing sherds and charcoal (p. 158). These caches noticeably differ from royal ones.

At Temple II, Miscellaneous Stone 54, originally a Preclassic sculptural decoration, was refit with another façade fragment from Late Classic temple

Table 6.3. Tikal Late Classic ritual deposits

Structure, Type	Ritual Type	Context and Materials	Date (AD)	Reference
Group 4F-1, 4F-3, small residence	D	Near structure; 3 manos	ca. 800	Haviland 1985:156–157
Group 4F-2, 4F-42, kitchen	D	Wall core; small bowl with sherds with charcoal inside	550–700	Haviland 1985:158
Temple II, south of North Acropolis	D	Roof comb fill: carved monument fragment (Misc. stone 54)	ca. 700	Coe 1965c
North Acropolis, 5D-33-2nd, temple	D	Fill, Rm. 2; Stela 31 (part of it burned), other carved monuments (pieces of Stela 37, Misc. stones 42, 45)	550–700	Coe 1990: 512–513
North Acropolis, 5D-26-1st, foot of temple	D	Pit in platform (central axis) fill; parts of Stela 32, 2 eccentric cherts, 10 obsidian eccentrics, 1 green obsidian fragment, 8 obsidian cores, 279 obsidian blades and fragments (49 green), 47 obsidian flakes, 7 green obsidian biface fragments, 4 chert blades, 138 chert flakes, 16 slate pieces, travertine metate, quartz metate fragment, quartzite metate fragment, 3 pieces of jade, 1 jade bead, 3 *Spondylus* beads, 10 jade mosaic pieces, 7 shell mosaic pieces, 20 polished, burned, perforated *Spondylus* fragments, 10+ marine shell species, bone imitation stingray spine fragments, 30 pieces of turtle carapaces, fauna (deer, crocodile), human bone, sherds	Late 7th century	Coe 1990: 324–325
Group 2G-1, 2G-58, small residence	AV	Burial 57; adult in bedrock grave; 3 vessels	700–900	Haviland 1988:125
Group 2G-1, 2G-59, small residence	AV	Burial 54; adult in bedrock grave; broken vessel, clay bead	700–900	Haviland 1988:125
Group 4F-1, 4F-43, small residence	AV	Burial 31; adult in fill; vase, tripod plate, killed bowl, retouched chert flake, jaw fragment, 9 chert flakes	700–800	Haviland 1985:132–133
Group 4G-1, Str. 4G-9, elite residence	AV	Burial 81; long bone fragment in masonry-block "box-like" crypt covered with slabs; 4 Ik vessels, a "smashed and incomplete Kau Incised cylinder bearing on its exterior a now-famous bird-with-fish motif and inscriptions," an unworked *Spondylus* valve, and other shell fragments	550–700	Becker 1999:12–13

(continued)

Table 6.3. (continued)

Structure, Type	Ritual Type	Context and Materials	Date (AD)	Reference
Group 4H-1, Str. 4H-4-2nd, elite residence	AV	Burial 89; adult male in fill; 3 vessels, an inverted and killed bowl under the skull, bowl, polychrome cylinder with a "four-vent rattle base containing 56 clay pellets"; corner-notched incisors	700–850	Becker 1999:24
Temple I, south of North Acropolis	AV	Burial 116; vaulted chamber; tomb of ruler Hasaw Chan K'awil, laid to rest on jaguar pelt; cinnabar painted circular design on capstone; lidded jade mosaic vase, jade necklace, bracelets, anklets, and ear flares (16 lbs. of jade), pearls, alabaster dish, marine shell, slate plaque, stingray spines, over 20 ceramic vessels, etc.	ca. 734	Harrison 1999:143–145
5D-73, temple south of Temple II	AV	Burial 196; possible chamber tomb of ruler Yik'in Chan K'awil; 25+ vessels, carved jade baby jaguar, lidded jade mosaic vase, jade necklace and bracelets, marine shell, stingray spines, etc.	ca. 750	Harrison 1999:162–164
Group 4F-1, 4F-4, small residence	T	Surface; tripod plate sherds, chert biface, burning	ca. 800	Haviland 1985:155
Group 4F-1, 4F-42, kitchen	T	On floor; burned	ca. 650	Haviland 1985:73
Group 4F-2, Platform 4F-8	T	Shallow pit in terrace steps; burned inside, burned jar fragment nearby	550–700	Haviland 1985:83
North Acropolis, 5D-33-1st, temple	T	Stairway surface; 10 cm layer of marl; lower steps burned	650–700	Coe 1990:529
North Acropolis, 5D-22-1st, temple	T	Surface; 2–3 cm layer of charcoal and dirt with censer sherds, monument pieces	550–700	Coe 1990:513
North Acropolis, Platform 5D-4-1st	T	Surface: censer sherds on burned floor	550–650	Coe 1990:151

fill 800 years later (Coe 1965c). In another example of the caching of older monumental pieces, the Early Classic Stela 31 was cached under the floor of Str. 5D-33-2nd prior to the Late Classic construction of Temple 5D-33-1st (Coe 1990:512–513). Other offerings included large chert eccentrics, incised obsidian, stingray spines, jade items of all shapes and sizes, hematite objects, coral, various species of marine shell, and stuccoed objects (e.g., Temple 5D-26-1st).

Late Classic royal burials are quite spectacular. One of the most imposing temples at Tikal, Temple I, served as the funerary temple of Tikal's most powerful ruler, Hasaw Chan K'awil (Heavenly Standard Bearer), who ruled from AD 682 until about AD 734 (Burial 116) (Harrison 1999:143−145). It overlooks a large plaza where subjects likely witnessed the interment of their deceased king. With him were entombed over twenty vessels, slate plaques, alabaster dishes, carved and incised bone, and more than sixteen pounds of jade items, including a mosaic-lidded vase. His family members and priests laid him to rest on a jaguar pelt, the major symbol of Maya kingship. In contrast, Late Classic burials found beneath the floors of one of the five structures of Group 2G-1, a nonroyal Tikal residence less than 2 km northeast of the North Acropolis, were quite simple and involved family members only. Burial 57 consisted of a male placed in a "bedrock grave containing three vessels"; another male (Burial 54) was buried with only "a single broken vessel and a clay bead" (Haviland 1988: 125). A similar pattern is found at residences located less than 1 km northeast of the North Acropolis. For example, Groups 4F-1 and 4F-2 burials yielded polychrome bowls and some small jade pieces (Haviland 1985).

Commoner and elite burials are similar to those described for Saturday Creek and Altar de Sacrificios. In the summit of Str. 4G-9 of Group 4G-1, the eastern structure (shrine) of an elite residence, archaeologists came upon a masonry-block "box-like" crypt sealed with slabs (Burial 81) (Becker 1999:12). It consists of a long bone fragment, four Ik vessels, a "smashed and incomplete Kau Incised cylinder bearing on its exterior a now-famous bird-with-fish motif and inscriptions" (p. 12), an unworked *Spondylus* valve, and other shell fragments. At another elite burial (Burial 89), dating to ca. AD 700−850 in the fill of Str. 4H-4-2nd of Group 4H-1, the Maya interred an adult male who had corner-notched incisors, with three vessels, an inverted and killed bowl underneath the skull, a bowl, and a polychrome cylinder with a "four-vent rattle base containing 56 clay pellets" (Becker 1999:24).

Termination rites at Tikal, especially indicated by burned plaster floors and broken items, are evidenced throughout small houses and monumental buildings. For example, tripod sherds and a chert biface were found on a burned floor of Str. 4F-4, a commoner residence (Haviland 1985:155). A residential platform (4F-8) contained a pit with burning on the inside and half a burned jar (p. 83). At the North Acropolis, Coe (1990:525) writes, "Fire and presumably incense appear to have been a functional constant." The Maya burned copal in censers and then broke them (e.g., Temple 5D-22-1st, Platform 5D-4-1st).

Summary and Discussion

Site formation processes similar to those at Saturday Creek and Altar de Sacrificios shaped small and monumental structures at Tikal. In "almost constant renovation, razing, and renewed construction" (Coe 1965c:13), ever-larger temple complexes grew over these early deposits. This process clearly resembles household rituals, albeit on an increasingly grand and public scale. Caches, burials, burned deposits, and destroyed objects are found throughout the depositional history of the North Acropolis and other monumental architecture. Through time in elite and later royal contexts, ritual activities became more labor intensive, exotic, political, and public but materially remained tied to traditions, including those supplicating gods and ancestors for water and other critical elements in life.

Rulers of Tikal conducted the same rituals as elsewhere but on a much larger and public scale. The life histories of monumental public buildings demonstrate ritual replication and expansion of dedication, ancestor veneration, and termination rites. These buildings face large plazas in which hundreds, if not thousands, of people witnessed and participated in ritual events. Further, because of their location these public arenas function as acoustic marvels. One can stand on top of Temple II, for example, speak, and be heard by all below. Aptly, the title *ahaw* can be translated as "he who shouts" (Houston and Stuart 2001), which would go well with the idea of the king performing, communicating important information, and conducting rites for the people below. Elite and commoner residences show the same depositional histories but on a smaller scale, more in line with those seen at Saturday Creek, Barton Ramie, Altar de Sacrificios, and Cuello. The goods that elites and commoners interred or destroyed as offerings, however, were not as ornate as the items found in royal contexts.

Kings at Tikal and comparable nonriver and river centers were vulnerable to changing material conditions because of seasonal water fluctuations and reliance on large-scale water/agricultural systems. Ritual can only go so far in bringing people into the political system. Kings need to feed and entertain farmers as well as provide water during seasonal drought and/or capital to repair water/agricultural systems damaged by heavy rains. When they could no longer do so, they lost their major means of extracting food and services from subjects. People voted with their feet and withdrew their support of Classic Maya kings. A few hardy souls reoccupied royal homes ("squatters") or remained in hinterland areas; they all continued to conduct traditional rites, at least through ca. AD 1000 (e.g., at Temples I, II, and III and other buildings) (Valdés and Fahsen 2004).

CHAPTER 7

The Rise and Fall of Classic Maya Rulers

The main question I have attempted to address in this book is how a few people get others to contribute labor and services without compensating them equally. In Chapter 1, I have presented a model of how emerging rulers use several types of traditional rituals in various settings to acquire and maintain political power, as well as how such power eventually can be lost. In brief, while the means of acquiring political power vary, the general processes of situating political change typically do not, and material support is a must—namely, surplus goods and labor. Ritual expansion occurs in tandem with political change and expresses and explains it within familiar cultural constructs. Ritual thus advances political agendas through presenting the new mixed in with the old. When surplus and labor are no longer available, political power is lost. In times of trouble, no matter how many ornate rituals rulers perform, they clearly no longer have special ties to the supernatural world. Indeed, rituals without results only highlight royal failures (e.g., Weber 1964 [1951]; Wortman 1985).

Maya rituals have a long history. The beliefs surrounding them, of course, no doubt varied at any given time as well as changed through time. There is little doubt that ritual scale and settings transformed as well. What did not change, however, is the fact that everyone performed traditional rites in the home as well as community, elite, and, in some cases, royal ones. The only difference is that the Maya conducted rites in the home and community before, during, and after the appearance and disappearance of kingship.

In this chapter, I document the rise and fall of Maya kings by integrating the history of Maya rulership (Chapter 2) and ritual (Chapters 4, 5, and 6). I detail the Maya collapse and conclude with a brief discussion of the aftermath and a possible scenario for the emergence and demise of Classic Maya rulers.

Water and Ritual: The Emergence of Maya Rulers

The archaeological evidence presented in the previous chapters indicates that (1) small and large Maya structures have structurally and functionally similar depositional histories consisting of caches under floors, burials with grave goods, and burned and broken objects on floors; (2) there is a gradual and incremental increase in scale of ritual activities through time, particularly at central, monumental public buildings; and (3) rituals never left the home. Commoners, elites, and royals conducted the "same" rites, albeit at an increasingly grand and public scale spatially (from house to elite compound to palace and temple) and chronologically, from the Late Preclassic through Classic periods. These rites were particularly suited for political appropriation because they concern life, death, and renewal, elements important in the lives of all Maya. Emerging Maya leaders replicated and expanded rituals and other traditional rites, including water ceremonies and those revolving around other crucial elements in life.

Maya elites and royals used more expensive and exotic ritual items as well as continued to use the same (or similar) objects as commoners did. For example, sherds with a molded face design found at Saturday Creek and small residences at Altar de Sacrificios transformed into pottery masks and shell or jade mosaic masks in royal contexts at Altar de Sacrificios and Tikal. Notched obsidian and chert flakes and tools were elaborated into beautifully chipped eccentrics. All Maya deposited human finger bones and fauna phalanges and other bones; the only difference is the container in which the Maya placed bones—sherds, lip-to-lip vessels, or royal tombs. A similar pattern of elaboration is seen in jade beads (from small spherical jade beads to large multishaped ones and mosaic objects), fragments of decorated items (small figurines to pieces of monumental architectural features, stelae, and altars), sherd clusters (undecorated to fancy decorated smashed vessels), killed ceramics (rimless vessels to those with kill holes), and other objects (e.g., ceramic and stone discs, stone balls, mica, and miniature vessels).

One type of artifact used for ritual purposes by all Maya is metates and manos. They are found fragmented or whole in commoner, elite, and royal contexts. The Maya sacrificed tools critical in everyone's life, which represent the never-ending importance of maize in daily life—economically, socially, politically, and religiously. Elites and royals also found ways to distinguish themselves physically from the majority, especially in their own person and in death. Cranial deformation and inlaid teeth were common means, though some commoners filed their teeth, and a few even had inlaid teeth. Distinctions were maintained after death; commoners were buried in house floors, elites interred in shrines, and royals entombed in burial crypts and tombs. Stingray spines seem to have been an elite and royal prerogative, though commoners had access to other marine items, especially plain or simply carved shells.

Conducting the same rites with the same items and behaviors promoted what Kertzer (1988:67–76) labels "solidarity without consensus." People did not have to have the same beliefs. Membership was based on Maya participation in events that benefited them all—propitiating the gods, not to mention forging a link between Maya farmers and political agents through debt relations and obligations. Commoners participated and contributed to their own political domination—as long as kings met their side of the bargain. This was made possible in part by royal persons' advancing and situating political change in traditional formats. Such events increasingly solidified and institutionalized a ruler's ability to acquire surplus through the creation of long-term obligations. While it is not possible to assess whether or not the earliest political rites were a conscious effort on the part of elites, I am certain that they soon realized the political benefits of successfully reaching the gods.

Pathways to political power in the southern Maya lowlands were similar. The scale on which rulers conducted rituals, however, the number of people they integrated, and the amount of surplus they acquired varied and were influenced by material factors and historical circumstances. Material factors include seasonal vagaries and the amount of surplus at hand; historical factors include the density of centers and rulers in any given area. While the variable distribution of land, water, and people presented a challenge to those seeking power, the strategies used by rulers to situate and advance political power were the same, entailing the replication and expansion of traditional rituals. These material factors and social strategies worked as long as there was enough water and food. When there was not, farmers blamed rulers, who had in the past claimed intimacy with supernatural forces.

For Saturday Creek and Barton Ramie—located on broad alluvial soils—community leaders sponsored local ceremonies, and occupants may or may not have been beholden to rulers at secondary or regional centers. Elites could not demand surplus labor and goods from community members because resources and water were plentiful year-round and accessible to all. Farmers thus were more self-sufficient and did not have to rely on royal or elite capital, food, or water systems. Consequently, elites did not have the means to exact tribute. As members of a larger society, however, residents interacted with their counterparts elsewhere socially (e.g., marriage) and economically (e.g., exchange). Elites sponsored traditional ceremonies at small temples to allay conflict in the face of wealth differences, to increase their prestige, and to promote solidarity.

It is almost counterintuitive that rulers did not emerge in areas with such plentiful, year-round resources (e.g., Kirch 1994). In addition to the reasons cited above, specific historic circumstances might account for the lack of rulers at minor centers; for example, their peripheral location on the eastern frontier of the southern Maya lowlands made it more difficult to interact with central and western polities. In essence, elites interested in becoming kings could not offer anything that people could not attain themselves. In other words, there were no obvious inducements for commoners to gift their valuable surplus to political leaders. Group effort, not corvée labor, thus built small temples and ball courts.

Rulers with varying amounts of power, however, arose at secondary centers. The major material difference between minor and secondary centers was that occupants of the latter had more noticeable seasonal issues with which to contend, a patchy distribution of agricultural soils, and a greater reliance on small-scale water/agricultural systems, which were also scattered. At Altar de Sacrificios, kings owned or controlled land in the immediate vicinity, from which they generated enough wealth to maintain a royal lifestyle. Farmers near the center probably worked royal lands in exchange for a portion of the crop. Rulers also acquired power and prestige through their participation in the royal interaction sphere (e.g., marriage and prestige-goods exchange). They did not acquire the degree of power held by kings at regional centers because they did not have the means to attract farmers from beyond the site core and immediate environs; basically, kings did not have much of a role in assisting commoners in maintaining water/agricultural systems, which did not bode well for the support of primary rulers. The situation was similar at other secondary centers. Farmers did not have to rely as much on capital provided by rulers, since water and agricultural systems were repaired and maintained at the household and community levels. Kings thus invested much wealth in public ceremonies and feasts to attract as many farmers as they could, as reflected in their ornate public iconography and buildings. Integrative events also served to define social membership in a larger community and provided the opportunity to exchange goods, visit friends and family, participate in ceremonies, games, and feasts, and look for potential mates.

A major difference between secondary and primary rulers was that the latter were involved in the building and maintenance of large-scale water systems (most of which are found next to royal architecture), on which many commoners relied during annual drought. The main difference between nonriver and river regional centers, other than location, is the distribution of agricultural land (concentrated alluvium or large dispersed plots). At Tikal and other nonriver centers, rulers replicated and expanded traditional rituals on an increasingly grand scale in public forums to attract and integrate dispersed farmers, to promote solidarity, situate political change, and legitimate their rights to exact tribute. Through ceremonies, kings demonstrated their close ties with important deities and ancestors and their involvement in the continuity of vital ele-

ments of life such as rain and fertility. Consequently, their power extended beyond the duration of ceremonies and ultimately sanctified tribute obligations.
At river centers such as Copán, rulers relied on water management as a means
to appropriate surplus, and they also had access to nearby densely settled farmers. Inadequate water supply was less of an issue for Palenque's kings; their concern was to divert and control water to prevent overflow and flooding. Water
was plentiful for surrounding farmers in the dry season. Palenque's kings conducted large-scale rituals to integrate people, justify their rights to demand
tribute, and promote solidarity in the face of political and economic inequality. Rulers of Copán and Palenque also provided capital to repair water/agri-
cultural systems during and after each rainy season and dealt with water allocation issues.

A History of Maya Ritual and Rulership

In Chapter 2, I have detailed the history of Maya rulership. In this section
I present highlights of this history and tie them into ritual replication and
expansion.

In the Late Preclassic period (ca. 250 BC–AD 250), high-ranking lineages
were transformed into royal ones. Elites and the earliest kings began to replicate and expand traditional rites in relatively grand settings. Elite tombs and
expensive items distinguish offerings of emerging political leaders from the rest
of the Maya, who continued to conduct the same rites in the home in a more
private and simpler manner. Monumental architecture served as arenas for public ceremonies and feasts. Inscriptions also focused on ceremonial events, not
on individuals. However, early kings were distinguished with the title of *ahaw*
as well as their use of Olmec royal iconography.

Minor centers were well established, while regional ones were just emerging. Not all nonriver elites and kings succeeded politically, for various material and historical reasons. For example, nascent rulers at Uaxactún, Nakbé, El
Mirador, and other centers were subsumed into political systems of powerful
neighbors at an early stage, for various reasons—Uaxactún to Tikal and Nakbé
and El Mirador to Calakmul. In some cases, lack of agricultural land prevented
large groups of people from settling in areas (e.g., Fedick and Ford 1990; Ford
1991b). El Mirador, with the largest and earliest Preclassic temple (El Tigre),
lost most of its inhabitants at the end of the Late Preclassic (ca. AD 250) (Matheny 1987), perhaps due to problems with reservoirs silting up (Hansen et al.
2002; Scarborough 1993), drought (Dahlin 1983), or political subjugation (Marcus 2003). If the first kings could have dealt with the reservoir and other problems at El Mirador, they no doubt would have become some of the most powerful rulers in the southern Maya lowlands.

The Early Classic period (ca. AD 250–550) witnessed full-blown Maya ruler-ship and the continued importance of domestic rituals conducted at home, within the community, and in public political forums. Inscriptions detailed the lives of kings, especially their esoteric knowledge and ties to the supernatural realm and distant places such as Teotihuacan. Royal dynasties represented them-selves as descent groups writ large, as visibly depicted on public monumental stelae as well as on royal architecture. Rulers emphasized the importance of royal ancestors in the lives of all through large public ceremonies with large au-diences and their closer ties to major deities such as Chac and the maize god. Inscriptions indicate the dedication of monumental buildings as well as new features, including conquests and capture of royal persons, royal visitations, heir accession, and bloodletting and period-ending rites.

The power of rulers at regional centers grew. Secondary rulers emerged, of-ten with the help of powerful neighbors and allies, typically through marriage alliances. Maya at minor centers continued essentially the same, other than deal-ing with the natural progression of things, including the growing number of farmers. Wealthy individuals increasingly participated in the elite interaction sphere.

The Late Classic period (ca. AD 550–850) witnessed the pinnacle of royal public rituals, not to mention the continuation of traditional rites in the home and community. Kings expanded traditional rites to their greatest extent and performed ornate royal rituals to highlight their ties to Maya deities and to the otherworld. Rulers also reached heights of power never before witnessed, as ev-idenced by the title *k'ul ahaw*. Persons of royal blood were entombed in funer-ary temples that faced large and open plazas. Inscriptions and iconography il-lustrate the proliferation of both private and public royal or nondomestic rites in addition to pan-Maya ones, including ball games, royal marriages, deity im-personations, period-ending rites, royal anniversaries, royal visitations, heir ac-cession, sacrifice of royal captives, bloodletting, and other rites.

Regional powerhouses jockeyed for more power, especially Tikal and Ca-lakmul and their respective allies. Battles and the capture of enemy kings were increasingly common themes in the iconographic and written records. If cir-cumstances allowed, secondary rulers took advantage of competition among primary rulers to expand their political horizons (e.g., Quiriguá).

Throughout the Terminal Classic period (ca. AD 850–950), Maya kings lost political power. Clearly, royal rituals no longer benefited people, who thus were no longer obligated to pay taxes. Several secondary rulers built monuments on their own, independent of major centers, and some experienced a brief flo-rescence. Farmers abandoned regional centers and either lived permanently in hinterland areas or left the southern Maya lowlands altogether. They still con-tinued to perform domestic and community rites, however. The last known inscriptions at many centers mention warfare, which probably resulted from problems that rulers no longer could solve. Many later Terminal Classic inscriptions no longer incorporate rulers or dynasties but instead emphasize deities, such as those witnessed at Chichén Itzá. Newcomers to the southern lowlands, perhaps attracted to weakening polities, came for a time, only to leave due to the same reason that caused indigenous kings to lose power—inadequate water supplies.

Discussion

Adopting and expanding familiar traditional rites allowed Maya kings to build and maintain an unequal relationship of sanctified rights and obligations that primarily benefited the sponsor. Emphasizing the positive aspects of unequal relations through ritual (being better able to propitiate and communicate with ancestors, rain deities, and other supernatural forces) was not so much manipulative as it was integrative. The Maya were not being led blindly—they had choices. For example, some dispersed into the hinterlands or contributed to other kings. Many farmers, though, participated in redefining their rights and obligations only because kings demonstrated their success in acquiring wealth, funding larger ceremonies, and contacting the supernatural realm to bring forth rain and bountiful crops.

Maya kings undoubtedly instituted new practices, such as the use of hieroglyphic writing to record dynastic histories, ritual warfare, human sacrifice, the deification of royal ancestors, the dedication of stelae (caching beneath them and the caching of stelae themselves), the use of Olmec and Teotihuacan imagery to bolster rulers' claims of special knowledge and skill, the use of special buildings as astronomical observatories, and the wearing of special costumes that allowed them to personify deities and demonstrate their closer ties to the gods as living ancestors of apotheosized kings (Houston and Stuart 1996). It was all about display and interacting—political theater (Demarest 1992; Inomata 2001a). Sponsoring traditional rites promoted solidarity, since rulers and subjects performed the same rituals. New rites, in contrast, distinguished royal persons from others. As long as these rites served to show the powers of kings, they still promoted integration and political agendas.

At the height of their power, regional kings conducted restricted rites for a select few in their palaces and public rites on top of temples and on lower palace platforms. New and restricted royal rites typically were performed in the small rooms on top of temples, not visible to the Maya below. But the people below knew that rulers conducted these secretive rites, after which they would emerge and perform rites more suitable for public consumption and participation. Most restricted royal rites, however, were limited to small-scale activities not necessarily appropriate for nonroyal viewing or participation. For example, many of the Late Classic painted vessels depict private royal activities that took place inside palaces, probably for court members and a few invited guests (e.g., Inomata 2001b), and include eating, drinking a ritual cacao beverage, making offerings, and greeting royal personages from other centers (Reents-Budet 1994: 84 – 99). Other events recorded on vessels include tribute payments, hunts, ball games, auto-sacrifice, and the sacrifice of captives (Reents-Budet 1994:262 – 264). Kings also performed and recorded events more conducive to public display, including human sacrifice carried out on the top of temples and recorded on stelae and ball games played in the ball courts (Freidel et al. 1993:259, 355). Most monumental architecture reflects the importance of royal and nonroyal interaction, usually fronting large plazas for feasts, festivals, performances, ceremonies, social gatherings, alliance building, and exchange. There were also ball courts for reenactments of the origin myth, intercenter ball games, local ball games, and feasts (e.g., Fox 1996).

Some kings may have been so powerful that they did not have to perform traditional rites, though they still performed public royal ones. For example, Chase and Chase (1998) note that not all Late Classic palace deposits at Caracol have ritual caches, particularly Ca'ana, one of the most restricted Maya temple-palace complexes, especially the upper platforms (Chase and Chase 2001). Instead, caches are typically found in front of structures in plazas. The lack of palace caches may indicate that rulers no longer had to perform public dedication ceremonies for palaces but instead performed public rituals in plazas. Or perhaps the massive size of Ca'ana prevented audiences below from being able to see royal performances, and thus kings had to move the show down to the plaza level. In another possible example, William Fash (1998:261) notes that while center layout varies from site to site, later construction styles more or less mirror earlier ones; and a consistent pattern exists throughout Classic Maya royal architecture, having to do with the "renewal of tried and trusted religious themes." Consequently, anything that varies from this pattern signifies a different message. "This makes the massive redesign of the Copan Acropolis by Waterlily Jaguar [early sixth century AD] . . . and the shifting of the triadic plan from the North Acropolis to the Great Plaza by Ruler A [Hasaw Chan K'awil] of Tikal . . . stand out as the daring work of visionaries" (Fash 1998:259 – 260). Change may also indicate, as in the Caracol case, a lessening need for kings to follow the status quo and explore new—nontraditional—ideas and styles in light of their ability to do so.

Traditional public rites conducted by royals were not exclusive but were superimposed on domestic and community ones. Consequently, they were not under royal or central authority: everyone could and did perform them in the home and community. The core royal rituals focused on the same issues of daily survival—fertility, rain, and ancestors—but according to a ritual calendar. Hinterland and commoner Maya conducted traditional rites in their homes in accordance with their own needs and schedules and also participated in elite community and royal ceremonies at set times in public arenas. Even though all Maya conducted the same traditional rites, this does not mean that traditional rituals did not change or that new ones were not added in response to political, social, or economic changes (Gossen and Leventhal 1993; Ringle 1999). Rituals, however, are more conservative than the beliefs that revolve around them (see Robertson Smith 1956 [1894]:18).

In sum, Maya kings demonstrated that they had special ties to the supernatural world that benefited everyone, and this enabled them to appropriate the surplus of others. As long as benefits continued, all was well. If farmers perceived that rulers were not keeping their side of the bargain, however, there was no longer any reason for them to participate in royal events and, more significantly, to contribute labor and goods.

Water and Ritual: The Political Collapse

As mentioned in Chapter 1, a collapsed society can be defined as one that is "suddenly smaller, less differentiated and heterogeneous, and characterized by fewer specialized parts; it displays less social differentiation; and it is able to exercise less control over the behavior of its members" (Tainter 1988:38). There is little doubt that this is what happened in the southern Maya lowlands, especially in regard to the loss of control over others. As briefly mentioned earlier, cases where a political vacuum remains are rare. What happened to cause such a drastic response, where centers were abandoned and some hinterland areas were for all intents and purposes largely deserted?

Before addressing this question, it is important to define the term "collapse." To begin with, not everyone defines Terminal Classic events as a collapse. For example, Sabloff (1992) suggests that better economic opportunities, such as salt trade, attracted people to the northern Yucatán lowlands. Marcus (1993, 1998), using ethnohistoric accounts of Postclassic and colonial Maya political histories, proposes that there were neither "golden ages" nor "collapses," but rather cycles of "peaks" and "troughs." Peaks were periods when regional centers politically incorporated a number of secondary centers. Troughs were periods when secondary rulers "broke away" from regional centers because they were able to attract more supporters. There is no doubt that cycles occurred, as Marcus details. However, the Terminal Classic "trough" resulted in the abandonment of large parts of the southern Maya lowlands and did not just reflect a period of decentralization. Indeed, earlier periods did witness cycles of some degree of centralization and fragmentation. The major difference is that this cycle or process took place in the southern Maya lowlands; in contrast, Terminal Classic political centralization occurred in an entirely new area—the northern lowlands—and consisted of joint rule, and the Classic period powerhouses of the southern lowlands were no longer part of the political landscape. In other words, peaks and troughs do happen, but usually within the same general area. When the entire cycle fails altogether, however, this needs explaining, especially since it is a rare occurrence.

I define "collapse" in political terms: societies do not fail; political institutions do. In the case of the Maya, kings disappeared; people did not. Basically, rulers lost their means of support, which resulted in their being unable to maintain a royal lifestyle. Elites and commoners were affected to various degrees. Events occurring during the Terminal Classic period at regional centers had various effects or no effect at all on lower-order centers: some were abandoned, some became independent, some experienced a brief spurt of power, and some continued as they had (Marcus 1976:186–190, 1994; Webster 2002:212–214). After the Terminal Classic, traditional ceremonies continued; rituals vital in defining Classic Maya rulership, however, disappeared in the southern lowlands, along with the power that had allowed kings to maintain such a rich ritual and political lifestyle.

What set in motion the erosion of Classic Maya rulership in the Terminal Classic (ca. AD 850–950)? Numerous explanations have been suggested, which I have also listed elsewhere (Lucero 2002a). These include climate change or drought (Brenner et al. 2002; Curtis et al. 1996; Dahlin 1983; Folan et al. 1983; Gill 2000; Gunn et al. 1995; Hodell et al. 1995, 2001; Lowe 1985); increased mono-cropping (Atran 1993); environmental and ecological degradation in the face of increasing population (Abrams and Rue 1988; Culbert 1977; Hosler et al. 1977; Sabloff and Willey 1967; Santley et al. 1986); foreign intrusion (Cowgill 1964); internal warfare (Demarest 1997); increasing competition (Bove 1981; Cowgill 1979); peasant revolt (Hamblin and Pitcher 1980; Thompson 1966); failures in management (Willey and Shimkin 1973), trade (Rathje 1973; Webb 1973), and subsistence (Culbert 1988; Turner 1974); yellow fever (Wilkinson 1995); and diminishing subsistence returns (Tainter 1988). Recently, David Webster (2002:327–328) has combined some of these explanations and argues that the collapse

> . . . was fundamentally triggered by three interrelated and dynamic factors, in the following order of importance: one, a worsening relationship of Maya populations to their agricultural and other resources; two, the destabilizing effects of warfare and competition, and three, the rejection of the ideology and institution of kingship. These in turn created or exacerbated a series of

secondary stresses, including increased vulnerability to drought, peasant unrest, and disease.

Increasingly, however, studies show that climate change occurred at the end of the Classic period, beginning in the late AD 700s (e.g., Curtis and Hodell 1993; Curtis et al. 1996; Dahlin 1983; Folan et al. 1983; Gill 2000; Gunn et al. 1995; Haug et al. 2003; Hodell et al. 1995; Leyden et al. 1996; Messenger 1990). I have argued elsewhere that this may have set in motion several of the "causes" mentioned above or exacerbated existing local problems (Lucero 2002a), such as environmental degradation (e.g., Copán area) and/or political competition (e.g., Petexbatún area).

While local climate patterns varied, evidence indicates that long-term climate change affected the entire Maya lowlands, especially the southern lowlands (Brenner et al. 2002). For example, based on current global climate patterns, Joel Gunn, William Folan, and Hubert Robichaux (1995) propose a model in which periods of florescence in Maya history are related to periods when there was an optimal balance between wet and dry seasons. The Maya collapse therefore occurred in a period when an *imbalance* existed between wet and dry seasons that adversely impacted agricultural schedules. Pollen data from the lakes region in the Petén suggest that deforestation was already in place by the Early Classic, which may further have added to the burden of unstable seasonal patterns, not to mention a steadily increasing population (Deevey et al. 1979; Rice 1993, 1996). David Hodell, Jason Curtis, and Mark Brenner (1995; see also Curtis et al. 1996), using lake core date from Lake Chichancanab and Punta Laguna in the Yucatán to assess temporal changes in oxygen isotopes and sediment composition, argue for an arid period beginning ca. AD 750 and lasting through ca. AD 1000, perhaps due to periodic episodes of increased solar activity that occurred about every 200 years (Hodell et al. 2001).

In a recent study in the Cariaco Basin of northern Venezuela, Gerald Haug and others (2003:1732) use results from measuring bulk sediment chemistry to explore the relationship between rainfall and riverine detrital, one that is recorded in "annually laminated sediments." They argue that they have been able to refine the time-line of Maya droughts. Their results show a gradual drying trend interspersed with short periods of intense drought at about AD 760, 810, 860, and 910. How do these dates correspond to events recorded in the southern Maya lowlands? The last-known inscriptions from nonriver centers date from AD 810 to 869 (a 59-year time span), river centers from AD 799 to 822 (a 23-year time span), and secondary centers from AD 742 to 909 (a 167-year time span). Not surprisingly, given their particular histories, secondary centers show the longest time span. River centers, even if one includes Piedras Negras (last date: AD 810) and Yaxchilán (last date: AD 808) as regional centers, cluster within a relatively short time span, perhaps reflecting a greater reliance on the annual rising and subsiding of the river. Archaeological evidence, however, indicates that the majority of centers were abandoned by the AD 900s.

Richardson Gill (2000:325) also breaks down the last inscribed dates, but by date and area: "Most of the 760–810 sites are grouped together in the west and southwest. The 811–860 sites are in the southeast and the 861–910 sites are concentrated in the core and in the north." When one looks closely at the distribution of sites and their last inscribed date, however, this relationship is not so obvious. I suspect that historical circumstances came into play more often than not in regard to the last known dates at several centers (e.g., Seibal, Dos Pilas, Toniná, and Palenque).

In a recent edited volume on the Terminal Classic in the Maya lowlands, Demarest and others (2004a) argue against any global, single cause such as drought, especially since some centers were abandoned before evidence of a drought exists, which suggests that warfare led to the political collapse— not drought (though some climate specialists place the drought beginning at ca. AD 750–760; Haug et al. 2003; Hodell et al. 1995). For example, Demarest (2004) shows that western centers in the Petexbatún and Pasión region were some of the first centers to show clear evidence for loss of political power, which he argues was due to political competition and warfare, not drought. As a consequence, trade patterns were disrupted, particularly trade involving exotic and wealth items that were critical in defining *k'ul ahaw* rulership. The effects of this disruption and the migration of people out of western kingdoms north, east, and elsewhere had major repercussions and eventually brought down other powerhouses. Demarest (2004) argues that population displacement resulted in the over-use of resources in areas with recent immigrants; and Tourtellot and Sabloff (2004) suggest that brigandry became a problem. There is no doubt that the Petexbatún area witnessed conflict (e.g., evidence for defensive works and violent death). Dos Pilas is a case in point; its last king, currently known as Ruler 4, was defeated in AD 761 by a ruler from Tamarandito (Demarest 1997, 2004). Afterward, the Maya attempted to defend their capital by stripping temples and palaces of stone façades and building walls around the epicenter in a failed attempt to keep their enemies at bay. Defensive works, violence, and destruction are seen elsewhere in the region as well (e.g., Aguateca, Punto de Chimino, and other centers).

It is possible, however, that changing seasonal patterns set in motion a series of events, including conflict over water, or exacerbated existing problems that eventually resulted in the demise of rulership. Thus it is not surprising that there was a "mosaic" pattern of political failure during the Terminal Classic (Demarest et al. 2004a). A crucial question that needs to be addressed, though, is *why* the political vacuum remained. As mentioned in Chapter 1, political fragmentation or replacement is the norm in the aftermath of political collapse; the utter and complete disappearance of political systems is rare. Long-term climate change, such as increasing drought in the form of shorter rainy seasons, explains why rulership did not emerge again in the southern Maya lowlands. Another fact worth noting is that the most powerful kings at regional centers, river and nonriver, lasted 40 to 100 years after the capture of Ruler 4 at Dos Pilas in AD 761; warfare and disrupted trade had no impact on these centers. Finally, the reasons why warfare was so widespread in the Petexbatún need to be addressed; O'Mansky and Dunning (2004) find no obvious evidence for environmental degradation; nor is there evidence for declining health (Wright 1997).

If material conditions were changing, however—such as decreasing annual rainfall or a change in the timing of the rainy season enough to interfere with surplus production—that could have been just the catalyst to set in motion competition over water rights. People fought over water, but victory was short-lived since water supplies were inadequate to support anything of a royal nature. Prudence Rice and others (2004:10) state that the evidence "largely argues against the concept of a uniform, chronologically aligned collapse or catastrophe in all regions of the lowlands or even a uniform 'decline' in population of political institutions." I agree that it is neither uniform nor catastrophic in the sense that only kings vanished, not people, and that they disappeared at different times.

Decreasing rainfall undermined the institution of rulership when existing ceremonies and water systems failed to provide sufficient water. Even a slight decrease in annual rainfall could have a dramatic impact on water levels, as Brian Fagan (2004) shows in cases throughout the globe. Farmers blamed decreasing food and water on kings, who had previously claimed a close intimacy with supernatural powers associated with rain, crops, and fertility. Lessening rainfall and its probable effects, such as increased disease and decreasing health, set in motion the erosion of political power, as Webster has noted (2002:327–328). As a result, the foundation of political power dissipated, with the final outcome of farmers emigrating from the interior or permanently living in hinterland areas; there might also have been some population loss due to decreasing health and fertility (Culbert 1977, 1988; Lowe 1985:62; Santley et al. 1986; Willey and Shimkin 1973). Maya kings could not reach and politically integrate farmers who permanently dispersed into hinterland areas (e.g., hinterland Copán; Freter 1994; Webster and Gonlin 1988) or migrated to the Yucatán, southeastern Petén, east to Belize, or west and south to the highlands (e.g., Culbert 1977; Laporte 2004; Lowe 1985:208; McAnany et al. 2004; Mock 2004; Santley et al. 1986; Willey and Shimkin 1973).

Drier conditions particularly affected areas lacking rivers and lakes and those in higher elevations with relatively low annual rainfall (see Figure 4.1). Minor and secondary centers show a gradual trend from lower to higher elevations and less so for annual rainfall, whereas regional centers represent the extremes in rainfall (the highest or lowest annual amounts, but typically the lowest) and elevation (highest). These patterns indicate that rainfall and elevation both influenced agricultural regimes (e.g., different temperatures) (see Akin 1991:47).

Kings' loss of power at regional centers had various impacts on smaller centers. Some secondary rulers began to build monuments on their own, independent of their previous overlords (Marcus 1976; Pohl and Pohl 1994); rulers not heavily dependent on water systems survived the drought, at least for a brief time. In addition, political fallout for secondary kings varied and was related to their level of involvement with regional rulers. The Maya at minor centers without water systems continued performing daily activities, largely unaffected by what was happening elsewhere.

Nonriver Centers

In areas without lakes or rivers, artificial reservoirs no longer adequately fulfilled daily water needs. As a result, commoners stopped congregating at center reservoirs and paying to get in. Eventually, Tikal's core was largely abandoned in the 900s, as was Calakmul's (Marcus 1998; Pinceman et al. 1998). Calakmul's abandonment was associated not only with drought but possibly with incursions from the Putún Maya from the Gulf Coast of Tabasco, Mexico, taking advantage of a weakened rulership. After ca. AD 790 Caracol was still occupied by "elite" Maya until ca. AD 895 (A. Chase and D. Chase 2004). Caracol's epicenter was abruptly abandoned by ca. AD 890 and burned, though a remnant population remained another 200 years or so (A. Chase and D. Chase 1996, 2001; D. Chase and A. Chase 2000). Exacerbating rulers' problems was the lack of stored goods that could have been used to allay famine and garner continued support for rulership.

River Centers

Concentrated alluvium clearly was not enough to prevent many farmers of Copán and Palenque from abandoning their kings to search for better areas to live. As was the case with similarly organized archaic states elsewhere, over-use of resources also contributed to problems caused by drought. There are indications that decreasing subsistence resources played a role in the disintegration of power, as indicated at Copán, where leaders were faced not only with depleting resources (Davis-Salazar 2003; Fash 1991:170–183; Paine and Freter 1996; Webster 1999; Wingard 1996) but also with competition between elite and royal lineages (Fash 1998; Fash et al. 2004; Fash and Stuart 1991; Freter 1994). These factors might explain why their last inscribed date (AD 822) is noticeably earlier than Tikal's (AD 869) and Caracol's (AD 859). Stelae were no longer carved in these times of trouble; instead, inscriptions were carved and painted on portable items (Fash 1998), similar to the Late Preclassic period. Another factor affecting Copán more than other river centers was similar to the situation at nonriver regional centers: changing rainfall patterns. Copán's annual rainfall is significantly less than at most other major centers, just over 130 cm, indicating that reservoirs probably dried up as well. Copán's hinterland population, however, while decreasing in number, did not completely abandon the region (Webster 2002:310).

While annual rainfall at Palenque is over 360 cm (one of the highest), kings still lost power when changing conditions exacerbated internal political instability as a result of their defeat twice in the 700s at the hands of rulers from Toniná, a secondary center 65 km to the south (Martin and Grube 2000:172–174, 182). These losses may also explain why Palenque had one of the earliest last-known inscribed dates in the southern lowlands (AD 799), much earlier than Toniná, which has the latest last-known inscribed date in the southern Maya lowlands (AD 909). And even if kings provided drinking water, rainfall-dependent farming practices in surrounding areas did not produce enough food, storage or not.

Secondary Centers

The disruption in the royal interaction sphere variously affected secondary centers but eventually resulted in the disappearance of royal hallmarks, including monumental architecture, inscriptions, and royal iconography. Small-scale water/agricultural systems and scattered resources did not provide kings with the same means to acquire political power as at regional centers. As a result of increasing drought, Maya kings lost what power they had. At centers with higher annual rainfall and small-scale water/agricultural systems, the disruption felt elsewhere did not automatically result in dramatic change; instead restructuring may have taken place, and in some cases a florescence.

Lamanai's location on a lagoon with fertile land coupled with trade with the Yucatán Maya provided its inhabitants with the means to outlast the political disintegration through the seventeenth century (Loten 1985; Pendergast 1986); kings, though, did not survive. Lamanai's inhabitants also benefited from runoff, as one of the eastern-most major centers in the southern Maya lowlands. The Maya continued to live for a time at Quiriguá, perhaps due to "its apparent isolation, its self sufficiency within the rich lower Motagua Valley, and a continued control over the lucrative highland-Caribbean trade route" (Sharer 1978:69). Kings of Seibal and Xunantunich witnessed a brief florescence. Seibal's rulers probably took advantage of the upheavals happening throughout the Pasión region, perhaps with a little impetus from the northeast (Ucanal), and Xunantunich's rulers took advantage of the waning power at Naranjo (LeCount et al. 2002; Mathews and Willey 1991; Tourtellot and González 2004). For example, the last-known dated inscriptions at Xunantunich date to AD 849 and at Seibal to AD 889, some of the latest. Altar de Sacrificios, with its last inscribed date of AD 849, was abandoned for a short time in the early AD 900s (Mathews and Willey 1991); was briefly reoccupied, perhaps by a different Maya or foreign group ca. A.D. 909–948; and was abandoned for good after AD 950 (Adams 1973; Smith 1972:6).

Even though Dos Pilas is in a resource-rich zone, historic circumstances (specifically, its location in a region with several competing kingdoms) resulted in its eventual abandonment after Ruler 4 was defeated in AD 761 by a neighboring king from Tamarandito (Demarest 1997). Recent paleoecological research on landscape changes conducted by Kevin Johnston, Andrew Breckenridge, and Barbara Hansen (2001), however, indicates that Laguna Las Pozas in the Pasión drainage of Guatemala was occupied in the Early Postclassic (ca. AD 900–1200), after nearby centers including Dos Pilas and Aguateca were abandoned (see also Palka 1997).

Classic political life eventually ceased at most secondary river centers due to the disruption in the royal interaction sphere and decreasing surplus.

Minor Centers

In areas with plentiful land and water where farmers did not rely on water systems or kings, the drought's impact was different than elsewhere. Of course the Maya, as members of a larger society, knew of events taking place in other places. On a day-to-day basis, however, not much necessarily changed. The Maya who lived at minor centers were the least affected by the dramatic events taking place at larger, more politically integrated centers. For example, the Maya who lived at Saturday Creek until at least AD 1500 (Conlon and Ehret 2002) did not have to face failing water/agricultural systems. A similar scenario took place at Barton Ramie, which was also occupied into the Postclassic until at least ca. AD 1200 and likely longer (Willey et al. 1965). Their location along a major river with runoff from the west and plentiful alluvium provided the means to weather changing climate and to continue with community life.[1] Local elites indeed had less access to exotic goods, since the interaction sphere was disrupted, but they soon obtained long-distance wares through different routes, particularly sea trade from the north and east. Political shifts occurring elsewhere in the southern Maya lowlands had little impact on a community that was not much involved in Classic Maya politics to begin with.

Summary Remarks

Having access to wealth or capital and critical resources in conjunction with the use of integrative strategies such as ceremonies provided a powerful centripetal political tool for Maya rulers. Climatic changes had a major impact on centers lacking permanent or adequate water sources in higher elevations with relatively low rainfall, where water systems and ritual were vital to political life. As drier conditions became more common, water and agricultural systems and crops failed, as did ceremonies that previously had resulted in bountiful rain and food. Combined with increasing soil depletion and deforestation, these factors resulted in the migration and dispersal of Maya farmers who once nucleated around centers. In the end, people blamed kings for all the mishaps occurring as a result of climate change.

The majority of Maya did not disappear or die off after the political collapse; they only permanently left the fold of the royal tribute system, since rulers no longer provided them with a strong inducement to remain. Postcollapse reorganization in the interior is thus best understood as a process unfolding at the community level. In the southern Maya lowlands after the Terminal Classic, former subjects no longer had to supply tribute to a ruling class; they only had to work for their families and the community to which they belonged, including local elites. After rulers lost power, farmers and elites continued to conduct traditional rites where they began, in the home and community, as Terminal Classic (ca. AD 850–950) and Early Postclassic (ca. AD 950–1200) residential deposits throughout the Maya lowlands illustrate (e.g., D. Chase and A. Chase 2004; Lucero 2003).

The Aftermath

What happened to former royal subjects? Some or even many farmers remained in the southern Maya lowlands. At first glance it may seem that there was massive population loss during and after the collapse. But increasing evidence from hinterland studies suggests that what might have happened instead was both migration out of these areas *and* a reversion to nonplatform houses constructed of thatch and/or wattle-and-daub, resulting in the "invisible" mounds of the archaeological record (e.g., Johnston 2004a, 2004b; Rice 1996; Webster 2002: 215). The collapse of Classic Maya political systems resulted in people organizing at the community level in some areas, especially near permanent water sources (e.g., Johnston et al. 2001; Masson 1997; Masson and Mock 2004). For example, the Maya inhabited the Petén Itzá lakes region until the conquest (Rice 1996; Rice and Rice 2004). Ford (1986) has recorded a notable presence of Terminal Classic occupation in the intercenter area between Tikal and Yaxhá, 29 km apart, after the Maya had abandoned the centers. Juan Antonio Laporte (2004) has noted a noticeable increase in population in the southeastern Petén, beginning in the Terminal Classic and decreasing somewhat in the Postclassic. McAnany and others (2004) note the same for the Sibun Valley in east-central Belize.

Another hallmark often used as a gauge of the abandonment of the southern lowlands is the noticeable decrease in ceramics. It is possible that the Maya began using more decorated gourds rather than ceramics (Hayden 1994), as do several Postclassic and modern Maya groups (e.g., Bunzel 1952:42; Hayden and Cannon 1984:172; Redfield and Villa Rojas 1934:75, 128; Tozzer 1907:122, 1941:90; Vogt 1970:54). Prudence Rice and Donald Forsyth (2004) also note that polychrome ceramics decrease in number and vessels become smaller and simpler in design and form. The lack of polychromes would make distinguishing plain vessels from different periods difficult. In sum, different building patterns and the increasing use of perishable goods and monochrome or unslipped ceramics all would have left less telling evidence in the archaeological record, which would appear to represent population loss and migration rather than population dispersal and migration.

Some of the Maya who migrated went north, attracted by a new religion revolving around Kukulcan and trade centered at Chichén Itzá;[2] others headed to Belize and to the highlands of Chiapas. Coastal areas provided marine resources, and shallow lakes the means for wetland agriculture—two types of resources less dependent upon rainfall. For the Yucatán, archaeologists have proposed an outmigration at the end of the Late Preclassic due to drier climate and later due to flooding salt pans (Santley et al. 1986); the area was not to see increased settlement until later in the Classic period at centers such as Chichén Itzá and Dzibilchaltún (Cobos 2004), when both climate change and lowering sea levels provided inducements to return. The Puuc area witnessed a peak in population in the Terminal Classic (Carmean et al. 2004). Other areas of the Yucatán peninsula, such as the southern areas of Quintana Roo, incorporated the use of canals to support the growing immigrant populations. As mentioned earlier, the Maya may have been attracted to the northern lowlands not only due to better economic opportunities but also because of a new religion centered on Kukulcan, the feathered serpent, as well as traditional Maya deities. They may have looked to new gods, since some of the traditional ones failed them, especially those associated with Classic Maya rulership (e.g., K'awil), which largely disappeared in Postclassic rites and iconography. In parts of the northern lowlands that experienced a florescence from ca. AD 750 to 1000 (Demarest et al. 2004a), however, the Maya still continued performing traditional rites, a practice which has persisted to the present.

To conclude, southern lowland Maya kings were around for nearly a millennium, a testament to their skills in integrating people. Their history, as they wrote it themselves, involved almost daily supplications to gods and ancestors, especially royal ones. It also records battles, the sacrifice of vanquished and captured rulers, accession rites, marriage alliances, bloodletting, and several other royal events and rites. What it does not mention is the nonreligious and nonritual means of power. I have attempted to fill this gap. The following section presents a possible scenario of how Maya kings acquired political power, as well as how they eventually lost it.

A Scenario: The Ancient Maya

In the Middle Preclassic period the Maya began more and more to move away from coasts, rivers, and lakes into interior areas with plentiful land that may or may not have had permanent water sources. First settlers or founders were also first served; the implications of this were not obvious until increasingly more people moved into these areas. Everyone conducted rituals in the home, which came from a long-standing tradition.

In the Late Preclassic first founders started to distinguish themselves from others by building larger houses and small public temples and acquiring exotics. Elites continued to practice the same rites as everyone else but began to use more expensive items as offerings—they could afford to relinquish them forever. They compensated laborers with food, exotics, and/or access to resources. Elites had to pay their workers well, since the latter could choose to work for other families who could afford to pay. To show their gratitude, patrons sponsored traditional rites and feasts for workers and their families and invited the entire community to attend and participate. Such events offered a break from work and a time to socialize, not to mention the opportunity to increase the prestige of elites in the eyes of farmers and to compete with other elites for prestige and labor.

This scenario was repeated again and again throughout the southern Maya lowlands. Why did the Maya no longer have a choice but to acquiesce to tribute demands instituted by rulers? Why and how did Maya elites transform into rulers? What circumstances, which should come as no surprise at this point, allowed rulers to emerge in some areas but not in others?

Even if *bajos* had once been wetlands or lakes, by the beginning of the Classic period they had transformed into seasonal swamps. In areas without surface water, initially *aguadas* provided enough water for the earliest settlers. Later, especially beginning in the Early Classic, large artificial reservoirs became critical; quarrying provided the construction materials to build temples and palaces next to reservoirs. Along or near rivers in Mexico, Guatemala, and western Honduras, growing numbers of people still needed access to potable water, especially at the height of the dry season, when rivers were low, murky, and disease-ridden. Rulers, when necessary, provided capital to repair water or agricultural systems damaged during the rainy season. Providers did not perform these services for free. Maya leaders, who emerged from wealthy founding lineages, realized that they could demand payment above and beyond equal compensation. Maya rulers could not demand too much from farmers because they could flee into the jungle or to other realms. Consequently, the average Maya was not powerless but had some leverage.

Areas with noticeable seasonal issues or problems provided the ideal circumstances for rulers to emerge. Many farmers relied on reservoirs—and on the rulers who built them and who lived and worshiped next to them. And when the rainy season began each year, it was clearly due to successful supplication of gods and ancestors by everyone, especially kings. Thirsty farmers thus had a stake in constructing and maintaining increasingly larger and sophisticated reservoirs. The continually growing numbers of farmers attracted to fertile areas were incorporated into the political system because of their need for water and because of a ruler's ability to secure enough water for everyone through supernatural connections.

Consequently, the most powerful kings arose in areas where people relied the most on large-scale water/agricultural systems—as well as on the plentiful agricultural land that yielded enough food to maintain royals and their subjects. Rulers used their wealth to maintain reservoirs and agricultural systems throughout the year. In areas without rulers (for example, along the Belize River), the availability of ample land and water (even in the dry season, due to runoff from Guatemala and Mexico) prevented elites from attracting lots of people and exacting tribute. Elites, however, sponsored community-wide ceremonies to offset potential conflict in the face of wealth differences. Kings at secondary centers could have built large-scale water/agricultural systems as well if their agricultural land had not been dispersed in relatively small pockets. These lands could not support large enough numbers of people to maintain a primary royal lifestyle, which they were able to witness on their visits to regional centers as subordinates or independent secondary kings. Further, when small-scale agricultural and/or water systems were damaged by heavy rainfall, farmers and communities repaired them without royal assistance.

Rulers realized that since most people lived dispersed throughout the hinterlands, they could choose to whom and at which center they contributed surplus goods and labor in exchange for access to water and capital. Consequently, political aspirants needed to fulfill more than just material needs. They responded through replicating and expanding traditional rites in plazas facing large temples and ball courts. The strategy of "bread and circuses" was not used only by Roman emperors. The rulers' success as landowners and providers of water and capital demonstrated to on-the-fence farmers that their special ties to gods and ancestors benefited them all. And since farmers had to pay anyway, why not pay successful aspirants? Why not contribute surplus goods and labor to kings who sponsored impressive ceremonies and feasts? Why not pay homage to rulers who captured and sacrificed fellow kings? Those who were unwilling to pay could flee to marginal areas that yielded little surplus and were thus of no interest to rulers.

Political domains expanded throughout the Late Classic, when Maya kings reached their apogee of power. And the system worked for nearly a millennium. But all things come to an end. The more Maya rulers depended on large-scale water systems to support their royal lifestyle, the more vulnerable they were to changing rainfall patterns. While political systems were somewhat fluid and flexible, one aspect of the subsistence system was not: their rainfall dependency and reliance on water/agricultural systems. Rituals no longer worked in the face of changing material conditions—namely, a long-term drought. Kings failed in their supplications to supernatural entities. Close ties to the otherworld brought both benefits and risks. When water was plentiful, rulers benefited; when it was not, rulers lost their edge—and power. They no longer paid into a system that did not work. Commoners either made their way out of centers into hinterland areas or left the region altogether in search of wetter pastures.

CHAPTER 8

Water, Ritual, and Politics
in Ancient Complex Societies

. . . since Fortune changes and men stand fixed in their old ways, they are prosperous
so long as there is congruity between them, and the reverse when there is not.
MACHIAVELLI (1994 [1514]:82)

In Chapter 1, I have presented a scenario on the emergence of rulers. My goal throughout this book has been to address a key question—how do a few people get others to contribute labor and goods without compensating them equally? To appreciate how political leaders emerge, it is first critical to understand—in addition to social and historical circumstances—material issues, namely, the amount and distribution of agricultural land, seasonal water issues, and where people live and work across the landscape. Together they influence the amount of available surplus in any given area. Uniting political power and the material world is ritual. As long as there is a balance among these features, all is well (politically anyway). When conditions change, so do political fortunes, for better or worse. And as I have attempted to demonstrate in this work, these processes occur cross-culturally. Surplus and ritual both are vital for political survival.

The replication and the expansion of familiar traditional rites allow rulers to bring people together to demonstrate their abilities in propitiating and communicating with ancestors and gods. The ultimate practical goal is to provide protection and capital, water, and food when necessary in exchange for surplus labor and goods. Subjects thus benefit materially (e.g., Service 1975:8); rulers' ability to fulfill material obligations only highlights their closer ties to supernatural entities. People also have options; they can contribute to another leader or in some cases leave political realms altogether and live in marginal areas unsuitable for surplus extraction. People participate in redefining their rights and obligations *because* rulers demonstrate their success in the material and spiritual realms.

The fact that rituals alone do not support political leaders goes a long way in explaining the different types of political systems as well as demonstrating the relatively limited number of responses to varied material and social conditions. Community organizations have several leaders (e.g., lineage heads, village chiefs, or elite Maya lineage heads) who cannot demand tribute but who use their wealth to distinguish themselves materially and to sponsor local integrative events. Farmers are extensive and/or intensive agriculturalists who rely on seasonal rainfall but do not rely on water/agricultural systems. Consequently, people are better able to deal with changing conditions and thus have long and relatively stable histories. Further, plentiful resources available year-round are not conducive to expanding the political economy. Household and public rites take place to honor ancestors, not the living.

The main differences between community organizations and local polities are that the latter include denser settlements, a greater reliance on water/agricultural systems, and the presence of one major institutionalized leader (e.g., a paramount chief or secondary Maya king). Political leaders acquire surplus labor and goods from people in return for what they provide in services—centripetal events such as feasts and ceremonies (e.g., Maya kings) and/or food during famine or capital to repair small-scale water/agricultural systems damaged during the rainy season (e.g., Hawaiian paramount chiefs). Political power often is linked to external ties (e.g., trade, esoteric information, and the elite/royal interaction sphere), whose duration is quite varied, while the subsistence economy largely is stable. In cases where external ties are not as significant (e.g., Hawaii), other factors (e.g., island setting and population size) can limit extent and affect duration. The greater importance of leaders in the lives of all is expressed in public rites that include thanking chiefly or royal ancestors. People perform rites in the home to honor their own ancestors.

The height of political power is achieved in centralized polities, where there is little doubt that royal intercession with supernatural entities is critical, because densely settled people rely on seasonal rainfall, intensive agriculture, and/or large-scale water or agricultural systems (e.g., Maya river regional centers, Egypt, and Mesopotamian city-states). Royal success—for example, in ensuring adequate river flooding for agriculture (e.g., Egypt and China)—is publicized in large-scale ceremonies with roots in traditional rites. Everyone worships ancestors and gods in the home and community as well. As long as surplus is stable, so are political systems (though the political system may change hands, as it did several times in Egypt). In integrative polities, the primary ruler has a similar role. The distinguishing feature is that key resources and settlement are more dispersed, which adds an additional challenge for rulers to reach people, not to mention their surplus (e.g., Maya nonriver regional centers and precolonial Balinese kingdoms). Rulers reach people, and their surplus, through sponsoring frequent ceremonies, feasts, and other integrative events and displays. Kings also play a large role in providing water through funding the building of large reservoirs and performing water rites. Seasonal fluctuations are always a concern in centralized and integrative polities, so long-term seasonal changes can and do bring down royal dynasties temporarily (e.g., precolonial Bali and Egypt) or permanently (e.g., southern Maya lowlands and southern Mesopotamia).

Another crucial issue that I have attempted to address is the types of changes that can cause rulers to lose their right to exact tribute. Seasonal vagaries are challenges enough to deal with—providing water during annual drought, allocating water, repairing water/agricultural systems damaged by flooding, and supplying food in times of scarcity. Climate change lasting more than a few seasons is another matter entirely. In *Floods, Famines, and Emperors: El Niño and the Fate of Civilizations*, Brian Fagan (1999) details how climate change has affected political histories throughout the world. For example, in the Moche case in Peru (pp. 119–138), he notes that an inflexible government and subsistence technology ("elaborate irrigations systems"; p. 138) lessened farmers' ability to survive long-term droughts and torrential rains and destructive floods caused by El Niño events. A series of several El Niño events damaged the large-scale irrigation systems repeatedly in the late AD 600s, eventually resulting in the demise of Moche political power. He presents several other instances where climate change had a dramatic impact on social, political, and economic institutions (e.g., Egypt and Europe and the "Little Ice Age"). While he does not discuss ritual, it is obvious that royal ceremonies failed. Fagan concludes his book by highlighting recent instances where the lack of foresight and articulation of institutions, resources, and changing rainfall patterns have had devastating results, as witnessed at present in parched east Africa.

Crumley (see Chapter 1) provides a more in-depth account of one particular area, western Europe, showing how certain climate regimes suited Roman expansion; centuries of success resulted in tried-and-true subsistence and political institutions that eventually were unable to cope with long-term climate change. Fagan (2004) further details the effects of climate change on societies in *The Long Summer: How Climate Changed Civilization*. In this work, he highlights how short-term or immediate responses (e.g., spending more resources to propitiate the gods) to changing climate can make societies more vulnerable in the long run—a lesson we are increasingly learning at present.

The point is that not being able to respond efficiently to climate change eventually can have drastic and unforeseen consequences, especially in situations where political and subsistence systems are not flexible enough to adjust to changing conditions. Short-term responses—including, for example, the elaboration of rituals in a last-ditch effort to appease the gods or using up stores of food and grain without taking into consideration future needs such as continuing famine and the need of seeds for planting—have long-lasting impacts, not usually beneficial (e.g., Hosler et al. 1977). More often than not, the response was to reorganize or adapt. The Roman Empire, for example, broke apart; "emperors" began relying on new rituals and gods, since the old ones had failed them. Many of the traditional Roman deities concerned crops and fertility (e.g., Juno and Diana), "weather and elements," and war (Minerva and Jupiter) (Crumley 2001). Roman emperors were closely tied to ritual and ceremony involving these deities, as was everyone else. Climate change changed all this and

. . . challenged sacred imperial authority. To account for widespread economic failures, Roman emperors were forced to reinterpret traditional religion or to embrace the mystical religious traditions of the eastern Mediterranean. Beginning with Aurelian (AD 215–275), who imported Persian worship of the Unconquered Sun, the search culminated with Constantine's (AD 285–337) conversion to Christianity. (Crumley 2001:31)

If responses are inadequate, people are more susceptible to foreign invasions, for example, or at least a new regime. Political institutions can also fragment into their constituent autonomous parts and later regenerate (e.g., Egypt, China, and Mesopotamia) (Cowgill 1988). Rarely does everyone abandon an area altogether;[1] people leave the only life they know when they have no other choice. If people previously have been willing to contribute to political coffers rather than leave, whatever makes them abandon their rulers, homes, and land must be extreme.

In the Maya area, kings rose and fell in areas with plentiful farming land and noticeable seasonal vagaries. Replicating and expanding traditional rituals brought people together and provided the arena for rulers to show off their various powers. Audience members had a say in their success, because kings knew that people could choose to whom to gift their tribute. In some cases farmers left kingdoms and settled in marginal areas where surplus was inadequate for political purposes. In many cases, however, this option was not available because of farmers' need for capital, water, or food in times of need. The average Maya commoner in the Classic period thus had little choice but to acquiesce to tribute demands but likely could choose which ruler to pay, as reflected in the prevalent and public monumental architecture that served as a backdrop for rulers to attract and entertain supporters and collect tribute.

The Maya political system worked for nearly a millennium, an amazing feat. It would take something drastic to bring it down. And something drastic indeed happened. Long-term climate change played a large part in bringing an end to Classic Maya *royal* life. Maya kings attempted to prevent the inevitable and used strategies that had worked for centuries. Rituals that once highlighted their successes now only emphasized their failures, since they could not bring forth enough water for daily needs and agricultural fields. Commoners responded by abandoning rulers and centers. Some permanently remained in the hinterlands or noncenter areas, where they could subsist in small family groups and communities; others fled the southern lowlands in all four directions. The situation was extreme enough to prevent the replacement of Maya kingship with a comparable political system.

The Maya reoccupied some centers, but in small numbers. And none of their members became kings. Rulers were gone forever in the southern Maya lowlands, not to mention much of their "great tradition" (the northern Maya lowlands are another story). Elites and commoners remained and continued to perform the daily social, religious, and economic tasks that they had always performed before and during the time of rulership.

Concluding Remarks

The goal of this book has been to explain the emergence and demise of political leadership in terms of the same two factors—water and ritual. While these topics are often discussed on their own, there can be little doubt that they are inextricably and dialectically linked. It is their articulation that plays a key role in the creation and dissolution of political power. Plentiful rain at the right time, which results in bountiful crops that feed everyone, is the direct result of kings' successful propitiation of gods and ancestors through traditional rituals writ large. Water and surplus sustain the body and rituals; rituals sustain the mind and spirit. Water and surplus provide the means to fund political systems, and rituals the arena to promote solidarity and political agendas. Participants or audience members have a voice in who becomes a leader and who does not. People also express disapproval when rulers fail in providing material necessities and vote with their feet and pocketbooks. Rulers cannot curtail the loss of tribute-payers in the face of their rituals failing.

Simply stated, water and ritual are crucial in the development and demise of political power.

Notes

Chapter 1

1. Drastic change or revolution (e.g., the French and Russian revolutions) usually occurs when current religious, political, social, and/or economic systems fail, or as a result of external causes such as conquest.

Chapter 2

1. Maya dates are based on regional ceramic chronologies, many of which have been refined with radiocarbon dates (Andrews 1990). Most political events are based on deciphered inscriptions.

2. While prehispanic annual rainfall may have been different than at present, the relative differences of rainfall between areas should be similar.

Chapter 4

1. This section is an expanded version of the ritual history of Saturday Creek presented in Lucero (2003).

2. This feature also might be the remnants of a hearth that the Maya cleaned out and covered.

Chapter 6

1. This section is an expanded version of the ritual history of Tikal presented in Lucero (2003).

Chapter 7

1. The question is why the Maya eventually abandoned these areas one or several centuries before the arrival of the Spanish.

2. It is interesting to note that Chichén Itzá iconography has a noticeable presence of water-lily motifs associated with monumental public architecture (see Rands 1953: Tables 1–4). Yet water lilies cannot grow in the deep waters of sacred cenotes but can grow in shallow lakes and cenotes.

Chapter 8

1. Also relatively rare are revolutions or a total replacement of political systems caused by the masses. For example, in France "what fell in 1789 was not a state, but a system of government" (Cowgill 1988:257). The Russian revolution did not result in equality for all but in a replacement of one bureaucracy with another.

References Cited

Abrams, Elliot M., and David J. Rue

1988. The Causes and Consequences of Deforestation among the Prehistoric Maya. *Human Ecology* 16:377–395.

Adams, Richard E. W.

1971. *The Ceramics of Altar de Sacrificios*. Papers of the Peabody Museum of Archaeology and Ethnology, Vol. 3, No. 1. Cambridge, MA: Harvard University.

1973. Maya Collapse: Transformation and Termination in the Ceramic Sequence at Altar de Sacrificios. In *The Classic Maya Collapse*, edited by T. P. Culbert, pp. 133–163. Albuquerque: University of New Mexico Press.

1995. Early Classic Maya Civilization: A View from Río Azul. In *The Emergence of Classic Maya Civilization*, edited by N. Grube, pp. 35–48. Acta Mesoamericana 8. Möckmühl: Verlag von Flemming.

Adams, Robert McC.

1966. *The Evolution of Urban Society: Early Mesopotamia and Prehispanic Mexico*. New York: Aldine de Gruyter.

Adas, Michael

1981. From Avoidance to Confrontation: Peasant Protest in Precolonial and Colonial Southeast Asia. *Comparative Studies in Society and History* 23:217–247.

Akin, Wallace E.

1991. *Global Patterns: Climate, Vegetation, and Soils*. Norman: University of Oklahoma Press.

Allen, Jane

1999. Managing a Tropical Environment: State Development in Early Historical-Era Kedah, Malaysia. In *Complex Polities in the Ancient Tropical World*, edited by E. A. Bacus and L. J. Lucero, pp. 131–150. Archeological Papers of the American Anthropological Association Number 9. Arlington, VA: American Anthropological Association.

Anderson, Richard L.

1989 [1979]. *Art in Small-Scale Societies*. Englewood Cliffs, NJ: Prentice-Hall.

Andres, Christopher R., and K. Anne Pyburn

2004. Out of Sight: The Postclassic and Early Colonial Periods at Chau Hiïx, Belize. In *The Terminal Classic in the Maya Lowlands: Collapse, Transition, and Transformation*, edited by A. A. Demarest, P. M. Rice, and D. S. Rice, pp. 402–423. Boulder: University Press of Colorado.

Andrews, E. Wyllys, V

1990. The Early Ceramic History of the Lowland Maya. In *Vision and Revision in Maya Studies*, edited by F. S. Clancy and P. D. Harrison, pp. 1–19. Albuquerque: University of New Mexico Press.

Andrews, George F.

1975. *Maya Cities: Placemaking and Urbanization.* Norman: University of Oklahoma Press.

Aoyama, Kazuo

2001. Classic Maya State, Urbanism, and Exchange: Chipped Stone Evidence of the Copán Valley and Its Hinterland. *American Anthropologist* 103:346–360.

Arie, Jane C.

2001. Sun Kings and Hierophants: Geocosmic Orientation and the Classic Maya. M.A. thesis. Las Cruces: New Mexico State University.

Ashmore, Wendy

1981. Precolumbian Occupation at Quiriguá Guatemala: Settlement Patterns in a Classic Maya Center. Ph.D. dissertation, University of Pennsylvania. Ann Arbor: University Microfilms International.

1984. Quirigua Archaeology and History Revisited. *Journal of Field Archaeology* 11: 365–386.

1990. Ode to a Dragline: Demographic Reconstruction at Classic Quirigua. In *Precolumbian Population History in the Maya Lowlands*, edited by T. P. Culbert and D. S. Rice, pp. 63–82. Albuquerque: University of New Mexico Press.

1991. Site-Planning Principles and Concepts of Directionality among the Ancient Maya. *Latin American Antiquity* 2:199–226.

Ashmore, Wendy, and Jeremy A. Sabloff

2002. Spatial Orders in Maya Civic Plans. *Latin American Antiquity* 13:201–215.

Ashmore, Wendy, Jason Yaeger, and Cynthia Robin

2004. Commoner Sense: Late and Terminal Classic Social Strategies in the Xunantunich Area. In *The Terminal Classic in the Maya Lowlands: Collapse, Transition, and Transformation*, edited by A. A. Demarest, P. M. Rice, and D. S. Rice, pp. 302–323. Boulder: University Press of Colorado.

Atran, Scott

1993. Itza Maya Tropical Agro-Forestry. *Current Anthropology* 34:633–700.

Baines, John, and Norman Yoffee

1998. Order, Legitimacy, and Wealth in Ancient Egypt and Mesopotamia. In *Archaic States*, edited by G. M. Feinman and J. Marcus, pp. 199–260. Santa Fe: School of American Research Press.

Barnhart, Edwin E.

2001. The Palenque Mapping Project: Settlement and Urbanism at an Ancient Maya City. Ph.D. dissertation. Austin: University of Texas.

Becker, Marshall
1992.   Burials as Caches; Caches as Burials: A New Interpretation of the Meaning of Ritual Deposits among the Classic Period Lowland Maya. In *New Theories on the Ancient Maya*, edited by R. J. Sharer, pp. 185–196. Philadelphia: University Museum, University of Pennsylvania.
1999.   *Excavations in Residential Areas of Tikal: Groups with Shrines*. With contributions by Christopher Jones and John McGinn. Tikal Report No. 21. University Museum Monograph 104. Philadelphia: University of Pennsylvania.

Bell, Catherine
1997.   *Ritual: Perspectives and Dimensions*. New York: Oxford University Press.

Blanton, Richard E.
1998.   Beyond Centralization: Steps toward a Theory of Egalitarian Behavior in Archaic States. In *Archaic States*, edited by G. M. Feinman and J. Marcus, pp. 135–172. Santa Fe: School of American Research Press.

Blanton, Richard E., Gary M. Feinman, Stephen A. Kowalewski, and Peter N. Peregrine
1996.   A Dual-Processual Theory for the Evolution of Mesoamerican Civilization. *Current Anthropology* 37:1–14.

Bloch, Maurice
1986.   *From Blessing to Violence: History and Ideology in the Circumcision Ritual of the Merina of Madagascar*. Cambridge: Cambridge University Press.
1987.   The Ritual of the Royal Bath in Madagascar: The Dissolution of Death, Birth and Fertility into Authority. In *Rituals of Royalty: Power and Ceremonial in Traditional Societies*, edited by D. Cannadine and S. Price, pp. 271–297. Cambridge: Cambridge University Press.

Bourdieu, Pierre
1977.   *Outline of a Theory of Practice*. Translated by R. Nice. Cambridge: Cambridge University Press.
1990.   *The Logic of Practice*. Translated by R. Nice. Stanford: University of Stanford Press.

Bove, Frederick J.
1981.   Trend Surface Analysis and the Lowland Classic Maya Collapse. *American Antiquity* 46:93–112.

Bradley, Richard
1990.   *The Passage of Arms: An Archaeological Analysis of Prehistoric Hoards and Votive Deposits*. Cambridge: Cambridge University Press.

Brady, James E., Ann Scott, Allan Cobb, Irma Rodas, John Fogarty, and Monica Urquizú Sánchez
1997.   Glimpses of the Dark Side of the Petexbatún Project: The Petexbatún Regional Cave Survey. *Ancient Mesoamerica* 8:353–364.

Braswell, Geoffrey E., Joel D. Gunn, María del Rosario Domínguez Carrasco, William J. Folan, Laraine A. Fletcher, Abel Morales López, and Michael D. Glascock
2004.   Defining the Terminal Classic at Calakmul, Campeche. In *The Terminal Classic in the Maya Lowlands: Collapse, Transition, and Transformation*, edited by A. A. Demarest, P. M. Rice, and D. S. Rice, pp. 162–194. Boulder: University Press of Colorado.

Brenner, Mark, Michael F. Rosenmeier, David A. Hodell, and Jason H. Curtis
  2002. Paleolimnology of the Maya Lowlands: Long-Term Perspectives on Inter-
    actions among Climate, Environment, and Humans. *Ancient Mesoamerica* 13:
    141–157.
Bright, John
  1981. *A History of Israel.* 3rd ed. Philadelphia: Westminster Press.
Brown, Clifford T.
  n.d.   Water Sources of Mayapán, Yucatán, Mexico. In *Precolumbian Water Man-
    agement: Ideology, Ritual, and Politics,* edited by L. J. Lucero and B. Fash. Tuc-
    son: University of Arizona Press. In press.
Bunzel, Ruth
  1952. *Chichicastenango: A Guatemalan Village.* Publications of the American Ethno-
    logical Society, No. 23. Locust Valley, NY: J. J. Augustin Publishers.
Burton, Thomas M., Darrell L. King, Robert C. Ball, and Thomas G. Baker
  1979. Utilization of Natural Ecosystems for Waste Water Renovation. United States
    Environmental Protection Agency, Region V. Chicago: Great Lakes National
    Programs Office.
Carmean, Kelli, Nicholas Dunning, and Jeff Karl Kowalski
  2004. High Times in the Hill Country: A Perspective from the Terminal Classic
    Puuc Region. In *The Terminal Classic in the Maya Lowlands: Collapse, Transi-
    tion, and Transformation,* edited by A. A. Demarest, P. M. Rice, and D. S.
    Rice, pp. 424–449. Boulder: University Press of Colorado.
Carmean, Kelli, and Jeremy A. Sabloff
  1996. Political Decentralization in the Puuc Region, Yucatán, Mexico. *Journal of
    Anthropological Research* 52:317–330.
Carneiro, Robert L.
  1970. A Theory of the Origin of the State. *Science* 169:733–738.
Chang, K. C.
  1983. *Art, Myth, and Ritual: The Path to Political Authority in Ancient China.* Cam-
    bridge, MA: Harvard University Press.
Chase, Arlen F., and Diane Z. Chase
  1989. The Investigation of Classic Period Maya Warfare at Caracol, Belize. *Mayab*
    5:5–18.
  1995. External Impetus, Internal Synthesis, and Standardization: E Group Assem-
    blages and the Crystallization of Classic Maya Society in the Southern Low-
    lands. In *The Emergence of Classic Maya Civilization,* edited by N. Grube,
    pp. 87–101. Acta Mesoamericana 8. Möckmühl: Verlag von Flemming.
  1996. A Mighty Maya Nation: How Caracol Built an Empire by Cultivating Its
    Middle Class. *Archaeology* 49(5):66–72.
  2001. The Royal Court of Caracol, Belize: Its Palaces and People. In *Royal Courts of
    the Ancient Maya Volume II: Data and Case Studies,* edited by T. Inomata and
    S. D. Houston, pp. 102–137. Boulder: Westview Press.
  2004. Terminal Classic Status-Linked Ceramics and the Maya "Collapse": De Facto
    Refuse at Caracol, Belize. In *The Terminal Classic in the Maya Lowlands: Col-
    lapse, Transition, and Transformation,* edited by A. A. Demarest, P. M. Rice,
    and D. S. Rice, pp. 343–366. Boulder: University Press of Colorado.

Chase, Diane Z., and Arlen F. Chase

1998. Architectural Context of Caches, Burials, and Other Ritual Activities for the Classic Period Maya (as Reflected at Caracol, Belize). In *Function and Meaning in Classic Maya Architecture*, edited by S. D. Houston, pp. 299–332. Washington, D.C.: Dumbarton Oaks.

2000. Inferences about Abandonment: Maya Household Archaeology and Caracol, Belize. *Mayab* 13:67–77.

2004. Santa Rita Corozal: Twenty Years Later. In *Archaeological Investigations in the Eastern Maya Lowlands: Papers of the 2003 Belize Archaeology Symposium*, edited by J. Awe, J. Morris, and S. Jones, pp. 243–255. Research Reports in Belizean Archaeology, Vol. 1. Belmopan, Belize: Institute of Archaeology, National Institute of Culture and History.

Chase, Diane Z., and Arlen F. Chase, eds.

1992. *Mesoamerican Elites: An Archaeological Perspective*. Norman: University of Oklahoma Press.

Childe, Gordon

1951 [1936]. *Man Makes Himself*. New York: New American Library.

Cobos Palma, Rafael

2004. Chichén Itzá: Settlement and Hegemony during the Terminal Classic Period. In *The Terminal Classic in the Maya Lowlands: Collapse, Transition, and Transformation*, edited by A. A. Demarest, P. M. Rice, and D. S. Rice, pp. 517–544. Boulder: University Press of Colorado.

Coe, William R.

1959. *Piedras Negras Archaeology: Artifacts, Caches, and Burials*. Philadelphia: University Museum, University of Pennsylvania.

1965a. Caches and Offertory Practices of the Maya Lowlands. In *Handbook of Middle American Indians*, Vol. 2, *Archaeology of Southern Mesoamerica, Part 1*, edited by G. R. Willey, pp. 462–468. Austin: University of Texas Press.

1965b. Tikal, Guatemala, and Emergent Maya Civilization. *Science* 147:1401–1419.

1965c. Tikal: Ten Years of Study of a Maya Ruin in the Lowlands of Guatemala. *Expedition* 8:5–56.

1990. *Excavations in the Great Plaza, North Terrace and North Acropolis of Tikal*. Tikal Report No. 14. The University Museum. Philadelphia: University of Pennsylvania.

Cohen, Abner

1974. *Two-Dimensional Man: An Essay on the Anthropology of Power and Symbolism in Complex Society*. Berkeley: University of California Press.

Conlon, James M., and Jennifer J. Ehret

2002. Time and Space: The Preliminary Ceramic Analysis for Saturday Creek and Yalbac, Cayo District, Belize, Central America. In *Results of the 2001 Valley of Peace Archaeology Project: Saturday Creek and Yalbac*, edited by L. J. Lucero, pp. 8–20. Report submitted to the Department of Archaeology, Ministry of Tourism and Culture, Belize.

Conrad, Henry S.

1905. *The Waterlilies: A Monograph of the Genus Nymphaea*. Publication No. 4. Washington, D.C.: Carnegie Institute of Washington.

Cowgill, George L.

1964. The End of Classic Maya Culture: A Review of Recent Evidence. *Southwestern Journal of Anthropology* 20:145–159.

1979. Teotihuacan, Internal Militaristic Competition, and the Fall of the Classic Maya. In *Maya Archeology and Ethnohistory*, edited by N. Hammond and G. R. Willey, pp. 51–62. Austin: University of Texas Press.

1988. Onward and Upward with Collapse. In *The Collapse of Ancient States and Civilizations*, edited by N. Yoffee and G. L. Cowgill, pp. 244–276. Tucson: University of Arizona Press.

Crumley, Carole L.

1993. Analyzing Historic Ecotonal Shifts. *Ecological Applications* 3:377–384.

1994. The Ecology of Conquest: Contrasting Agropastoral and Agricultural Societies' Adaptation to Climatic Change. In *Historical Ecology: Cultural Knowledge and Changing Landscapes*, edited by C. L. Crumley, pp. 183–201. Santa Fe: School of American Research Press.

1995a. Building an Historical Ecology of Gaulish Polities. In *Celtic Chiefdom, Celtic State: The Evolution of Complex Social Systems in Prehistoric Europe*, edited by B. Arnold and D. B. Gibson, pp. 26–33. Cambridge: Cambridge University Press.

1995b. Heterarchy and the Analysis of Complex Societies. In *Heterarchy and the Analysis of Complex Societies*, edited by R. M. Ehrenreich, C. L. Crumley, and J. E. Levy, pp. 1–5. Archeological Papers of the American Anthropological Association No. 6. Arlington, VA: American Anthropological Association.

2001. Communication, Holism, and the Evolution of Sociopolitical Complexity. In *From Leaders to Rulers*, edited by J. Haas, pp. 19–33. New York: Plenum Publishers.

2003. Alternative Forms of Social Order. In *Heterarchy, Political Economy, and the Ancient Maya: The Three Rivers Region of the East-Central Yucatán Peninsula*, edited by V. L. Scarborough, F. Valdez, Jr., and N. Dunning, pp. 136–145. Tucson: University of Arizona Press.

Culbert, T. Patrick

1977. Maya Development and Collapse: An Economic Perspective. In *Social Process in Maya Prehistory*, edited by N. Hammond, pp. 509–530. London: Academic Press.

1988. The Collapse of Classic Maya Civilization. In *The Collapse of Ancient States and Civilizations*, edited by N. Yoffee and G. L. Cowgill, pp. 69–101. Tucson: University of Arizona Press.

1991. Maya Political History and Elite Interaction: A Summary View. In *Classic Maya Political History: Hieroglyphic and Archaeological Evidence*, edited by T. P. Culbert, pp. 311–346. Cambridge: Cambridge University Press.

1997. Agricultura maya en los humedales de las tierras bajas mayas. *Los Investigadores de la Cultura Maya* 5:14–19. Campeche: Universidad Autónoma de Campeche, México.

Culbert, T. Patrick, Laura J. Kosakowsky, Robert E. Fry, and William A. Haviland

1990. The Population of Tikal, Guatemala. In *Precolumbian Population History in the Maya Lowlands*, edited by T. P. Culbert and D. S. Rice, pp. 103–121. Albuquerque: University of New Mexico Press.

Culbert, T. Patrick, and Don S. Rice, eds.
1990. *Precolumbian Population History in the Maya Lowlands.* Albuquerque: University of New Mexico Press.

Curtis, Jason H., and David A. Hodell
1993. An Isotopic and Trace Element Study of Ostracods from Lake Miragoane, Haiti: A 10,500-Year Record of Paleosalinity and Paleotemperature Changes in the Caribbean. In *Climate Change in Continental Isotopic Records,* edited by P. K. Swart, K. C. Lohmann, J. McKenzie, and S. Savin, pp. 135–152. Geophysical Monograph 78. Washington, D.C.: American Geophysical Union.

Curtis, Jason H., David A. Hodell, and Mark Brenner
1996. Climate Variability on the Yucatan Peninsula (Mexico) during the Past 3500 Years, and Implications for Maya Cultural Evolution. *Quaternary Research* 46:37–47.

Dahlin, Bruce H.
1983. Climate and Prehistory on the Yucatan Peninsula. *Climatic Change* 5:245–263.

D'Altroy, Terence N., and Timothy K. Earle
1985. Staple Finance, Wealth Finance, and Storage in the Inka Political Economy. *Current Anthropology* 26:187–206.

Davis-Salazar, Karla L.
2003. Late Classic Water Management and Community Organization at Copan, Honduras. *Latin American Antiquity* 14:275–299.

Deal, Michael
1988. Recognition of Ritual Pottery in Residential Units: An Ethnoarchaeological Model of the Maya Family Altar Tradition. In *Ethnoarchaeology among the Highland Maya of Chiapas, Mexico,* edited by T. A. Lee, Jr., and B. Hayden, pp. 61–89. Papers of the New World Archaeological Foundation No. 56. Provo: Brigham Young University.

Deevey, E. S., Don S. Rice, Prudence M. Rice, H. H. Vaughn, Mark Brenner, and M. S. Flannery
1979. Mayan Urbanism: Impact on a Tropical Karst Environment. *Science* 206: 298–306.

de la Garza, Mercedes
1992. *Palenque.* Chiapas Eterno. Gobierno del Estado de Chiapas, Mexico.

Demarest, Arthur A.
1992. Ideology in Ancient Maya Cultural Evolution: The Dynamics of Galactic Polities. In *Ideology and Pre-Columbian Civilizations,* edited by A. A. Demarest and G. W. Conrad, pp. 135–157. Santa Fe: School of American Research Press.
1997. The Vanderbilt Petexbatun Regional Archaeological Project 1989–1994: Overview, History, and Major Results of a Multidisciplinary Study of the Classic Maya Collapse. *Ancient Mesoamerica* 8:209–227.
2004. After the Maelstrom: Collapse of the Classic Maya Kingdoms and the Terminal Classic in the Western Petén. In *The Terminal Classic in the Maya Lowlands: Collapse, Transition, and Transformation,* edited by A. A. Demarest, P. M. Rice, and D. S. Rice, pp. 102–124. Boulder: University Press of Colorado.

Demarest, Arthur A., Prudence M. Rice, and Don S. Rice

2004a.   The Terminal Classic in the Maya Lowlands: Assessing Collapse, Transitions, and Transformations. In *The Terminal Classic in the Maya Lowlands: Collapse, Transition, and Transformation*, edited by A. A. Demarest, P. M. Rice, and D. S. Rice, pp. 545–572. Boulder: University Press of Colorado.

Demarest, Arthur A., Prudence M. Rice, and Don S. Rice, eds.

2004b.   *The Terminal Classic in the Maya Lowlands: Collapse, Transition, and Transformation*. Boulder: University Press of Colorado.

DeMarrais, Elizabeth, Luis Jaime Castillo, and Timothy Earle

1996.   Ideology, Materialization, and Power Strategies. *Current Anthropology* 37: 15–31.

de Montmollin, Olivier

1989.   *The Archaeology of Political Structure: Settlement Analysis in a Classic Maya Polity*. Cambridge: Cambridge University Press.

Drennan, Robert D.

1988.   Household Location and Compact versus Dispersed Settlement in Prehispanic Mesoamerica. In *Household and Community in the Mesoamerican Past*, edited by R. R. Wilk and W. Ashmore, pp. 273–293. Albuquerque: University of New Mexico Press.

Dunning, Nicholas P.

1996.   A Reexamination of Regional Variability in the Prehistoric Agricultural Landscape. In *The Managed Mosaic: Ancient Maya Agriculture and Resource Use*, edited by S. L. Fedick, pp. 53–68. Salt Lake City: University of Utah Press.

Dunning, Nicholas P., Timothy Beach, Pat Farrell, and Sheryl Luzzadder-Beach

1998.   Prehispanic Agrosystems and Adaptive Regions in the Maya Lowlands. *Culture and Agriculture* 20: 87–101.

Dunning, Nicholas P., Timothy Beach, and Sheryl Luzzadder-Beach

n.d.   Environmental Variability among *Bajos* in the Southern Maya Lowlands and Its Implications for Ancient Maya Civilization and Archaeology. In *Precolumbian Water Management: Ideology, Ritual, and Politics*, edited by L. J. Lucero and B. Fash. Tucson: University of Arizona Press. In press.

Dunning, Nicholas P., Timothy Beach, and David Rue

1997.   The Paleoecology and Ancient Settlement of the Petexbatun Region, Guatemala. *Ancient Mesoamerica* 8: 255–266.

Dunning, Nicholas P., John G. Jones, Timothy Beach, and Sheryl Luzzadder-Beach

2003.   Physiography, Habitats, and Landscapes of the Three Rivers Region. In *Heterarchy, Political Economy, and the Ancient Maya: The Three Rivers Region of the East-Central Yucatán Peninsula*, edited by V. L. Scarborough, F. Valdez, Jr., and N. Dunning, pp. 14–24. Tucson: University of Arizona Press.

Durkheim, Emile

1995 [1912].   *The Elementary Forms of Religious Life*. Translated by K. E. Fields. New York: Free Press.

Earle, Timothy

1978.   *Economic and Social Organization of a Complex Chiefdom: The Halelea District, Kaua'i Hawaii*. Anthropological Papers, Museum of Anthropology, No. 63. Ann Arbor: University of Michigan.

1989. The Evolution of Chiefdoms. *Current Anthropology* 30:84–88.
1997. *How Chiefs Come to Power: The Political Economy in Prehistory.* Stanford: Stanford University Press.

Elson, Christina M., and Michael E. Smith
2001. Archaeological Deposits from the Aztec New Fire Ceremony. *Ancient Mesoamerica* 12:1–18.

Engels, Friedrich
1964 [1957]. Engels to Bloch, London, September 21–22, 1890. In *On Religion,* by K. Marx and F. Engels (introduction by R. Niebuhr), pp. 273–277. New York: Schocken Books.
1978 [1884]. The Origin of the Family, Private Property, and the State: Selections. In *The Marx-Engels Reader,* edited by R. C. Tucker, pp. 734–759. 2nd ed. New York: W. W. Norton.

Evans, Susan Toby, and David L. Webster, eds.
2001. *Archaeology of Ancient Mexico and Central America: An Encyclopedia.* New York: Garland Publishing.

Evans-Pritchard, E. E.
1940. The Nuer of the Southern Sudan. In *African Political Systems,* edited by M. Fortes and E. E. Evans-Pritchard, pp. 272–296. International African Institute. London: Oxford University Press.

Fagan, Brian
1999. *Floods, Famines, and Emperors: El Niño and the Fate of Civilizations.* New York: Basic Books.
2004. *The Long Summer: How Climate Changed Civilization.* New York: Basic Books.

Farriss, Nancy
1984. *Maya Society under Colonial Rule: The Collective Enterprise of Survival.* Princeton: University of Princeton Press.

Fash, Barbara W.
2005. Iconographic Evidence for Water Management and Social Organization at Copán. In *Copán: History of an Ancient Maya Kingdom,* edited by E. W. Andrews and W. L. Fash, pp. 103–138. Santa Fe: School of American Research.

Fash, Barbara W., and Karla L. Davis-Salazar
n.d. Copán Water Ritual and Management: Imagery and Sacred Place. In *Precolumbian Water Management: Ideology, Ritual, and Politics,* edited by L. J. Lucero and B. Fash. Tucson: University of Arizona Press. In press.

Fash, William L.
1991. *Scribes, Warriors and Kings: The City of Copán and the Ancient Maya.* London: Thames and Hudson.
1998. Dynastic Architectural Programs: Invention and Design in Classic Maya Buildings at Copán and Other Sites. In *Function and Meaning in Classic Maya Architecture,* edited by S. D. Houston, pp. 223–270. Washington, D.C.: Dumbarton Oaks.

Fash, William L., E. Wyllys Andrews, and T. Kam Manahan
2004. Political Decentralization, Dynastic Collapse, and the Early Postclassic in the Urban Center of Copán, Honduras. In *The Terminal Classic in the Maya Low-*

lands: Collapse, Transition, and Transformation, edited by A. A. Demarest, P. M. Rice, and D. S. Rice, pp. 260–287. Boulder: University Press of Colorado.

Fash, William L., and David S. Stuart
1991. Dynastic History and Cultural Evolution at Copan, Honduras. In *Classic Maya Political History: Hieroglyphic and Archaeological Evidence,* edited by T. P. Culbert, pp. 147–179. Cambridge: Cambridge University Press.

Faust, Betty B.
1998. *Mexican Rural Development and the Plumed Serpent: Technology and Cosmology in the Tropical Forest of Campeche, Mexico.* Foreword by B. Meggers. Westport, CT: Bergin and Garvey.

Fedick, Scott L.
1994. Ancient Maya Agricultural Terracing in the Upper Belize River Area: Computer-Aided Modeling and the Results of Initial Field Investigations. *Ancient Mesoamerica* 5:107–127.
1996. An Interpretive Kaleidoscope: Alternative Perspectives on Ancient Agricultural Landscapes of the Maya Lowlands. In *The Managed Mosaic: Ancient Maya Agriculture and Resource Use,* edited by S. L. Fedick, pp. 107–131. Salt Lake City: University of Utah Press.

Fedick, Scott L., and Anabel Ford
1990. The Prehistoric Agricultural Landscape of the Central Maya Lowlands: An Examination of Local Variability in a Regional Context. *World Archaeology* 22:18–33.

Feinman, Gary M.
1998. Scale and Social Organization: Perspectives on the Archaic State. In *Archaic States,* edited by G. M. Feinman and J. Marcus, pp. 95–133. Santa Fe: School of American Research Press.

Fields, Virginia M.
1989. The Origins of Divine Kingship among the Lowland Classic Maya. Ph.D. dissertation. Austin: University of Texas.

Flannery, Kent V.
1972. The Cultural Evolution of Civilizations. *Annual Review of Ecology and Systematics* 3:399–426.
1976. Contextual Analysis of Ritual Paraphernalia from Formative Oaxaca. In *The Early Mesoamerican Village,* edited by K. Flannery, pp. 333–345. New York: Academic Press.

Flannery, Kent V., ed.
1982. *Maya Subsistence: Studies in Memory of Dennis E. Puleston.* New York: Academic Press.

Folan, William J., Joel Gunn, Jack D. Eaton, and Robert W. Patch
1983. Paleoclimatological Patterning in Southern Mesoamerica. *Journal of Field Archaeology* 10:453–468.

Folan, William J., Joyce Marcus, Sophia Pincemin, María del Rosario Domínguez Carrasco, Laraine Fletcher, and Abel Morales López
1995. Calakmul: New Data from an Ancient Maya Capital in Campeche, Mexico. *Latin American Antiquity* 6:310–334.

Ford, Anabel
1986. *Population Growth and Social Complexity: An Examination of Settlement and Environment in the Central Maya Lowlands.* Anthropological Papers No. 35. Tempe: Arizona State University.
1990. Settlement and Environment in the Upper Belize River Area and Variability in Household Organization. In *Prehistoric Population History in the Maya Lowlands,* edited by T. P. Culbert and D. S. Rice, pp. 167–182. Albuquerque: University of New Mexico Press.
1991a. Economic Variation of Ancient Maya Residential Settlement in the Upper Belize River Area. *Ancient Mesoamerica* 2:35–46.
1991b. Problems with Evaluation of Population from Settlement Data: Examination of Ancient Maya Residential Patterns in the Tikal-Yaxhá Intersite Area. *Estudios de Cultura Maya* 18:157–186.
1996. Critical Resource Control and the Rise of the Classic Period Maya. In *The Managed Mosaic: Ancient Maya Agriculture and Resource Use,* edited by S. L. Fedick, pp. 297–303. Salt Lake City: University of Utah Press.

Fortes, M.
1940. The Political System of the Tellensi of the Northern Territories of the Gold Coast. In *African Political Systems,* edited by M. Fortes and E. E. Evans-Pritchard, pp. 239–271. International African Institute. London: Oxford University Press.

Fortes, M., and E. E. Evans-Pritchard
1940. Introduction. In *African Political Systems,* edited by M. Fortes and E. E. Evans-Pritchard, pp. 1–23. International African Institute. London: Oxford University Press.

Fox, John Gerard
1996. Playing with Power: Ballcourts and Political Ritual in Southern Mesoamerica. *Current Anthropology* 37:483–509.

Fox, John W., and Garrett W. Cook
1996. Constructing Maya Communities: Ethnography for Archaeology. *Current Anthropology* 37:811–821.

Fox, John W., Garrett W. Cook, Arlen F. Chase, and Diane Z. Chase
1996. Questions of Political and Economic Integration: Segmentary versus Centralized States among the Ancient Maya. *Current Anthropology* 37:795–801.

Fox, Richard G.
1977. *Urban Anthropology: Cities in their Cultural Settings.* Englewood Cliffs, NJ: Prentice-Hall.

Frazer, James George
1920 [1890]. *The Golden Bough: A Study in Magic and Religion.* Vol. 1. 3rd ed. London: Macmillan.

Freidel, David
1986. Maya Warfare: An Example of Peer Polity Interaction. In *Peer Polity Interaction and Socio-Political Change,* edited by C. Renfrew and J. F. Cherry, pp. 93–108. Cambridge: Cambridge University Press.

Freidel, David, and Linda Schele

1988.   Kingship in the Late Preclassic Maya Lowlands: The Instruments and Places of Ritual Power. *American Anthropologist* 90:547–567.

1989.   Dead Kings and Living Temples: Dedication and Termination Rituals among the Ancient Maya. In *Word and Image in Maya Culture: Explorations in Language, Writing, and Representation*, edited by W. F. Hanks and D. S. Rice, pp. 233–243. Salt Lake City: University of Utah Press.

Freidel, David, Linda Schele, and Joy Parker

1993.   *Maya Cosmos: Three Thousand Years on the Shaman's Path.* New York: William Marrow.

French, Kirk D.

2002.   Creating Space through Water Management at the Classic Maya Site of Palenque, Chiapas, Mexico. M.A. thesis. Cincinnati: University of Cincinnati.

French, Kirk, David S. Stuart, and Alfonso Morales

n.d.   Archaeological and Epigraphic Evidence for Water Management and Ritual at Palenque. In *Precolumbian Water Management: Ideology, Ritual, and Politics*, edited by L. J. Lucero and B. Fash. Tucson: University of Arizona Press. In press.

Freter, AnnCorinne

1994.   The Classic Maya Collapse at Copan, Honduras: An Analysis of Maya Rural Settlement Trends. In *Archeological Views from the Countryside: Village Communities in Complex Society*, edited by G. M. Schwartz and S. E. Falconer, pp. 160–176. Washington, D.C.: Smithsonian Institution Press.

Fried, Morton H.

1967.   *The Evolution of Political Society.* New York: Random House.

Friedman, Jonathan

1975.   Tribes, States, and Transformations. In *Marxist Analyses and Social Anthropology*, edited by M. Bloch, pp. 161–202. New York: Wiley and Sons.

1998.   *System, Structure, and Contradiction: The Evolution of "Asiatic" Social Formations.* 2nd ed. Walnut Creek, CA: Altamira Press.

Friedman, Jonathan, and Michael J. Rowlands

1978.   Notes toward an Epigenetic Model of the Evolution of "Civilisation." In *The Evolution of Social Systems*, edited by J. Friedman and M. J. Rowlands, pp. 201–267. London: Duckworth.

Fry, Robert

1990.   Disjunctive Growth in the Maya Lowlands. In *Precolumbian Population History in the Maya Lowlands*, edited by T. P. Culbert and D. S. Rice, pp. 285–300. Albuquerque: University of New Mexico Press.

Garber, James F.

1986.   The Artifacts. In *Archaeology at Cerros, Belize, Central America, Volume I*, edited by R. A. Robertson and D. A. Freidel, pp. 117–126. Dallas: Southern Methodist University Press.

1989.   *The Artifacts: Archaeology at Cerros, Belize, Central America, Volume II.* Dallas: Southern Methodist University Press.

Garber, James F., W. David Driver, Lauren A. Sullivan, and David M. Glassman

1998. Bloody Bowls and Broken Pots: The Life, Death, and Rebirth of a Maya House. In *The Sowing and the Dawning: Termination, Dedication, and Transformation in the Archaeological and Ethnographic Record of Mesoamerica*, edited by S. B. Mock, pp. 125–133. Albuquerque: University of New Mexico Press.

Geertz, Clifford

1980. *Negara: The Theatre State in Nineteenth-Century Bali.* Princeton: Princeton University Press.

Giddens, Anthony

1979. *Central Problems in Social Theory: Action, Structure and Contradiction in Social Analysis.* Berkeley: University of California Press.

1984. *The Constitution of Society: Outline of a Theory of Structuration.* Berkeley: University of California Press.

Giesey, Ralph E.

1985. Models of Rulership in French Royal Ceremonial. In *Rites of Power: Symbolism, Ritual, and Politics since the Middle Ages*, edited by S. Wilentz, pp. 41–64. Philadelphia: University of Pennsylvania Press.

Gifford, James C., Robert J. Sharer, Joseph W. Ball, Arlen F. Chase, Carol A. Gifford, Muriel Kirkpatrick, and George H. Myer

1976. *Prehistoric Pottery Analysis and the Ceramics of Barton Ramie in the Belize Valley.* Peabody Museum of Archaeology and Ethnology Memoirs, Vol. 18. Cambridge, MA: Harvard University.

Gill, Richardson B.

2000. *The Great Maya Droughts: Water, Life, and Death.* Albuquerque: University of New Mexico Press.

Gillespie, Susan D.

2000a. Maya "Nested Houses": The Ritual Construction of Place. In *Beyond Kinship: Social and Material Production in House Societies*, edited by R. A. Joyce and S. D. Gillespie, pp. 135–160. Philadelphia: University of Pennsylvania Press.

2000b. Rethinking Ancient Maya Social Organization: Replacing "Lineage" with "House." *American Anthropologist* 102:467–484.

2001. Personhood, Agency, and Mortuary Ritual: A Case Study from the Ancient Maya. *Journal of Anthropological Archaeology* 20:73–112.

Gilman, Antonio

1981. The Development of Social Stratification in Bronze Age Europe. *Current Anthropology* 22:1–23.

Godelier, Maurice

1977. *Perspectives in Marxist Anthropology.* Translated by R. Brain. Cambridge: Cambridge University Press.

1978. Infrastructures, Societies, and History. *Current Anthropology* 19:763–771.

Gómez-Pompa, Arturo, José Salvador Flores, and Mario Aliphat Fernández

1990. The Sacred Cacao Groves of the Maya. *Latin American Antiquity* 1:247–257.

Gossen, Gary H., and Richard M. Leventhal

1993. The Topography of Ancient Maya Religious Pluralism: A Dialogue with the Present. In *Lowland Maya Civilization in the Eighth Century A.D.*, edited by

J. A. Sabloff and J. S Henderson, pp. 185–217. Washington, D.C.: Dumbarton Oaks.

Graham, Elizabeth

1994.   *The Highlands of the Lowlands: Environment and Archaeology in the Stann Creek District Belize, Central America.* Monographs in World Archaeology 19. Madison: Prehistory Press.

Graham, John A.

1972.   *The Hieroglyphic Inscriptions and Monumental Art of Altar de Sacrificios.* Papers of the Peabody Museum of Archaeology and Ethnology, Vol. 64, No. 2. Cambridge, MA: Harvard University.

Grube, Nikolai, and Simon Martin

2001.   The Dynastic History of the Maya. In *Maya: Divine Kings of the Rain Forest,* edited by N. Grube, pp. 149–174. Cologne: Könemann Verlagsgesellschaft.

Gunn, Joel D.

1994.   Global Climate and Regional Biocultural Diversity. In *Historical Ecology: Cultural Knowledge and Changing Landscapes,* edited by C. L. Crumley, pp. 67–97. Santa Fe: School of American Research Press.

Gunn, Joel D., William J. Folan, and Hubert R. Robichaux

1995.   A Landscape Analysis of the Candeleria Watershed in Mexico: Insights into Paleoclimate Affecting Upland Horticulture in the Southern Yucatan Peninsula Semi-Karst. *Geoarchaeology* 10:3–42.

Gunn, Joel, Ray T. Matheny, and William J. Folan

2002.   Climate-Change Studies in the Maya Area. *Ancient Mesoamerica* 13:79–84.

Hamblin, Robert L., and Brian L. Pitcher

1980.   The Classic Maya Collapse: Testing Class Conflict Hypotheses. *American Antiquity* 45:246–267.

Hammer, David E., and Robert H. Kadlec

1980.   *Wetland Utilization for Management of Community Water: Concepts and Operation in Michigan.* Industrial Development Division, Institute of Science and Technology. Ann Arbor: University of Michigan.

Hammond, Norman

1995.   Ceremony and Society at Cuello: Preclassic Ritual Behavior and Social Differentiation. In *The Emergence of Classic Maya Civilization,* edited by N. Grube, pp. 49–60. Acta Mesoamericana 8. Möckmühl: Verlag von Flemming.

1999.   The Genesis of Hierarchy: Mortuary and Offertory Ritual in the Pre-Classic at Cuello, Belize. In *Social Patterns in Pre-Classic Mesoamerica,* edited by D. C. Grove, pp. 49–66. Washington, D.C.: Dumbarton Oaks.

Hammond, Norman, and Juliette Cartwright Gerhardt

1991.   Offertory Practices. In *Cuello: An Early Maya Community in Belize,* edited by N. Hammond, pp. 225–231. Cambridge: University of Cambridge Press.

Hammond, Norman, Juliette Cartwright Gerhardt, and Sara Donaghey

1991.   Stratigraphy and Chronology in the Reconstruction of Preclassic Developments. In *Cuello: An Early Maya Community in Belize,* edited by N. Hammond, pp. 23–69. Cambridge: University of Cambridge Press.

Hansen, Richard D.
   1998.   Continuity and Disjunction: The Pre-Classic Antecedents of Classic Architecture. In *Function and Meaning in Classic Maya Architecture,* edited by S. D. Houston, pp. 49–122. Washington, D.C.: Dumbarton Oaks.

Hansen, Richard D., Steven Bozarth, John Jacob, David Wahl, and Thomas Schreiner
   2002.   Climatic and Environmental Variability in the Rise of Maya Civilization: A Preliminary Perspective from Northern Peten. *Ancient Mesoamerica* 13: 273–295.

Hardesty, Donald L., and Don D. Fowler
   2001.   Archaeology and Environmental Changes. In *New Directions in Anthropology and Environment: Intersections,* edited by C. L. Crumley, pp. 72–89. Walnut Creek, CA: Altamira Press.

Harris, Edward C.
   1989.   *Principles of Archaeological Stratigraphy.* 2nd ed. San Diego: Academic Press.

Harrison, Peter D.
   1993.   Aspects of Water Management in the Southern Maya Lowlands. *Research in Economic Anthropology* 7: 71–119.
   1999.   *The Lords of Tikal: Rulers of an Ancient Maya City.* New York: Thames and Hudson.

Harrison, Peter D., and B. L. Turner II, eds.
   1978.   *Pre-Hispanic Maya Agriculture.* Albuquerque: University of New Mexico Press.

Hassan, Fekri
   1994.   Population Ecology and Civilization in Ancient Egypt. In *Historical Ecology: Cultural Knowledge and Changing Landscapes,* edited by C. L. Crumley, pp. 155–181. Santa Fe: School of American Research Press.

Haug, Gerald H., Detlef Günther, Larry C. Peterson, Daniel M. Sigman, Konrad A. Hughen, and Beat Aeschlimann
   2003.   Climate and the Collapse of Maya Civilization. *Science* 299 : 1731–1735.

Hauser-Schäublin, Brigitta
   2003.   The Precolonial Balinese State Reconsidered: A Critical Evaluation of Theory Construction on the Relationship between Irrigation, the State, and Ritual. *Current Anthropology* 44 : 153–181.

Haviland, William A.
   1970.   Tikal, Guatemala, and Mesoamerican Urbanism. *World Archaeology* 2 : 186–197.
   1981.   Dower Houses and Minor Centers at Tikal, Guatemala: An Investigation into the Identification of Valid Units in Settlement Hierarchies. In *Lowland Maya Settlement Patterns,* edited by W. Ashmore, pp. 89–117. Albuquerque: University of New Mexico Press.
   1985.   *Excavations in Small Residential Groups of Tikal: Groups 4F-1 and 4F-2.* Tikal Report No. 19. University Monograph 58. The University Museum. Philadelphia: University of Pennsylvania.
   1988.   Musical Hammocks at Tikal: Problems with Reconstructing Household Composition. In *Household and Community in the Mesoamerican Past,* edited

by R. R. Wilk and W. Ashmore, pp. 121–134. Albuquerque: University of New Mexico Press.

1997. The Rise and Fall of Sexual Inequality: Death and Gender at Tikal, Guatemala. *Ancient Mesoamerica* 8:1–12.

2003. Settlement, Society, and Demography at Tikal. In *Tikal: Dynasties, Foreigners, and Affairs of State*, edited by J. A. Sabloff, pp. 111–142. Santa Fe: School of American Research Press.

Hayden, Brian

1994. Village Approaches to Complex Society. In *Archeological Views from the Countryside: Village Communities in Complex Society*, edited by G. M. Schwartz and S. E. Falconer, pp. 198–206. Washington, D.C.: Smithsonian Institution Press.

1995. Pathways to Power: Principles for Creating Socioeconomic Inequalities. In *Foundations of Social Inequality*, edited by T. D. Price and G. M. Feinman, pp. 15–86. New York: Plenum Press.

Hayden, Brian, and Aubrey Cannon

1984. *The Structure of Material Systems: Ethnoarchaeology in the Maya Highlands.* Society for American Archaeology Papers No. 3. Washington, D.C.: Society for American Archaeology.

Hayden, Brian, and Rob Gargett

1990. Big Man, Big Heart?: A Mesoamerican View of the Emergence of Complex Society. *Ancient Mesoamerica* 1:3–20.

Healy, Paul F., John D. H. Lambert, J. T. Arnason, and Richard J. Hebda

1983. Caracol, Belize: Evidence of Ancient Maya Agricultural Terraces. *Journal of Field Archaeology* 10:397–410.

Hellmuth, Nicholas N.

1987. *The Surface of the Underworld: Iconography of the Gods of Early Classic Maya Art in Peten, Guatemala.* 2 vols. Culver City: Foundation for Latin American Anthropological Research.

Helms, Mary W.

1979. *Ancient Panama: Chiefs in Search of Power.* Austin: University of Texas Press.

1993. *Craft and the Kingly Ideal: Art, Trade, and Power.* Austin: University of Texas Press.

1998. *Access to Origins: Affines, Ancestors, and Aristocrats.* Austin: University of Texas Press.

Hendon, Julia A.

1999. The Pre-Classic Maya Compound as the Focus of Social Identity. In *Social Patterns in Pre-Classic Mesoamerica*, edited by D. C. Grove, pp. 97–125. Washington, D.C.: Dumbarton Oaks.

Hocart, Arthur M.

1970 [1936]. *Kings and Councillors: An Essay in the Comparative Anatomy of Human Society.* Edited by R. Needham. Chicago: University of Chicago Press.

Hodell, David A., Mark Brenner, Jason H. Curtis, and Thomas Guilderson

2001. Solar Forcing of Drought Frequency in the Maya Lowlands. *Science* 292: 1367–1370.

Hodell, David A., Jason H. Curtis, and Mark Brenner
1995. Possible Role of Climate in the Collapse of Classic Maya Civilization. *Nature* 375:391–394.

Hosler, Dorothy, Jeremy A. Sabloff, and Dale Runge
1977. Simulation Model Development: A Case Study of the Classic Maya Collapse. In *Social Process in Maya Prehistory*, edited by N. Hammond, pp. 553–590. London: Academic Press.

Houston, Stephen D.
1993. *Hieroglyphs and History at Dos Pilas: Dynastic Politics of the Classic Maya.* Austin: University of Texas Press.
1998. On the River of Ruins: Explorations at Piedras Negras, Guatemala, 1997. *Mexicon* 20:16–22.

Houston, Stephen, Héctor Escobedo, Mark Child, Charles Golden, and René Muñoz
2003. The Moral Community: Maya Settlement Transformation at Piedras Negras, Guatemala. In *The Social Construction of Ancient Cities*, edited by M. L. Smith, pp. 212–253. Washington, D.C.: Smithsonian Institution Press.

Houston, Stephen, Héctor Escobedo, Mark Child,
Charles Golden, René Muñoz, and Mónica Urquizú
1998. Monumental Architecture at Piedras Negras, Guatemala: Time, History, and Meaning. *Mayab* 11:40–56.

Houston, Stephen, and David Stuart
1996. Of Gods, Glyphs and Kings: Divinity and Rulership among the Classic Maya. *Antiquity* 70:289–312.
2001. Peopling the Classic Maya Court. In *Royal Courts of the Ancient Maya, Volume I: Theory, Comparison, and Synthesis*, edited by T. Inomata and S. D. Houston, pp. 54–83. Boulder: Westview Press.

Houston, Stephen, and Karl Taube
2000. An Archaeology of the Senses: Perception and Cultural Expression in Ancient Mesoamerica. *Cambridge Archaeological Journal* 10:261–294.

Iannone, Gyles
2002. Annales History and the Ancient Maya State: Some Observations on the "Dynamic Model." *American Anthropologist* 104:68–78.

Ibn Khaldun, Abu Zayd Abd ar-Rahman
1967 [ca. 1382–1404]. *The Muqaddimah: An Introduction to History.* Vol. 1. Translated by Franz Rosenthal. Princeton: Princeton University Press.

Inomata, Takeshi
2001a. The Classic Maya Royal Palace as a Political Theater. In *Ciudades mayas: Urbanización y organización espacial*, edited by A. Ciudad Ruiz, pp. 341–362. Madrid: Sociedad Española de Estudios Mayas.
2001b. King's People: Classic Maya Courtiers in a Comparative Perspective. In *Royal Courts of the Ancient Maya, Volume I: Theory, Comparison, and Synthesis*, edited by T. Inomata and S. D. Houston, pp. 27–53. Boulder: Westview Press.

Inomata, Takeshi, and Lawrence S. Coben
n.d. Overture: An Invitation to the Archaeological Theater. In *Archaeology of Performance: Theater, Power and Community*, edited by T. Inomata and L. S. Coben. Walnut Creek, CA: AltaMira Press. In press.

Jacobsen, Thorkild, and Robert M. Adams
1958. Salt and Silt in Ancient Mesopotamian Agriculture. *Science* 128:1251–1258.

Jeakle, Julie E.
2002. Social Integration and the Maya: The Multifunctionality of Mesoamerican Ball Courts. M.A. thesis. Las Cruces: New Mexico State University.

Jeakle, Julie, Lisa J. Lucero, and Sarah Field
2002. SC-3: A Minor Center Temple Ball Court. In *Results of the 2001 Valley of Peace Archaeology Project: Saturday Creek and Yalbac*, edited by L. J. Lucero, pp. 47–64. Report submitted to the Department of Archaeology, Ministry of Tourism and Culture, Belize.

Johnson, Allen W., and Timothy Earle
2000. *The Evolution of Human Societies: From Foraging Group to Agrarian State.* 2nd ed. Stanford: Stanford University Press.

Johnston, Kevin J.
2004a. The "Invisible" Maya: Minimally Mounded Residential Settlement at Itzán, Petén, Guatemala. *Latin American Antiquity* 15:145–175.
2004b. Lowland Maya Water Management Practices: The Household Exploitation of Rural Wells. *Geoarchaeology* 19:265–292.

Johnston, Kevin J., Andrew J. Breckenridge, and Barbara C. Hansen
2001. Paleoecological Evidence of an Early Postclassic Occupation in the Southwestern Maya Lowlands: Laguna Las Pozas, Guatemala. *Latin American Antiquity* 12:149–166.

Jones, Christopher
1991. Cycles of Growth at Tikal. In *Classic Maya Political History: Hieroglyphic and Archaeological Evidence*, edited by T. P. Culbert, pp. 102–127. Cambridge: Cambridge University Press.

Jones, Christopher, William R. Coe, and William A. Haviland
1981. Tikal: An Outline of Its Field Study (1956–1970) and a Project Bibliography. In *Archaeology, Handbook of Middle American Indians*, Supplement 1, edited by J. A. Sabloff, pp. 296–312. Austin: University of Texas Press.

Jones, Grant D.
1989. *Maya Resistance to Spanish Rule: Time and History on a Colonial Frontier.* Albuquerque: University of New Mexico Press.

Joyce, Arthur A.
2000. The Founding of Monte Albán: Sacred Propositions and Social Practices. In *Agency in Archaeology*, edited by M. Dobres and J. Robb, pp. 71–91. London: Routledge Press.
2004. Sacred Space and Social Relations in the Valley of Oaxaca. In *Mesoamerican Archaeology*, edited by J. Hendon and R. Joyce, pp. 192–216. Oxford: Blackwell.

Joyce, Arthur A., Laura Arnaud Bustamante, and Marc N. Levine
2001. Commoner Power: A Case Study from the Classic Period Collapse on the Oaxaca Coast. *Journal of Archaeological Method and Theory* 8:343–385.

Joyce, Rosemary A.
2000. Heirlooms and Houses: Materiality and Social Memory. In *Beyond Kinship: Social and Material Production in House Societies*, edited by R. A. Joyce and S. D. Gillespie, pp. 189–212. Philadelphia: University of Pennsylvania Press.

Kaufman, Herbert

1988. The Collapse of Ancient States and Civilizations as an Organizational Problem. In *The Collapse of Ancient States and Civilizations*, edited by N. Yoffee and G. L. Cowgill, pp. 219–235. Tucson: University of Arizona Press.

Kemp, Barry J.

1991. *Ancient Egypt: Anatomy of a Civilization*. London and New York: Routledge.

Kertzer, David I.

1988. *Ritual, Politics, and Power.* New Haven: Yale University Press.

Killion, Thomas W.

1990. Cultivation Intensity and Residential Site Structure: An Ethnoarchaeological Examination of Peasant Agriculture in the Sierra de los Tuxtlas, Veracruz, Mexico. *Latin American Antiquity* 1:191–215.

Kirch, Patrick V.

1984. *The Evolution of the Polynesian Chiefdoms.* Cambridge: Cambridge University Press.

1994. *The Wet and the Dry: Irrigation and Agricultural Intensification in Polynesia.* Chicago: University of Chicago Press.

Kirch, Patrick V., and Roger C. Green

2001. *Hawaiki, Ancestral Polynesia: An Essay in Historical Anthropology.* Cambridge: Cambridge University Press.

Klejn, Leo S.

1982. *Archaeological Typology.* BAR International Series 153. Oxford: British Archaeological Reports.

Krejci, Estella, and T. Patrick Culbert

1995. Preclassic and Classic Burials and Caches in the Maya Lowlands. In *The Emergence of Classic Maya Civilization*, edited by N. Grube, pp. 103–116. Acta Mesoamericana 8. Möckmühl: Verlag von Flemming.

Kunen, Julie L.

n.d. Water Management, Ritual, and Community in Tropical Complex Societies. In *Precolumbian Water Management: Ideology, Ritual, and Politics*, edited by L. J. Lucero and B. Fash. Tucson: University of Arizona Press. In press.

Kunen, Julie L., Mary Jo Galindo, and Erin Chase

2002. Pits and Bones: Identifying Maya Ritual Behavior in the Archaeological Record. *Ancient Mesoamerica* 13:197–211.

Kunen, Julie L., and Paul J. Hughbanks

2003. Bajo Communities as Resource Specialists: A Heterarchical Approach to Maya Socioeconomic Organization. In *Heterarchy, Political Economy, and the Ancient Maya: The Three Rivers Region of the East-Central Yucatán Peninsula*, edited by V. L. Scarborough, F. Valdez, Jr., and N. Dunning, pp. 92–108. Tucson: University of Arizona Press.

Kus, Susan, and Victor Raharijaona

1998. Between Earth and Sky There Are Only a Few Large Boulders: Sovereignty and Monumentality in Central Madagascar. *Journal of Anthropological Archaeology* 17:53–79.

2000. House to Palace, Village to State: Scaling Up Architecture and Ideology. *American Anthropologist* 102:98–113.

Lansing, J. Stephen

1991. *Priests and Programmers: Technologies of Power in the Engineered Landscape of Bali.* Princeton: University of Princeton.

Laporte, Juan Antonio

2004. Terminal Classic Settlement and Polity in the Mopan Valley, Petén, Guatemala. In *The Terminal Classic in the Maya Lowlands: Collapse, Transition, and Transformation*, edited by A. A. Demarest, P. M. Rice, and D. S. Rice, pp. 195–230. Boulder: University Press of Colorado.

Leach, Edmund R.

1966. Ritualization in Man in Relation to Conceptual and Social Development. *Philosophical Transactions of the Royal Society of London* 251:403–408.

1970 [1954]. *Political Systems of Highland Burma: A Study of Kachin Social Structures.* London School of Economics Monographs in Social Anthropology No. 44. London: Athlone Press.

LeCount, Lisa J.

1996. Pottery and Power: Feasting, Gifting, and Displaying Wealth among the Late and Terminal Classic Lowland Maya. Ph.D. dissertation. Los Angeles: University of California, Los Angeles.

LeCount, Lisa J., Jason Yaeger, Richard M. Leventhal, and Wendy Ashmore

2002. Dating the Rise and Fall of Xunantunich, Belize. *Ancient Mesoamerica* 13: 41–63.

Lee, Daniel B.

1998. On the Social Meaning and Meaninglessness of Religion. Paper presented at the Annual Meetings of the American Sociological Association, August, San Francisco.

2000. *Old Order Mennonites: Rituals, Beliefs, and Community.* Chicago: Burnham Publishers.

Lewis, Brandon S.

2003. Environmental Heterogeneity and Occupational Specialization: An Examination of Lithic Tool Production in the Three Rivers Region of the Northeastern Petén. In *Heterarchy, Political Economy, and the Ancient Maya: The Three Rivers Region of the East-Central Yucatán Peninsula*, edited by V. L. Scarborough, F. Valdez, Jr., and N. Dunning, pp. 122–135. Tucson: University of Arizona Press.

Leyden, Barbara W., Mark Brenner, Tom Whitmore, Jason H. Curtis, Dolores R. Piperno, and Bruce H. Dahlin

1996. A Record of Long- and Short-Term Climatic Variation from Northwest Yucatán: Cenote San José Chulcacá. In *The Managed Mosaic: Ancient Maya Agriculture and Resource Use*, edited by S. L. Fedick, pp. 30–50. Salt Lake City: University of Utah Press.

Lincoln, Bruce

1994. *Authority: Construction and Corrosion.* Chicago: University of Chicago Press.

Looper, Matthew G.

1999. New Perspectives on the Late Classic Political History of Quirigua, Guatemala. *Ancient Mesoamerica* 10:263–280.

Loten, H. Stanley
    1985. Lamanai Postclassic. In *The Lowland Maya Postclassic*, edited by A. F. Chase and P. M. Rice, pp. 85–90. Austin: University of Texas Press.

Loten, H. Stanley, and David M. Pendergast
    1984. *A Lexicon for Maya Architecture*. Archaeology Monograph 8. Toronto: Royal Ontario Museum.

Lowe, John W. G.
    1985. *The Dynamics of Apocalypse: A Systems Simulation of the Classic Maya Collapse*. Albuquerque: University of New Mexico Press.

Lucero, Lisa J.
    1999a. Classic Lowland Maya Political Organization: A Review. *Journal of World Prehistory* 13:211–263.
    1999b. Water Control and Maya Politics in the Southern Maya Lowlands. In *Complex Polities in the Ancient Tropical World*, edited by E. A. Bacus and L. J. Lucero, pp. 34–49. Archeological Papers of the American Anthropological Association No. 9. Arlington, VA: American Anthropological Association.
    2001. *Social Integration in the Ancient Maya Hinterlands: Ceramic Variability in the Belize River Area*. Anthropological Research Paper No. 53. Tempe: Arizona State University.
    2002a. The Collapse of the Classic Maya: A Case for the Role of Water Control. *American Anthropologist* 104:814–826.
    2003. The Politics of Ritual: The Emergence of Classic Maya Rulers. *Current Anthropology* 44:523–558.
    2004. Exploring Classic Maya Politics: Yalbac, Central Belize. In *Archaeological Investigations in the Eastern Maya Lowlands: Papers of the 2003 Belize Archaeology Symposium*, edited by J. Awe, J. Morris, and S. Jones, pp. 83–91. Research Reports in Belizean Archaeology, Vol. 1. Belmopan, Belize: Institute of Archaeology, National Institute of Culture and History.
    n.d.a. Agricultural Intensification, Water and Political Power in the Southern Maya Lowlands. In *Structure, Agency, and Explanation in Models of Premodern Agricultural Intensification*, edited by J. Marcus and C. Stanish. Los Angeles: Cotsen Institute of Archaeology, UCLA. In press.
    n.d.b. The Power of Water in Ancient Maya Politics. In *Precolumbian Water Management: Ideology, Ritual, and Politics*, edited by L. J. Lucero and B. Fash. Tucson: University of Arizona Press. In press.

Lucero, Lisa J., ed.
    1997. *1997 Field Season of the Valley of Peace Archaeology (VOPA) Project*. Report submitted to the Department of Archaeology, Ministry of Tourism and the Environment, Belize.
    2002b. *Results of the 2001 Valley of Peace Archaeology Project: Saturday Creek and Yalbac*. Report submitted to the Department of Archaeology, Ministry of Tourism and Culture, Belize.

Lucero, Lisa J., and David L. Brown
    2002. SC-18: A Wealthy Maya Farming Residence. In *Results of the 2001 Valley of Peace Archaeology Project: Saturday Creek and Yalbac*, edited by L. J. Lucero, pp. 18–25. Report submitted to the Department of Archaeology, Ministry of Tourism and Culture, Belize.

Lucero, Lisa J., Scott L. Fedick, Andrew Kinkella, and Sean M. Graebner

  2004. Ancient Maya Settlement in the Valley of Peace Area, Belize. In *Archaeology of the Upper Belize River Valley: Half a Century of Maya Research*, edited by J. F. Garber, pp. 86–102. Gainesville: University Press of Florida.

Lucero, Lisa J., Sean M. Graebner, and Elizabeth Pugh

  2002. SC-78: The Eastern Platform Mound of an Elite Compound. In *Results of the 2001 Valley of Peace Archaeology Project: Saturday Creek and Yalbac*, edited by L. J. Lucero, pp. 33–46. Report submitted to the Department of Archaeology, Ministry of Tourism and Culture, Belize.

Lucero, Lisa J., Gaea McGahee, and Yvette Corral

  2002. SC-85: A Common Maya Farming Household. In *Results of the 2001 Valley of Peace Archaeology Project: Saturday Creek and Yalbac*, edited by L. J. Lucero, pp. 26–32. Report submitted to the Department of Archaeology, Ministry of Tourism and Culture, Belize.

Lundell, Cyrus

  1937. *The Vegetation of Petén*. Publication No. 478. Washington, D.C.: Carnegie Institute of Washington.

Machiavelli, Niccolo

  1994 [1514]. *The Prince*. New York: Barnes and Noble Books.

Malinowski, Bronislaw

  1984 [1922]. *Argonauts of the Pacific*. Prospect Heights, IL: Waveland Press.

Mann, Michael

  1986. *The Sources of Social Power, Volume I: A History of Power from the Beginning to A.D. 1760*. Cambridge: Cambridge University Press.

Marcus, George E.

  1983. "Elite" as a Concept, Theory, and Research Tradition. In *Elites: Ethnographic Issues*, edited by G. E. Marcus, pp. 7–27. Albuquerque: School of American Research and University of New Mexico Press.

Marcus, Joyce

  1976. *Emblem and State in the Classic Maya Lowlands: An Epigraphic Approach to Territorial Organization*. Washington, D.C.: Dumbarton Oaks.

  1978. Archaeology and Religion: A Comparison of the Zapotec and Maya. *World Archaeology* 10:172–191.

  1993. Ancient Maya Political Organization. In *Lowland Maya Civilization in the Eighth Century A.D.*, edited by J. A. Sabloff and J. S. Henderson, pp. 111–183. Washington, D.C.: Dumbarton Oaks.

  1994. The Collapse of Maya States: A Dynamic Model. Paper presented at the Annual Meetings of the American Anthropological Association, December, Atlanta, Georgia.

  1996. The Importance of Context in Interpreting Figurines. *Cambridge Archaeological Journal* 6:285–291.

  1998. The Peaks and Valleys of Ancient States: An Extension of the Dynamic Model. In *Archaic States*, edited by G. M. Feinman and J. Marcus, pp. 59–94. Santa Fe: School of American Research Press.

  2003. Recent Advances in Maya Archaeology. *Journal of Archaeological Research* 11:71–148.

Marcus, Joyce, and Kent V. Flannery
1996. *Zapotec Civilization: How Urban Society Evolved in Mexico's Oaxaca Valley.* London: Thames and Hudson.

Martin, Simon
2001. Court and Realm: Architectural Signatures in the Classic Maya Southern Lowlands. In *Royal Courts of the Ancient Maya, Volume I: Theory, Comparison, and Synthesis,* edited by T. Inomata and S. D. Houston, pp. 168–194. Boulder: Westview Press.
2003. In Line of the Founder: A View of Dynastic Politics at Tikal. In *Tikal: Dynasties, Foreigners, and Affairs of State,* edited by J. A. Sabloff, pp. 3–45. Santa Fe: School of American Research Press.

Martin, Simon, and Nikolai Grube
2000. *Chronicle of the Maya Kings and Queens: Deciphering the Dynasties of the Ancient Maya.* London: Thames and Hudson.

Marx, Karl, and Friedrich Engels
1977 [1932].   The German Ideology. In *Karl Marx: Selected Readings,* edited by D. McLellan, pp. 159–191. Oxford: Oxford University Press.

Masson, Marilyn A.
1997. Cultural Transformation at the Maya Postclassic Community of Laguna de On, Belize. *Latin American Antiquity* 8:293–316.

Masson, Marilyn A., and Shirley Boteler Mock
2004. Ceramics and Settlement Patterns at Terminal Classic-Period Lagoon Sites in Northeastern Belize. In *The Terminal Classic in the Maya Lowlands: Collapse, Transition, and Transformation,* edited by A. A. Demarest, P. M. Rice, and D. S. Rice, pp. 367–401. Boulder: University Press of Colorado.

Matheny, Ray T.
1987. An Early Maya Metropolis Uncovered: El Mirador. *National Geographic* 172: 317–339.

Mathews, Peter
1985. Maya Early Classic Monuments and Inscriptions. In *A Consideration of the Early Classic Period in the Maya Lowlands,* edited by G. R. Willey and P. Mathews, pp. 5–54. Institute for Mesoamerican Studies No. 10. Albany: State University of New York at Albany.

Mathews, Peter, and Gordon R. Willey
1991. Prehistoric Polities of the Pasion Region: Hieroglyphic Texts and Their Archaeological Settings. In *Classic Maya Political History: Hieroglyphic and Archaeological Evidence,* edited by T. P. Culbert, pp. 30–71. Cambridge: Cambridge University Press.

McAnany, Patricia A.
1990. Water Storage in the Puuc Region of the Northern Maya Lowlands: A Key to Population Estimates and Architectural Variability. In *Precolumbian Population History in the Maya Lowlands,* edited by T. P. Culbert and D. S. Rice, pp. 263–284. Albuquerque: University of New Mexico Press.
1995. *Living with the Ancestors: Kinship and Kingship in Ancient Maya Society.* Austin: University of Texas Press.

1998. Ancestors and the Classic Maya Built Environment. In *Function and Meaning in Classic Maya Architecture*, edited by S. D. Houston, pp. 271–298. Washington, D.C.: Dumbarton Oaks.

McAnany, Patricia A., Eleanor Harrison, Polly A. Peterson, Steven Morandi, Satoru Murata, Ben S. Thomas, Sandra L. López Varela, Daniel Finamore, and David G. Buck

2004. The Deep History of the Sibun River Valley. In *Archaeological Investigations in the Eastern Maya Lowlands: Papers of the 2003 Belize Archaeology Symposium*, edited by J. Awe, J. Morris, and S. Jones, pp. 295–310. Research Reports in Belizean Archaeology, Vol. 1. Belmopan, Belize: Institute of Archaeology, National Institute of Culture and History.

McGee, R. Jon

1990. *Life, Ritual and Religion among the Lacandon Maya*. Belmont, CA: Wadsworth.

1998. The Lacandon Incense Burner Renewal Ceremony: Termination and Dedication Ritual among the Contemporary Maya. In *The Sowing and the Dawning: Termination, Dedication, and Transformation in the Archaeological and Ethnographic Record of Mesoamerica*, edited by S. B. Mock, pp. 41–46. Albuquerque: University of New Mexico Press.

McKillop, Heather

1995. Underwater Archaeology, Salt Production, and Coastal Maya Trade at Stingray Lagoon, Belize. *Latin American Antiquity* 6:214–228.

1996. Ancient Maya Trading Ports and the Integration of Long-Distance and Regional Economies. *Ancient Mesoamerica* 7:49–62.

McMullen, David

1987. Bureaucrats and Cosmology: The Ritual Code of T'ang China. In *Rituals of Royalty: Power and Ceremonial in Traditional Societies*, edited by D. Cannadine and S. Price, pp. 181–236. Cambridge: Cambridge University Press.

Messenger, Lewis C., Jr.

1990. Ancient Winds of Change: Climatic Settings and Prehistoric Social Complexity in Mesoamerica. *Ancient Mesoamerica* 1:21–40.

Miksic, John N.

1999. Water, Urbanization, and Disease in Ancient Indonesia. In *Complex Polities in the Ancient Tropical World*, edited by E. A. Bacus and L. J. Lucero, pp. 167–184. Archeological Papers of the American Anthropological Association No. 9. Arlington, VA: American Anthropological Association.

Miller, Mary

2001. Life at Court: The View from Bonampak. In *Royal Courts of the Ancient Maya, Volume II: Data and Case Studies*, edited by T. Inomata and S. D. Houston, pp. 201–222. Boulder: Westview Press.

Miller, Mary, and Karl Taube

1993. *The Gods and Symbols of Ancient Mexico and the Maya*. London: Thames and Hudson.

Mock, Shirley B.

1998. Prelude. In *The Sowing and the Dawning: Termination, Dedication, and Transformation in the Archaeological and Ethnographic Record of Mesoamerica*, edited by S. B. Mock, pp. 3–18. Albuquerque: University of New Mexico Press.

2004. Maya Traders on the North-Central Belize Coast. In *Archaeological Investigations in the Eastern Maya Lowlands: Papers of the 2003 Belize Archaeology Symposium*, edited by J. Awe, J. Morris, and S. Jones, pp. 359–370. Research Reports in Belizean Archaeology, Vol. 1. Belmopan, Belize: Institute of Archaeology, National Institute of Culture and History.

Moore, Jerry D.
1996. The Archaeology of Plazas and the Proxemics of Ritual: Three Andean Traditions. *American Anthropologist* 98:789–802.

Neiman, Fraser D.
1997. Conspicuous Consumption as Wasteful Advertising: A Darwinian Perspective on Spatial Patterns in Classic Maya Terminal Monument Dates. In *Rediscovering Darwin: Evolutionary Theory and Archeological Explanation*, edited by C. M. Barton and G. A. Clark, pp. 267–290. Archeological Papers of the American Anthropological Association No. 7. Arlington, VA: American Anthropological Association.

Nelson, Stephen G., Barry D. Smith, and Bruce R. Best
1980. *Nitrogen Uptake by Tropical Freshwater Macrophytes*. Water Resources Research Center. Technical Report No. 10. Mangialo: University of Guam.

Olson, Kirsten A.
1994. Inclusive and Exclusive Mechanisms of Power: Obsidian Blade Production and Distribution among the Ancient Maya of the Belize River Area. M.A. thesis, University of California, Los Angeles.

O'Mansky, Matt, and Nicholas P. Dunning
2004. Settlement and Late Classic Political Disintegration in the Petexbatún Region, Guatemala. In *The Terminal Classic in the Maya Lowlands: Collapse, Transition, and Transformation*, edited by A. A. Demarest, P. M. Rice, and D. S. Rice, pp. 83–101. Boulder: University Press of Colorado.

Paine, Richard R., and AnnCorinne Freter
1996. Environmental Degradation and the Classic Maya Collapse at Copan, Honduras (A.D. 600–1250). *Ancient Mesoamerica* 7:37–47.

Palka, Joel W.
1997. Reconstructing Classic Maya Socioeconomic Differentiation and the Collapse at Dos Pilas, Peten, Guatemala. *Ancient Mesoamerica* 8:293–306.

Pauketat, Timothy R.
2000. The Tragedy of the Commoners. In *Agency in Archaeology*, edited by M. Dobres and J. Robb, pp. 113–129. London: Routledge Press.

Pendergast, David M.
1981. Lamanai, Belize: Summary of Excavation Results, 1974–1980. *Journal of Field Archaeology* 8:29–53.
1986. Stability through Change: Lamanai, Belize, from the Ninth to Seventeenth Century. In *Late Lowland Maya Civilization: Classic to Postclassic*, edited by J. A. Sabloff and E. W. Andrews V, pp. 223–249. Albuquerque: University of New Mexico Press.
1998. Intercessions with the Gods: Caches and Their Significance at Altun Ha and Lamanai, Belize. In *The Sowing and the Dawning: Termination, Dedication,*

and Transformation in the Archaeological and Ethnographic Record of Mesoamerica, edited by S. B. Mock, pp. 55–63. Albuquerque: University of New Mexico Press.

Peniche Rivero, Piedad
1990. *Sacerdotes y comerciantes: El poder de los mayas e itzaes de Yucatán en los siglos VII a XVI*. Mexico: Fondo de Cultura Económica.

Piehl, Jennifer
2002. The Skeletal Remains from the 2001 Field Season at Saturday Creek. In *Results of the 2001 Valley of Peace Archaeology Project: Saturday Creek and Yalbac*, edited by L. J. Lucero, pp. 84–94. Report submitted to the Department of Archaeology, Ministry of Tourism and Culture, Belize.

Pincemin, Sophia, Joyce Marcus, Lynda F. Folan, William J. Folan, Maria del R. Domínguez C., and Abel Morales L.
1998. Extending the Calakmul Dynasty Back in Time: A New Stela from a Maya Capital in Campeche, Mexico. *Latin American Antiquity* 9:310–327.

Pohl, Mary E. D., and John M. D. Pohl
1994. Cycles of Conflict: Political Factionalism in the Maya Lowlands. In *Factional Competition and Political Development in the New World*, edited by E. M. Brumfiel and J. W. Fox, pp. 138–157. Cambridge: Cambridge University Press.

Pope, Kevin O., and Bruce H. Dahlin
1989. Ancient Maya Wetland Agriculture: New Insights from Ecological and Remote Sensing Research. *Journal of Field Archaeology* 16:87–106.

Postgate, J. Nicholas
1992. *Early Mesopotamia: Society and Economy at the Dawn of History*. London and New York: Routledge.

Postgate, J. Nicholas, Tao Wang, and Toby Wilkinson
1995. The Evidence for Early Writing: Utilitarian or Ceremonial? *Antiquity* 69: 459–480.

Potter, Daniel R., and Eleonor M. King
1995. A Heterarchical Approach to Lowland Maya Socioeconomics. In *Heterarchy and the Analysis of Complex Society*, edited by R. M. Ehrenreich, C. L. Crumley, and J. E. Levy, pp. 17–32. Archeological Papers of the American Anthropological Association 6. Arlington, VA: American Anthropological Association.

Puleston, Dennis E.
1977. The Art and Archaeology of Hydraulic Agriculture in the Maya Lowlands. In *Social Process in Maya Prehistory: Studies in Honor of Sir Eric Thompson*, edited by N. Hammond, pp. 449–467. New York: Academic Press.

1983. *Settlement Survey of Tikal*. Tikal Report No. 13. University Museum Monograph 50. The University Museum. Philadelphia: University of Pennsylvania.

Pyburn, K. Anne
1997. The Archaeological Signature of Complexity in the Maya Lowlands. In *The Archaeology of City-States: Cross Cultural Approaches*, edited by D. L. Nichols and T. H. Charlton, pp. 155–168. Washington, D.C., and London: Smithsonian Institution Press.

Random House
1993. *Unabridged Dictionary.* 2nd ed. New York: Random House.

Rands, Robert L.
1953. *The Water Lily in Maya Art: A Complex of Alleged Asiatic Origin.* Bureau of American Ethnology Bulletin 151, Anthropological Papers No. 34. Washington, D.C.: Smithsonian Institution.

Rappaport, Roy A.
1971. Ritual, Sanctity, and Cybernetics. *American Anthropologist* 73:59–76.
1999. *Ritual and Religion in the Making of Humanity.* Cambridge: Cambridge University Press.

Rathje, William L.
1973. Classic Maya Development and Denouement: A Research Design. In *The Classic Maya Collapse,* edited by T. P. Culbert, pp. 405–454. Albuquerque: University of New Mexico Press.

Redfield, Robert, and Alfonso Villa Rojas
1934. *Chan Kom: A Maya Village.* Chicago: University of Chicago Press.

Reents-Budet, Dorie
1994. *Painting the Maya Universe: Royal Ceramics of the Classic Period.* Durham: Duke University Press.
2001. Classic Maya Concepts of the Royal Court. In *Royal Courts of the Ancient Maya, Volume I: Theory, Comparison, and Synthesis,* edited by T. Inomata and S. D. Houston, pp. 195–233. Boulder: Westview Press.

Reilly, F. Kent, III
1991. Olmec Iconographic Influences on the Symbols of Maya Rulership: An Examination of Possible Sources. In *Sixth Palenque Round Table, 1986,* edited by V. M. Fields, pp. 151–166. The Palenque Round Table Series, Vol. 8. Norman: University of Oklahoma Press.

Reina, Ruben E.
1967. Milpas and Milperos: Implications for Prehistoric Times. *American Anthropologist* 69:1–20.

Rice, Don S.
1986. The Peten Postclassic: A Settlement Perspective. In *Late Lowland Maya Civilization: Classic to Postclassic,* edited by J. A. Sabloff and E. W. Andrews V, pp. 301–344. Albuquerque: University of New Mexico Press.
1993. Eighth-Century Physical Geography, Environment, and Natural Resources in the Maya Lowlands. In *Lowland Maya Civilization in the Eighth Century A.D.,* edited by J. A. Sabloff and J. S. Henderson, pp. 11–63. Washington, D.C.: Dumbarton Oaks.
1996. Paleolimnological Analysis in the Central Petén, Guatemala. In *The Managed Mosaic: Ancient Maya Agriculture and Resource Use,* edited by S. L. Fedick, pp. 193–206. Salt Lake City: University of Utah Press.

Rice, Don S., and T. Patrick Culbert
1990. Historical Contexts for Population Reconstruction in the Maya Lowlands. In *Precolumbian Population History in the Maya Lowlands,* edited by T. P. Culbert and D. S. Rice, pp. 1–36. Albuquerque: University of New Mexico Press.

Rice, Prudence M.

1999. Rethinking Classic Lowland Maya Pottery Censers. *Ancient Mesoamerica* 10:25–50.

Rice, Prudence M., Arthur A. Demarest, and Don S. Rice

2004. The Terminal Classic and the "Classic Maya Collapse" in Perspective. In *The Terminal Classic in the Maya Lowlands: Collapse, Transition, and Transformation*, edited by A. A. Demarest, P. M. Rice, and D. S. Rice, pp. 1–11. Boulder: University Press of Colorado.

Rice, Prudence M., and Donald W. Forsyth

2004. Terminal Classic-Period Lowland Ceramics. In *The Terminal Classic in the Maya Lowlands: Collapse, Transition, and Transformation*, edited by A. A. Demarest, P. M. Rice, and D. S. Rice, pp. 28–59. Boulder: University Press of Colorado.

Rice, Prudence M., and Don S. Rice

2004. Late Classic to Postclassic Transformation in the Petén Lakes Region, Guatemala. In *The Terminal Classic in the Maya Lowlands: Collapse, Transition, and Transformation*, edited by A. A. Demarest, P. M. Rice, and D. S. Rice, pp. 125–139. Boulder: University Press of Colorado.

Richards, Colin, and Julian Thomas

1984. Ritual Activity and Structured Deposition in Later Neolithic Wessex. In *Neolithic Studies: A Review of Some Current Research*, edited by R. Bradley and J. Gardiner, pp. 189–218. BAR International Series 133. Oxford: British Archaeological Reports.

Ringle, William M.

1999. Pre-Classic Cityscapes: Ritual Politics among the Early Lowland Maya. In *Social Patterns in Pre-Classic Mesoamerica*, edited by D. C. Grove, pp. 183–223. Washington, D.C.: Dumbarton Oaks.

Robertson Smith, William

1956 [1894]. *The Religion of the Semites: The Fundamental Institutions.* 2nd ed. New York: Meridian Books.

Robin, Cynthia

2002. Outside of Houses: The Practices of Everyday Life at Chan Nòohol, Belize. *Journal of Social Archaeology* 2:245–268.

Robin, Cynthia, and Norman Hammond

1991. Burial Practices. In *Cuello: An Early Maya Community in Belize*, edited by N. Hammond, pp. 204–225. Cambridge: University of Cambridge Press.

Roosevelt, Anna C.

1999. The Development of Prehistoric Complex Societies: Amazonia, A Tropical Forest. In *Complex Polities in the Ancient Tropical World*, edited by E. A. Bacus and L. J. Lucero, pp. 13–33. Archeological Papers of the American Anthropological Association No. 9. Arlington, VA: American Anthropological Association.

Roscoe, Paul B.

1993. Practice and Political Centralisation: A New Approach to Political Evolution. *Current Anthropology* 34:111–140.

Russell, Bertrand

1938. *Power: A New Social Analysis.* New York: W. W. Norton.

Sabloff, Jeremy A.

1986. Interaction among Classic Maya Polities: A Preliminary Explanation. In *Peer Polity Interaction and Socio-Political Change,* edited by C. Renfrew and J. F. Cherry, pp. 109–116. Cambridge: Cambridge University Press.

1992. Interpreting the Collapse of Classic Maya Civilization: A Case Study of Changing Archeological Perspectives. In *Meta-Archaeology: Reflections by Archaeologists and Philosophers,* edited by L. Embree, pp. 99–119. Dordrecht, the Netherlands: Kluwer Academic Publisher.

Sabloff, Jeremy A., and Gordon R. Willey

1967. The Collapse of Maya Civilization in the Southern Lowlands: A Consideration of History and Process. *Southwestern Journal of Anthropology* 23:311–336.

Sahlins, Marshall

1968. *Tribesmen.* Englewood Cliffs: Prentice–Hall.

1972. *Stone Age Economics.* Chicago: Aldine-Atherton.

Sanchez, Gabriela, and Nick Chamberlain

2002. A Summary and Preliminary Analysis of Saturday Creek Burials. In *Results of the 2001 Valley of Peace Archaeology Project: Saturday Creek and Yalbac,* edited by L. J. Lucero, pp. 65–72. Report submitted to the Department of Archaeology, Ministry of Tourism and Culture, Belize.

Sanchez, Gabriela, and Jennifer Piehl

2002. Ancient Maya Household Ancestor Veneration at Saturday Creek, Belize. Paper presented at the 67th Annual Meetings of the Society for American Archaeology, March 20–24, Denver.

Sanders, William T.

1977. Environmental Heterogeneity and the Evolution of Lowland Maya Civilization. In *The Origins of Maya Civilization,* edited by R. E. W. Adams, pp. 287–297. Albuquerque: University of New Mexico Press.

Santley, Robert, S., Thomas W. Killion, and Mark T. Lycett

1986. On the Maya Collapse. *Journal of Anthropological Research* 42:123–159.

Scarborough, Vernon L.

1991. Water Management Adaptations in Non-Industrial Complex Societies: An Archaeological Perspective. In *Archaeological Method and Theory,* Vol. 3, edited by M. B. Schiffer, pp. 101–154. Tucson: University of Arizona Press.

1993. Water Management in the Southern Maya Lowlands: An Accretive Model for the Engineered Landscape. *Research in Economic Anthropology* 7:17–69.

1996. Reservoirs and Watersheds in the Central Maya Lowlands. In *The Managed Mosaic: Ancient Maya Agriculture and Resource Use,* edited by S. L. Fedick, pp. 304–314. Salt Lake City: University of Utah Press.

1998. Ecology and Ritual: Water Management and the Maya. *Latin American Antiquity* 9:135–159.

2003. *The Flow of Power: Ancient Water Systems and Landscapes.* Santa Fe: School of American Research Press.

Scarborough, Vernon L., and Gary C. Gallopin

1991. A Water Storage Adaptation in the Maya Lowlands. *Science* 251:658–662.

Scarborough, Vernon L., Fred Valdez, Jr., and Nicholas Dunning

2003. Introduction. In *Heterarchy, Political Economy, and the Ancient Maya: The Three Rivers Region of the East-Central Yucatán Peninsula*, edited by V. L. Scarborough, F. Valdez, Jr., and N. Dunning, pp. xiii–xx. Tucson: University of Arizona Press.

Schele, Linda, and David Freidel

1990. *A Forest of Kings: The Untold Story of the Ancient Maya*. New York: William Morrow and Company.

Schele, Linda, and Peter Mathews

1991. Royal Visits and Other Intersite Relationships among the Classic Maya. In *Classic Maya Political History: Hieroglyphic and Archaeological Evidence*, edited by T. P. Culbert, pp. 226–252. Cambridge: Cambridge University Press.

Schele, Linda, and Mary Ellen Miller

1986. *The Blood of Kings: Dynasty and Ritual in Maya Art*. New York: George Braziller.

Schiffer, Michael B.

1976. *Behavioral Archaeology*. New York: Academic Press.

Scott, James C.

1990. *Domination and the Arts of Resistance: Hidden Transcripts*. New Haven and London: Yale University Press.

Service, Elman R.

1962. *Primitive Social Organization: An Evolutionary Perspective*. New York: Random House.

1975. *Origins of the State and Civilization: The Process of Cultural Evolution*. New York: W. W. Norton.

Sharer, Robert J.

1978. Archaeology and History at Quirigua, Guatemala. *Journal of Field Archaeology* 5:51–70.

1994. *The Ancient Maya*. 5th ed. Stanford: Stanford University Press.

2003. Tikal and the Copan Dynastic Founding. In *Tikal: Dynasties, Foreigners, and Affairs of State*, edited by J. A. Sabloff, pp. 319–353. Santa Fe: School of American Research Press.

Small, David B.

1995. Heterarchical Paths to Evolution: The Role of External Economies. In *Heterarchy and the Analysis of Complex Societies*, edited by R. M. Ehrenreich, C. L. Crumley, and J. E. Levy, pp. 71–85. Archeological Papers of the American Anthropological Association No. 6. Arlington, VA: American Anthropological Association.

Smith, A. Ledyard

1972. *Excavations at Altar de Sacrificios: Architecture, Settlement, Burials, and Caches*. Papers of the Peabody Museum of Archaeology and Ethnology, Vol. 62, No. 2. Cambridge, MA: Harvard University Press.

Steward, Julian

1972 [1955]. *Theory of Culture Change: The Methodology of Multilinear Evolution*. Urbana and Chicago: University of Illinois Press.

Stross, Brian

1998. Seven Ingredients in Mesoamerican Ensoulment: Dedication and Termination in Tenejapa. In *The Sowing and the Dawning: Termination, Dedication, and Transformation in the Archaeological and Ethnographic Record of Mesoamerica*, edited by S. B. Mock, pp. 31–39. Albuquerque: University of New Mexico Press.

Stuart, David

1993. Historical Inscriptions and the Maya Collapse. In *Lowland Maya Civilization in the Eighth Century A.D.*, edited by J. A. Sabloff and J. S. Henderson, pp. 321–354. Washington, D.C.: Dumbarton Oaks.

1995. A Study of Maya Inscriptions. Ph.D. dissertation. Nashville: Vanderbilt University.

1996. Kings of Stone: A Consideration of Stelae in Ancient Maya Ritual and Representation. *Res* 29/30:148–171.

1998. "The Fire Enters His House": Architecture and Ritual in Classic Maya Texts. In *Function and Meaning in Classic Maya Architecture*, edited by S. D. Houston, pp. 373–425. Washington, D.C.: Dumbarton Oaks.

Stuart, David, and Stephen Houston

1994. *Classic Maya Place Names*. Studies in Pre-Columbian Art and Archaeology No. 33. Washington, D.C.: Dumbarton Oaks.

Tainter, Joseph A.

1988. *The Collapse of Complex Societies*. Cambridge: Cambridge University Press.

Tambiah, Stanley J.

1977. The Galactic Polity: The Structure of Traditional Kingdoms in Southeast Asia. *Annals of the New York Academy of Sciences* 293:69–97.

Taube, Karl

1992. *Major Gods of Ancient Yucatan*. Studies in Pre-Columbian Art and Archaeology No. 32. Washington, D.C.: Dumbarton Oaks.

1995. The Rainmakers: The Olmec and Their Contributions of Mesoamerican Belief and Ritual. In *The Olmec World: Ritual and Rulership*, edited by A. Rosenbaum, pp. 83–103. The Art Museum. Princeton: Princeton University Press.

Tedlock, Dennis

1985. *Popol Vuh: The Definitive Edition of the Mayan Book of the Dawn of Life and the Glories of Gods and Kings*. New York: Simon and Schuster.

Thomas, Julian

1991. *Rethinking the Neolithic*. Cambridge: Cambridge University Press.

Thompson, J. Eric S.

1966. *The Rise and Fall of Maya Civilization*. 2nd ed. Norman: University of Oklahoma Press.

1970. *Maya History and Religion*. Norman: University of Oklahoma Press.

Tourtellot, Gair

1990. Population Estimates for Preclassic and Classic Seibal, Peten. In *Precolumbian Population History in the Maya Lowlands*, edited by T. P. Culbert and D. S. Rice, pp. 83–102. Albuquerque: University of New Mexico Press.

1993. A View of Ancient Maya Settlements in the Eighth Century. In *Lowland Maya Civilization in the Eighth Century A.D.*, edited by J. A. Sabloff and J. S. Henderson, pp. 219–241. Washington, D.C.: Dumbarton Oaks.

Tourtellot, Gair, and Jason J. González

2004. The Last Hurrah: Continuity and Transformation at Seibal. In *The Terminal Classic in the Maya Lowlands: Collapse, Transition, and Transformation*, edited by A. A. Demarest, P. M. Rice, and D. S. Rice, pp. 60–82. Boulder: University Press of Colorado.

Tourtellot, Gair, and Jeremy A. Sabloff

2004. Seibal Revisited: The Crown Jewel in the Regional Necklace? Paper presented at the 69th Annual Meetings of the Society for American Archaeology, March 31–April 4, Montreal.

Toynbee, Arnold

1972. *A Study of History*. 1st abridged one-volume ed. New York: Weathervane Books.

Tozzer, Alfred M.

1907. *A Comparative Study of the Mayas and the Lacandones*. New York: Macmillan.

1941. *Landa's Relación de Las Cosas de Yucatán*. Papers of the Peabody Museum of American Archaeology and Ethnology, No. 28. Cambridge, MA: Harvard University.

Trigger, Bruce G.

1991. Distinguished Lecture in Archeology: Constraint and Freedom—A New Synthesis for Archeological Explanation. *American Anthropologist* 93:551–569.

2003. *Understanding Early Civilization: A Comparative Study*. Cambridge: Cambridge University Press.

Turner, B. L., II

1974. Prehistoric Intensive Agriculture in the Mayan Lowlands. *Science* 185:118–124.

Valdés, Juan Antonio, and Federico Fahsen

2004. Disaster in Sight: The Terminal Classic at Tikal and Uaxactun. In *The Terminal Classic in the Maya Lowlands: Collapse, Transition, and Transformation*, edited by A. A. Demarest, P. M. Rice, and D. S. Rice, pp. 140–161. Boulder: University Press of Colorado.

Vogt, Evon Z.

1970. *The Zinacantecos of Mexico: A Modern Maya Way of Life*. New York: Holt, Rinehart and Winston.

1993. *Tortillas for the Gods: A Symbolic Analysis of Zinacanteco Rituals*. Norman: University of Oklahoma Press.

Wagner, Gunther

1940. The Political Organization of the Bantu of Kavirondo. In *African Political Systems*, edited by M. Fortes and E. E. Evans-Pritchard, pp. 197–236. International African Institute. London: Oxford University Press.

Walker, William H.

1995. Ceremonial Trash? In *Expanding Archaeology*, edited by J. M. Skibo, W. H. Walker, and A. Neilsen, pp. 67–79. Salt Lake City: University of Utah Press.

1998. Where Are the Witches of Prehistory? *Journal of Archaeological Method and Theory* 5:245–308.

2002. Stratigraphy and Practical Reason. *American Anthropologist* 104:159–177.

Walker, William H., and Lisa J. Lucero

2000. The Depositional History of Ritual and Power. In *Agency in Archaeology*, edited by M. Dobres and J. Robb, pp. 130–147. London: Routledge Press.

Wauchope, Robert

1938. *Modern Maya Houses: A Study of Their Archaeological Significance*. Publication No. 502. Washington, D.C.: Carnegie Institution of Washington.

Webb, Malcolm C.

1973. The Peten Maya Decline Viewed in the Perspective of State Formation. In *The Classic Maya Collapse*, edited by T. P. Culbert, pp. 367–404. Albuquerque: University of New Mexico Press.

Weber, Max

1958 [1930]. *The Protestant Ethic and the Spirit of Capitalism*. Translated by Talcott Parsons. New York: Charles Scribner's Sons.

1964 [1951]. *The Religion of China: Confucianism and Taoism*. Translated by Hans H. Gerth. New York: Macmillan.

Webster, David L.

1976. On Theocracies. *American Anthropologist* 78:812–828.

1977. Warfare and the Evolution of Maya Civilization. In *The Origins of Maya Civilization*, edited by R. E. W. Adams, pp. 335–372. Albuquerque: University of New Mexico Press.

1998. Warfare and Status Rivalry: Lowland Maya and Polynesian Comparisons. In *Archaic States*, edited by G. M. Feinman and J. Marcus, pp. 311–351. Santa Fe: School of American Research Press.

1999. The Archaeology of Copán, Honduras. *Journal of Archaeological Research* 7:1–53.

2000. The Not So Peaceful Civilization: A Review of Maya War. *Journal of World Prehistory* 14:65–119.

2002. *The Fall of the Ancient Maya: Solving the Mystery of the Maya Collapse*. London: Thames and Hudson.

Webster, David L., and AnnCorinne Freter

1990. The Demography of Late Classic Copan. In *Precolumbian Population History in the Maya Lowlands*, edited by T. P. Culbert and D. S. Rice, pp. 37–61. Albuquerque: University of New Mexico Press.

Webster, David, AnnCorinne Freter, and Rebecca Storey

2004. Dating Copán Culture-History: Implications for the Terminal Classic and the Collapse. In *The Terminal Classic in the Maya Lowlands: Collapse, Transition, and Transformation*, edited by A. A. Demarest, P. M. Rice, and D. S. Rice, pp. 231–259. Boulder: University Press of Colorado.

Webster, David, and Nancy Gonlin

1988. Household Remains of the Humblest Maya. *Journal of Field Archaeology* 15:169–190.

Webster, David, William T. Sanders, and P. van Rossum

1992. A Simulation of Copán Population History and Its Implications. *Ancient Mesoamerica* 3:185–197.

Weiss-Krejci, Estella, and Thomas Sabbas
2002. The Potential Role of Small Depressions as Water Storage Features in the Central Maya Lowlands. *Latin American Antiquity* 13:343–357.

White, Leslie A.
1959. *The Evolution of Culture: The Development of Civilization to the Fall of Rome.* New York: McGraw-Hill.
1971 [1949]. *The Science of Culture: A Study of Man and Civilization.* New York: Farrar, Straus and Giroux.

Wiessner, Polly, and Akii Tumu
1998. *Historical Vines: Enga Networks of Exchange, Ritual, and Warfare in Papua New Guinea.* With translations and assistance by Nitze Pupu. Washington, D.C., and London: Smithsonian Institution Press.

Wilkinson, Robert L.
1995. Yellow Fever: Ecology, Epidemiology, and Role in the Collapse of the Classic Lowland Maya Civilization. *Medical Anthropology* 16:269–294.

Willey, Gordon R.
1973. *The Altar de Sacrificios Excavations: General Summary and Conclusions.* Papers of the Peabody Museum of Archaeology and Ethnology, Vol. 64, No. 3. Cambridge, MA: Harvard University.

Willey, Gordon R., William R. Bullard, John B. Glass, and James C. Gifford
1965. *Prehistoric Maya Settlements in the Belize Valley.* Peabody Museum of Archaeology and Ethnology Papers, Vol. 54. Cambridge, MA: Harvard University.

Willey, Gordon R., and Demitri B. Shimkin
1973. The Maya Collapse: A Summary View. In *The Classic Maya Collapse,* edited by T. P. Culbert, pp. 457–501. Albuquerque: University of New Mexico Press.

Willey, Gordon R., and A. Ledyard Smith
1969. *The Ruins of Altar de Sacrificios, Department of Peten, Guatemala: An Introduction.* Papers of the Peabody Museum of Archaeology and Ethnology, Vol. 62, No. 1. Cambridge, MA: Harvard University.

Wingard, John D.
1996. Interactions between Demographic Processes and Soil Resources in the Copán Valley, Honduras. In *The Managed Mosaic: Ancient Maya Agriculture and Resource Use,* edited by S. L. Fedick, pp. 207–235. Salt Lake City: University of Utah Press.

Wolf, Eric R.
1966. *Peasants.* Englewood Cliffs: Prentice-Hall.
1999. *Envisioning Power: Ideologies of Dominance and Crises.* Berkeley: University of California Press.

Wortman, Richard
1985. Moscow and Petersburg: The Problem of Political Center in Tsarist Russia, 1881–1914. In *Rites of Power: Symbolism, Ritual, and Politics Since the Middle Ages,* edited by S. Wilentz, pp. 244–271. Philadelphia: University of Pennsylvania Press.

Wren, Linnea H., and Peter Schmidt
1991. Elite Interaction during the Terminal Classic Period: New Evidence from Chichen Itza. In *Classic Maya Political History: Hieroglyphic and Archaeological*

Evidence, edited by T. P. Culbert, pp. 199–225. Cambridge: Cambridge University Press.

Wright, Lori E.
  1997. Biological Perspectives on the Collapse of the Pasión Maya. *Ancient Mesoamerica* 8:267–273.

Yoffee, Norman
  1988. The Collapse of Ancient Mesopotamian States and Civilization. In *The Collapse of Ancient States and Civilizations*, edited by N. Yoffee and G. L. Cowgill, pp. 44–68. Tucson: University of Arizona Press.

Index

Printed and bound by CPI Group (UK) Ltd, Croydon, CR0 4YY

13/04/2025

14656491-0003